RUN to the ROAR

JOE HURSTON
and Martha VanCise

D0951317

Charisma
HOUSE
A STRANG COMPANY

Most Strang Communications/Charisma House/Siloam/Realms/FrontLine products are available at special quantity discounts for bulk purchase for sales promotions, premiums, fund-raising, and educational needs. For details, write Strang Communications/Charisma House/Siloam/Realms/FrontLine, 600 Rinehart Road, Lake Mary, Florida 32746, or telephone (407) 333-0600.

Run to the Roar by Joe Hurston and Martha VanCise
Published by Charisma House
A Strang Company
600 Rinehart Road
Lake Mary, Florida 32746
www.charismahouse.com

Unless otherwise noted, all Scripture quotations are from the Holy Bible, New International Version. Copyright © 1973, 1978, 1984, International Bible Society. Used by permission.

Scripture quotations marked KJV are from the King James Version of the Bible.

Cover design by Rachel Campbell

AUTHOR'S NOTE: Due to issues of government security and religious persecution, some names and details of stories in this book have been changed for the privacy and protection of the persons involved.

Library of Congress Cataloging-in-Publication Data
Hurston, Joe.
  Run to the roar / Joe Hurston with Martha VanCise.
    p. cm.
  ISBN 1-59185-905-0 (paper back)
  1. Hurston, Joe. 2. Aeronautics in missionary work. 3. Missionaries--Biography. I. Van Cise, Martha. II. Title.
BV2082.A9H87 2006
266.0092--dc22
[B]
2006008055

First Edition

06 07 08 09 10 — 9 8 7 6 5 4 3 2 1
Printed in the United States of America

Acknowledgments

M^{Y DEEPEST THANKS} go to many more people than are listed below. Above all, I thank first and foremost my Lord Jesus, who has never, ever left me or forsaken me.

Thank you, Cindy, my beloved wife, for standing strong by my side and loving and encouraging me. To each of you, my seven children I give thanks and appreciation.

- Steve, for your courage and strength.
- Ben, for your brilliance and heart to serve.
- Cherie, my special dove, for your incredible commitment to Jesus.
- Christian, for your great faith and diligence. You will far surpass me in so many ways.
- Angelica, for your deep insight and sure convictions.
- Juliet, for your ability to make people smile. I love your smile.
- Peter, for your deep compassion. You bring joy to my heart.

I could fill many pages listing the friends who have stood by me over the years, but I can only list a few.

- Joe Polozola: Thank you, Joe, for leading me to Jesus.
- Larry Junker: You've been like the best dad anyone could have.
- Dr. Larry Linkous: My dear pastor, you have helped me soar!
- The Honorable Judge Robert Decatur: My Tuskegee Airman friend, you taught me so much and encouraged me again and again to *Run to the Roar*.
- Rolf Engelhard: Thank you, Rolf, for sharing your genius with me and the rest of the world.
- Martha VanCise: Thank you for helping me capture in print the mighty things that our Lord has done and is doing!

My family and friends have been an integral part of these stories and miracles. I hope these accounts of God at work will challenge you to *Run to the Roar*.

—JOE HURSTON

ACKNOWLEDGMENTS

A SPECIAL THANKS GOES to Jim (Cincy Kid) and Donna (Roomie) Hay. Jim prayed, and Donna gave the manuscript a preliminary editing. Thank you, Tom and Dorothy Endicott, for providing "Johnny's House," the ideal writer's retreat. I also want to thank my colleagues in the English as a Second Language Department at Indian River Community College. You allowed flexibility in my schedule to meet writing deadlines, you all cheered me on during the rewrites, and remember—you *promised* to buy a copy of the book. Thank you, Barbara Dycus, for showing Joe and me that *Run to the Roar* was much more than a collection of stories.

—MARTHA VANCISE

CONTENTS

Contents

INTRODUCTION

WHEN I LIVED in Haiti, I often heard of Joe Hurston, the missionary pilot, but I never met him until I returned to the United States. Joe was one of many missionaries with whom I had contact. He was also one of many missionaries who had exciting and inspiring stories, and whose friends had said, "You must write a book." As a writer, I knew that "missionary" stories were hard to market. Joe, as I would eventually learn, did not let ideas die quietly. If an idea had merit, he would pump life into it and make it walk. He sent me a couple stories, and I had to admit the stories held my interest, but I also knew they were not publishable in the current market. "I have many more," he told me. "Did I ever tell you about 'The Sea Rescue'? Or 'Dead Stick Landing'? Or 'The Saving of Dorothy Erdman'? She died...*and came back to life!*" He had already named the chapters.

I forgot about his stories until a couple years later when I was cleaning out files. Since I was in between projects, I reworked the two stories he had given me and mailed them to him. When the revised stories arrived, Joe opened the envelope while standing in the entrance hall of his home. "I started reading," he said. "I didn't even change out of my goon clothes—my suit and tie. I read and cried until I reached the end of the stories."

After reading the revised stories, Joe immediately called me. While we both knew that the stories might never be published, we both felt this was God's time for us to work on a book. "We must look for a theme," I told Joe. "As I work with the stories, I'll watch for a theme to emerge."

During the next two years I interviewed Joe, and he also recorded material as he drove to and from work. We felt that we had strong stand-alone short stories, but the stories would have to connect to form a book. Les Stobbe, a writer and editor told us, "The stories are like pearls that need to be threaded on a string."

"What about the Africa story?" I asked Joe.

Soon after lions had killed people in a Zimbabwe village, Joe and some missionary pilots had visited the village. When Joe and the pilots had started discussing how fast they would run if they heard a lion roar, their African guide had abruptly stopped the conversation. *"Never run from a lion,"* he said. *"Always run to the roar.* If you take a direct approach to the roar, all your senses will be tuned to finding out where the lion is located. Then you can maneuver away from the lion and escape."

Since Joe often likened his approach to problem solving as "running to the roar," we decided to string the stories on the tail of a lion. Initially, I wrote using the lion theme, and the stories ended with a narrow escape from a Bahamian killer storm. By the time we had come to the end of the manuscript, however, Joe's life had changed. He had moved from being a missionary pilot to an entrepreneur on the Space Coast of Florida. Each time he called, he excitedly told me of doors opening into new arenas of witness. He called one evening elated because he had been working inside one of the space shuttles at the Kennedy Space Center. I was in a quandary. God was moving in ways every bit as exciting as in the early missionary stories. Did we have one book and a great epilogue or the beginning of a second book?

As we hesitated, not knowing how to handle the manuscript, we both faced personal challenges. Along with expanding a cartridge recycling business, Joe was a man on a mission to restore damaged relationships with his adult children. And I was a bald-headed writer conducting interviews through a chemo-induced haze. During our personal battles, we found ourselves using principles in the stories to help us face new challenges. We found the lessons had applications beyond safe landings and showing the *JESUS* film in isolated Haitian villages. The story principles could be applied to health, family, business, and spiritual issues.

During the writing of the manuscript, Joe often spoke of a burning vision "...to take the gospel around the world." Although he had conducted *JESUS* film crusades in several countries, he felt God had a greater work in store for him. As each new door had opened in his business, Cartridge Source of America, he had been certain that "this was the door" to his dream. In 2004, however, God began to move pieces of His purpose into place and show Joe Hurston that his perception of the dream to "take the gospel around the world" paled in comparison with what God had in mind.

As you read *Run to the Roar,* you will see how Christ "is able to do immeasurably more than all we ask or imagine, according to his power that is at work within us" (Eph. 3:20). So now I invite you to come, join Joe on a spiritual safari. In *Run to the Roar*, he will show you how to face lions that roar, "Failure! Failure! You can't come here! Give up! It can't be done." Along the way, you will find helpful trail signs that say, "I've been here. This is what I learned. Maybe this will help you."

As you travel with Joe, he will challenge you to:

· Allow God to unstop your ears.
· Abandon the comfortable, predictable place.
· Engage and fully trust Christ to guide your life.
· Confidently wield the sword of God's Word.

You will find travel tips:

· Don't carry unnecessary weight.
· Take delight in the journey.
· Never allow fear to redirect your steps.

You will praise God as you witness the ways He extends His mercy:

· He preserves our lives when we make mistakes of ignorance.
· He uses many agents and methods to bring us to Himself.
· He is the God of second chances.

You will look at God's plan for your life in a new way:

· God never works with an outdated map for your life.
· On our small maps we see only God's obvious purposes. On His map He sees hidden purposes.
· Nothing can barricade the route God lays out for us.
· Little by little, God fits together His plan for your life.
· What appears to be a delay may be the beginning of a new path.

You will find courage for difficult hours that require great power and strength:

· God has placed you where you are for such a time as this.
· When you make difficult decisions, others may abandon

you, but Jesus will never leave you.

- Fear accompanies great danger. Accept its presence and face it.
- Great spiritual battles often precede great accomplishments.

Joe and I pray that *Run to the Roar* will challenge you to step off the safari bus and into God's great adventure of running to the roar.

—MARTHA VANCISE

PROLOGUE

WAS IT A cough?

I held a shallow breath of air, then slowly let it seep from my lungs. For hours I had been sipping air, never relaxing enough to take a deep breath. If the doorknob rattled or someone moved outside the house I had to know. On this dark night it was hard to separate reality from imagination. My sweat, a leftover symptom of the fever, intensified the odor of the filthy mattress. That smell, though, was nothing compared to what lay outside.

In the darkness I couldn't see the bedroom wall, but I could point to about where the tsunami marker was on the wall. A slight terrain elevation had spared the house, but the waters and mud had swept through leaving a line high on the walls.

Was the stench in my nostrils from the putrefying bodies in the muck beyond the walls or just a memory of what I had seen and which my mind struggled to comprehend?

I wanted to wipe the sweat from my brow. I wanted to stretch my legs. I wanted to move, but my wife, Cindy, and daughter Cherie seemed to be breathing evenly and relaxed. I lay quietly, holding my breath intermittently to sort out the night sounds. In all the years that I had "run to the roar," I had never faced a night like this one. I was afraid.

Why couldn't that landlord have allowed me to enter the house and count out the nineteen million rupiahs instead of asking me to peel off the money on the doorstep? The young men, who had shown great curiosity and stayed with us all day, had witnessed the transaction. They and others in the town knew that we had entered the house with expensive movie cameras, backpacks, and several square cases with unknown contents. In a city 80 percent destroyed by the tsunami a couple weeks before, the smallest undamaged item had high value.

And what about the insurgents? If they came that night, we would be the first target because our house lay outside the secure green zone. Besides all that, we were American Christians in an Islamic community that had been isolated from foreigners for years. The photos that I had seen that day of tortured members of the persecuted church had chilled me.

I knew that in the other rooms dirty, hungry, and apprehensive team members were sleeping fitfully. On this night, death permeated the air. I realized that I had purposely shut safe doors and lunged against closed doors to lead six trusting people deep into the lion's lair. These people included husbands and fathers, parents, and those dear to me—Cindy and Cherie.

Have I made a mistake in pressing into the center of the disaster? I wondered. *Should I have stayed with the original plan that guaranteed us a clean place to sleep, food, safety, and transportation? Is this the lion God wanted me to go after? Will God protect us through the night?*

CHAPTER 1

LIONS STILL PREFER CHRISTIANS

LION COUNTRY TRAVEL TIP

FACE REALITY: LION TERRITORY IS DANGEROUS TERRITORY.

FEAR DIVIDED THEIR attention. The adults watched the images on the film screen, but not only the screen—they also watched for movement in the darkness that surrounded the viewing area. Tension had even corralled the younger children. Instead of romping and ranging around the edges of the crowd, they stayed within touching distance of an elder. Toddlers snuggled in their mothers' arms. I must admit…apprehension stirred in my gut, too. Every rustle in the African bush seemed magnified.

I wanted to turn up the sound, drown the uneasiness, and relax the audience. After all, viewing one's first film should be remembered as an evening of pleasure, not a night of dread. I dared not increase the sound, though. If we missed the cue that a killer had entered our stage, one of us could be mauled or dragged to our death.

I was well into a two-week training blitz for Mission Aviation Fellowship (MAF) pilots who served in the southern countries of Africa. The life of a missionary pilot involves a few *minutes* of high-concentration landings, glorious takeoffs into the blue sky, and an occasional harrowing experience. But it also involves *hours* of strenuous loading and unloading of planes in tropical heat, brain-numbing watches over dials and digital numbers in the cockpit, and *hours* of reading the sky.

Knowing that many pilots longed to take a more active part in evangelization, I had approached MAF with a plan to train pilots in setting up and showing the *JESUS* film.* From my own experiences

---

* As of January 2006, the *JESUS* film has been translated into 924 languages.

1

with the film, I knew that the *JESUS* film accurately and succinctly presented the gospel in the language of the host people and in a manner that people of all cultures, education levels, and ages could understand. Since MAF pilots often served missionaries in primitive areas, in Africa we decided to travel to a remote settlement on a game reserve for our training session.

Maritz, a seasoned safari guide and a Christian, accompanied us and introduced us to the people. Maritz had long flowing locks of curly hair. A big man, he exuded power. Although he no doubt differed in size, this former member of the Rhodesian secret police, who was known for his warring exploits, reminded me of King David. Maritz drove us to the village in a battered Land Rover that looked like it was made for a Serengeti adventure movie. The Land Rover had no top, no seat belts, and had been modified for maximum visibility of wildlife. The three rows of seats were tiered like bleachers. From the dents and dings on the vehicle, I figured Maritz was either a wild driver or had used this vehicle in his warring exploits.

"I'm a good driver," he assured us. "Those dents are from wild animal attacks."

Our destination, a village of four hundred to five hundred people, was located on a game reserve, a truly gated community. The people lived within the confines of a ten- to twelve-foot high predator fence, which surrounded their homes and several thousand acres of garden plots and pasture. After passing through a portal, we saw primitive but adequate homes that were raised on short pilings above the ground. Neat and orderly, the wood and tin-roofed houses appeared to have been designed and laid out by the game reserve authorities.

We arrived as darkness was falling and hurriedly looked for a place to set up our equipment. Someone directed us to the center of the village, but the area was too small for the large crowd that was sure to gather. Quickly we moved to the edge of the village and an open area near the fence.

All activity ceased in the village as the people turned out to watch the strangers who had entered their settlement. We smiled and greeted some of the people, shook hands with the village leaders, and then hurriedly began unloading the equipment.

Although friendly, this crowd didn't seem to react as most groups did. Instead of standing close to each other and giggling about the white strangers, they watched and spoke in murmurs. Even the children took longer to press in and touch the equipment.

Whatever the reason for their reserved mood, my primary job was to train the pilots in the setup of the film. After having set up the film equipment more than 350 times, I had developed a time-tested routine.

"Remember, some people have never seen a light bulb," I told the pilots. "The people will trip on wires and cables. They don't understand the danger of electrical current from the generator. Sometimes the noise of the generator will frighten them."

I glanced at a nearby group of villagers. They still gazed at us gravely. "You never know what mood you'll find when you arrive," I said. "Usually the people exhibit a lot of curiosity and excitement. Occasionally a crowd will become rowdy and disrespectful." I couldn't quite figure out the people of this village. They seemed respectful but preoccupied, as if something bothered them.

As I continued explaining to the pilots how to protect both equipment and people, Maritz moved through the village greeting friends and explaining about the movie they would soon view. When he returned, he motioned for us to gather. "The people are very nervous," he said. "Four renegade lions have broken through the predator fence and have killed seven or eight people. Everyone is afraid." Now I understood the people's mood.

In spite of the tension and grief that tempered the evening, nearly everyone in the village gathered to view the film. Once I had the film rolling, I moved to the back of the crowd where Maritz and members of the mission team stood near the fence conversing quietly. The subject, of course, was *lions*.

"If I hear a lion roar, you'll see me running," one young man said.

"*Never run from a lion*," Maritz said quietly. "Run to the roar."

"Do what!" I said.

"Run to the roar."

"Everything inside of me would say, 'Run away from the roar,'" I said. The others nodded their heads in agreement.

"You want to know where that lion is," Maritz explained. "You don't want to be running blindly through the bush or through the village when a lion roars. If it's roaring, it has probably already seen you. That lion can run faster than you can. You don't want it to over-take you from behind while you're running in blind fear. You need to go toward the roar in order to figure out where the lion is, and then plan your escape. If you take a direct approach to the roar, all your senses will be tuned to finding out where the lion is located. Then you can maneuver away from the lion and escape."

Maritz could run to the roar, but I scanned the area looking for a good hiding place if a lion showed up.

LION COUNTRY TRAVEL TIP 2

BE FOREWARNED: WHEN THE LION ROARS, FEAR WILL USUALLY STOP YOU IN YOUR TRACKS AND MAKE YOUR HEART POUND.

In *The Chronicles of Narnia*, Mrs. Beaver tells the children about Aslan, the great and good lion. She says, "If there's anyone who can appear before Aslan without their knees knocking, they're either braver than most or else just silly."[1] In *The Pilgrim's Progress*, Christian cowers when lions appear on his path. Although he trembles with fear, he continues his journey.[2]

Lions appear in primitive art, mythology, and Scripture. They may be agents of good or evil. The apostle Peter said that the devil prowled like a roaring lion looking for someone to devour (1 Pet. 5:8). In the Book of Revelation, we see Christ as the Lion of the tribe of Judah. No matter what the lion represents, when it roars, it will usually stop you in your tracks and make your heart pound. You may prefer lion images of Aslan, Disney's *Lion King*, or the Lion of the tribe of Judah, but in real life, lions will likely represent Satan and confront you as ferocious soul-devouring beasts. Don't enter lion territory without facing the reality that you are entering dangerous territory.

LION COUNTRY TRAVEL TIP 3

KEEP IN MIND THAT THE LION RULES VAST TERRITORIES BY INTIMIDATION. THE LION LIES AND EXAGGERATES HIS POWER. (SEE JOHN 8:44.)

A lion's roar can be heard for five miles. The circle of intimidation covers a large area. As you near any accomplishment, you will hear the lion roar, "Failure! Failure! You can't come here! Give up! It can't be done." I won't deny that the roar has made my heart pound, but God's ever-present enabling has given me boldness to resist and overcome many lions. Have I always been victorious in every lion confrontation? If your idea of victory is standing unscathed with one foot on the lion's head—well, no, I haven't always been victorious. If your concept of victory is bearing the scars of conflict but still being committed to following the Guide through lion territory—the answer is yes.

LION COUNTRY TRAVEL TIP 4

TAKE A CLOSE LOOK AT WHAT IS ON THE MENU IN LION TERRITORY.

One African safari guide said, "There are more man-eating lions than the tourist bureaus would like to admit." In the Christian realm, more Christians are being devoured than the church would like to acknowledge. No matter your theology relating to the eternal home of these people, Satan and his pride of lions are devouring the joy, peace, marriages, Christian witness, influence, effectiveness, and even the emotional and physical lives of Christians all over the world.

> **In the spider-web of facts, many a truth is strangled.**[3]
> —PAUL ELDRIDGE

When you enter the kingdom of heaven, you also enter lion territory. Programs emphasizing "Celebrate Jesus" and "God wants you to be happy" often grow churches, but they fail to prepare the Christian for the realities of lion-infested country. Celebrate that your name has been entered in the Lamb's book of life; be aware, though, that your name has been penciled on the lion's menu as *"soup de jour."*

The lion disguises himself in discouragement, unfavorable circumstances, and unsolvable problems. When encountering these situations you can ignore them, retreat, or move toward the difficulty. The apostle Peter, who turned his back and ran at one lion encounter, tells us to resist the lion and to stand firm (1 Pet. 5:9). Only as you run to the roar by dealing with the problems and adversities that block your path can you grow spiritually and accomplish God's purpose for your life.

LION COUNTRY TRAVEL TIP 5

MAKE A CHOICE. SETTLE DOWN TO A RELAXING JAUNT THROUGH LION TERRITORY, OR STEP OFF THE BUS INTO THE GREAT ADVENTURE GOD HAS FOR YOU.

You can choose to stay in a spiritual reserve surrounded by like-minded friends, familiar traditions, and well-defined boundaries that separate you from lions. Or…you can venture into lion territory. Some people settle for mini-safaris. They travel through lion territory in an air-conditioned bus and sip lemonade as they listen to a twenty-minute Sunday morning travelogue. If they hear a lion roar, they treat the roar as a novel experience—not a call to action. Others hear the roar and dream of bringing home unimaginable trophies, but they never get off the bus to pursue their dreams.

> **There are risks and costs to a program of action. But they are far less than the long-range risks and costs of comfortable inaction.[4]**
> —JOHN F. KENNEDY

Run to the Roar is a call to get off the bus and venture beyond the safe spaces of our religious and personal worlds. Yes, you will attract the attention of the lion. The trophies for God, however, lie deep in lion territory—a place of danger, conflict, and glorious triumph. You, and you alone, can decide whether to stay on the bus or get off and follow God's best plan for your life.

CHAPTER 2

DO YOU HEAR THE ROAR?

ROAR RESPONSE 1

THE CALL TO FOLLOW THE ROAR OFTEN BEGINS
WHEN WE ARE CHILDREN. GOD-INSTILLED DESIRES
CALL US TO GREATER ACCOMPLISHMENTS.

RUNNING TO THE roar is more than some romantic achievement of a lifetime dream. As you venture into lion territory, God will open your eyes to many needs and plant desires to meet those needs in your heart. In the chapters ahead we will see how running to the roar involves commitment to follow these God-planted desires and embrace these attitudes:

· Confidence that He will never abandon us

· Respect for danger but courage to face difficulties to rescue the neglected

· Determination to engage in the necessary spiritual battles

· Perseverance to endure until the lion is tamed or defeated

Does God give all Christians the desire to run to the roar? Or does He assign some to stay in the safe spaces? I cannot answer for others, but I must respond to the call that I hear. And you must respond to the call that you hear. Take time to evaluate the desires of your heart. Early in life, God plants desires in our hearts to paint, write, fly, teach, nurture children, care for the sick, and minister in various ways. How have you treated those desires? Have you cultivated those desires or looked at the impossibilities that blocked your path? How often have you said, "I've always wanted to…"? How often have you brushed aside the desire or dream or call because you heard the roar of "You could never accomplish that," or "You don't have time for that"?

As you follow God-given dreams and keep them in proper perspective, they provide a means to travel deeper into lion territory. These desires often form the foundation blocks of your life's work and ministry. As you evaluate the desires that God has placed in your heart, look also at the barriers to pursuing those desires. Determine to face them. As you face the barriers and deal with them, you will move closer to accomplishing the purpose for which God created you.

> **No instinct can be put in you by the Holy Ghost but He purposes to fulfill. Let your faith then rise and soar away and claim all the land you can discover.[1]**
> —S. A. KEEN

I believe that God gave me the desire to fly to broaden my ministry. When I was three and a half years old, I saw my first airplane. At four, I ran away from home. My mother found me a half-mile down the road at the airport. She scolded me and took me home. I returned to the airport. Her father said, "Evelyn, you're going to have to cut a little willow switch and switch his legs all the way home. It's the only way you can get that boy to stay home."

She switched me all the way home, but I returned to the airport. I was absolutely smitten and in love with airplanes. After several calf-smarting trips back home from the airport, I said, "Momma, I don't want to disobey you. But you'll just have to keep switching me because I'm not going to stop going to the airport."

She threw up her hands in desperation and said, "Well, at least let me show you the safe way to get to the airport. I don't want you run over by a car."

By the time I was seven, I had taken possession of my first plane, and I was no longer of any use to anyone who didn't have something to do with airplanes. My mother never wondered where I was. She knew I was at the airport.

My first plane was a Bamboo Bomber. Nearly every bomber pilot in World War II trained in what was called the *Bamboo Bomber*. The Cessna, ugly as a mud fence, had a short fat nose and two big radial engines. After training in the Bamboo Bomber, pilots would go on to B17s, B24s, and B25s. An old Bamboo Bomber had been abandoned at the Baton Rouge Downtown Airport and tied down far away from the other planes. Made with a lot of wood (which gave it the *bamboo* tag), the plane's tail surfaces had rotted and the cushions had long since disappeared from the metal bucket seats. Some of the instruments had been removed, leaving holes on the dash, but several instruments and radios remained.

With an old book on flying tucked under my arm, I crawled into the Bamboo Bomber and began my flight training. Placing the book where I could read it, I moved the controls and taught myself to fly. I didn't spend one hour in the Bamboo Bomber...I didn't spend a hundred hours...I spent whole summers in the Bamboo Bomber. The Bamboo Bomber was *my* airplane.

Pilots and mechanics would see me going out to the plane and say, "Going for another flight lesson, Joe?"

"Yep," I would answer and tuck my flying book under my arm.

I figured out the ailerons and rudders, and I knew what the throttle was, but I was a little confused on the mixtures and the prop. It had two throttles, two mixtures, two props, and carburetor heat. Coordinating the movement of ten levers baffled me, but I read on in the book and flew on.

After a hard day of flying, I would talk my plane through one more flight. "OK now, let's go through this again. Set the brakes. Are the engines started and running? Now, advance the throttles. OK, I'm advancing the throttles." According to the book, I had to watch the airspeed. When it built up, I was supposed to pull up. When I thought the plane should be up, I cautioned myself, "Watch the airspeed. Careful of stall! Careful of stall!"

Habits are safer than rules; you don't have to watch them. And you don't have to keep them either. They keep you.[2]
—**FRANK CRANE, "ESSAYS"**

I wasn't getting off the ground yet, but the daily discipline of working the controls and following flight procedures established auto responses and prepared me for real flying later. During some stages of your spiritual life, you may feel that you're just going through the motions and not getting off the ground. The disciplines of prayer,

Bible study, and church attendance, however, will train you to stay the course when unexpected trials, temptations, or opportunities suddenly appear. A phrase from a song or a scripture (maybe one learned in childhood) will often guide your response and protect you from damage to or destruction of a God-given dream. Take time daily to tuck your Bible under your arm and find a place where you can go over the manual and the controls of your life with God.

ROAR RESPONSE 2

AS YOU RUN TO THE ROAR, GUARD THE DESIRES
OF YOUR HEART AND CALLS TO SERVICE.
KEEP THEM OUT OF THE LION'S REACH.

By age eight, I was spending every moment that I wasn't in school at the airport. That obsession with flying also led me into ungodly influences that nearly destroyed my life.

God plants desires in our hearts that He intends to make use of in later years. The great lion, Satan, though, constantly works to destroy or corrupt those desires. In the pursuit of dreams and calls of God you must, at every point, ask yourself, *Am I following the will of God or my own desires? Am I keeping this call to service in proper perspective? Are my choices dulling my relationship with God or destroying those whom I love?* You cannot leave a trail of bodies in the wake of your pursuit of a dream or a call to serve God.

Our idea of getting from point A to point B is a straight line. If God shows us where He wants us to go, we can take it from there. God, however, seems never to take a straight line to our goals. He leads us on detours, and on those side trails He often plants new desires in our hearts. Those desires may lie dormant, and we may struggle to find meaning for the detour. Then, like a surprise lily that springs up and blooms overnight, a new ministry or purpose for our life springs out of the needs we saw on the detour. In the late 1970s, my experiences as a first-responder to disaster victims appeared to be a ministry side trip. Several years later, relief ministries emerged as the primary focus of my ministry.

My introduction to relief ministries following a disaster came in 1979 when I was a missionary in Haiti. In the early months of my work in Haiti, I studied Creole, researched ways to "teach the people to fish" rather than rely on handouts, and assisted several mission organizations. Experience in radio and television enabled me to handle English language newscasts for Radio Lumiére in Port-au-Prince. Radio Lumiére, a ministry of World Team, did not have wire services, so I monitored newscasts on a series of very powerful short-wave radios.

In late August of 1979, I noticed that a tropical storm had formed to the east of us. It was steadily gaining strength as it worked its way across the Atlantic. The majority of storms track north, but this storm, now named *Hurricane David,* stayed in the low latitudes. I soon realized that, unless a very strong steering wind redirected David, it was coming our way. It had wiped out the tiny island of Dominica with 140-mph winds. Now, with winds exceeding 155 mph, it was classed as a Level 5 hurricane—the highest level of hurricanes.

Through the newscast, I kept the people updated on the storm track, which could hit Haiti. I felt like John the Baptist crying in the wilderness, "Prepare!" Instead of looking forward to salvation, though, the people were facing a hurricane of massive proportions. As I drove through business-as-usual Port-au-Prince, I cringed when I thought of what was going to happen if the storm hit. Tin roofs, held in place by rocks, would fly through the air like oversized razor blades, slicing people, animals, and property. Few people, however, seemed aware or concerned about the approaching storm.

Headed toward the island of Hispaniola, the storm appeared to bear down on Santo Domingo, the capital city of the Dominican Republic. While still abreast of Santo Domingo and about twenty-five miles off the coast, the storm veered sharply toward the coast and headed into San Cristobal, which lay on the coast just to the west of Santo Domingo.

Winds steady at 175 mph and gusting to over 200 mph heaped a tidal wave equivalent to a four-story building. The wave slammed into San Cristobal, killing twelve hundred people that night. From there, David charged up the middle of Hispaniola. Mountains ranging up to ten thousand feet helped disorganize the storm and reduce the winds to a little over 100 mph. Instead of dropping over the mountain into Port-au-Prince, the storm stayed on the eastern side of the mountain range and popped out on the north coast of Haiti. We had dodged the bullet this time, but the Dominican Republic had taken a direct hit.

Now I had grown up in Louisiana, and I had seen a lot of hurricane destruction. A number of serious hurricanes had come out of the Gulf of Mexico and traveled up the Mississippi River Valley. I remember as a child going outside and standing in the quiet of the eye of a hurricane after cowering through hours of howling, rain-slashing wind. I knew firsthand about the destruction of hurricane winds and tidal waves, but the news coming in from the Dominican Republic was horrifying even to me.

ROAR RESPONSE 3

THE ANSWER IS ALWAYS YES!

Being in the position of a news journalist, I received some of the earliest reports out of the Dominican Republic. The reports generated more than a desire to report breaking news. The stories from the Dominican Republic touched my heart in such a way that I felt I must do something to help the people.

Was this a *call* from God? I can't really say that it was a call, but it was a small and essential piece that would fit into the puzzle of my life at a later date. Christians often disagree over whether God calls people to a certain ministry and whether you must have a call to minister. The Bible is filled with stories of called people. Simply put, God called them to follow Him in obedience. God calls each of us to holy living and daily obedience to His correction and guidance. Our daily *yes* to God often prepares us to hear and respond to a more demanding and more specific call to service.

> **Our great danger may be to hold dogmatically to some "thing" associated with the divine plan for us. Every cup, however divinely appointed, should be held to very loosely. It is not that which claims us supremely, but the present will of our Father.[3]**
> —WATCHMAN NEE

When we sense God's direction to a specific ministry, is it a forever call to that one job? God calls some people to a one-time special project. Noah built an ark, and Mary bore Jesus. Others hear a call to many projects; David slew Goliath, ruled Israel, and left us many psalms. Abraham responded to a continual call to move and mark the boundaries of the Promised Land. No matter the length, breadth, or height of a call, we will only fulfill that call as we live in daily obedience to God.

As you can see, *the call* does not fit into a box. God calls each of us in His own way and for His own distinct purpose. We all are called to respond to God's leading—whether to bake a cherry pie for a sick neighbor, provide a shelter for the homeless in Cincinnati, or treat lepers in Africa.

How can you know if you are called by God to a ministry? Rather than trying to figure out if you are called to a ministry, move step by step as God leads and as He opens doors to you. Guard against shutting your mind to what God may be asking you to do. As you move forward in submission to God, you will sense God's peace. If it is a specific call from God, it will grow stronger and clearer.

My aviation career was in its first stages, and since I did not have a plane, I had to rely on commercial airlines to travel. Since Haiti shares the island of Hispaniola with the Dominican Republic, the airport in Port-au-Prince was both an escape route from the island and the means of reaching relatives in the Dominican Republic. On a normal day the airport was a madhouse. Following Hurricane David, all semblance of order disintegrated. It was no place for the timid. Seats on the airlines were given to people of importance and those able to take and hold a position at the check-in counter.

At 5 feet 10 inches and weighing less than 150 pounds, I wasn't going to force my way through the mobs to the front of the line, so I put together my "Important Person" package. I had a press card from a Christian writer's school, a card introducing me as an honorary citizen of Port-au-Prince, and documentation of my newscaster position with Radio Lumiére. To complete my "Important Person" package, I carried a small black-and-white video camera, which a supporter of my ministry had sent me. In the late 1970s, and especially in Haiti, video cameras were rare.

When I arrived at the airport, I slung my bag over my shoulder, hoisted the video camera to the side of my face with one hand, and waved my important papers with the other hand. I pressed through the crammed-full terminal calling out, "Press! Press! Press!"

No one noticed the press credentials. They saw the video camera and saw me as an *Important Person* who might put their faces on the news. A person-width seam opened before me, and soon I made my way to the reservation desk. It took talking and name dropping and flashing of credentials and every paper I could pull out of my wallet, but I managed to board a flight and land in Santo Domingo. Of course, Las Americas International in Santo Domingo was even more chaotic than François Duvalier International in Port-au-Prince.

By flashing the press card and keeping my camera on my shoulder, I was able to rent the last available car at the airport. From Las Americas, I drove the few kilometers into Santo Domingo. The city had been spared the brunt of the storm, but the hotels had no electricity or running water. Rates at the Hilton had been reduced, but only journalists had taken advantage of the prices.

ROAR RESPONSE 4

RECOGNIZE GOD'S HAND IN THE DETAILS. GOD OFTEN LAYS THE GROUNDWORK FOR A MINISTRY THROUGH OPENING SMALL DOORS.

Often small events take on greater significance when viewed from a distance. God is always viewing events in our lives as part of a larger purpose. To God, each event and circumstance is a vital part of the picture. From our limited perspective, some details are stray pieces carelessly tossed into the puzzle of our life. Unknown to me at this time, the Lord had orchestrated a phenomenal trip to the Dominican Republic that would unstop my ears and open my eyes to the needs of disaster victims. Each detail of the trip—a ticket to the Dominican Republic, a rental car, lodging at the Hilton, and meeting a top photojournalist—worked together to give me a close-up view of the intensity of a hurricane, the magnitude of the aftermath, and the resulting need for disaster assistance. Under ordinary circumstances these details would have been easy to arrange, but in the chaos following the hurricane, God surely had a hand in their arrangement.

Some of the top news and photojournalists in the industry were staying at the Hilton, and I listened intently to all the conversations around me. San Cristobal, where twelve hundred had died, was the main topic. In the buffet line, I struck up a conversation with Matt, a young journalist who wrote for the *New York Times.* Matt had a big shock of wild curly hair, was thin and gaunt, and looked every bit like the burrowing journalist. He knew how to find and penetrate the most sensitive and newsworthy aspect of an event.

"How can I get press clearance?" I asked. I knew that I would never get into the devastated area without proper authorization, and I wasn't about to flash my little bold-lettered PRESS card around these journalists.

"Do you know where I can rent a car?" Matt asked. He had his own concerns about getting a story and hadn't really heard my question.

"I got the last one," I said.

We loaded our plates and found a couple of empty chairs at a table. As the stories whirled around us, I was more intent than ever on getting to San Cristobal.

"Man!" I said. "If I just had clearance to get in."

"And if I just had a car," Matt said.

"I've got a car."

"I've got clearance."

"Let's go!" we both said, leaping to our feet.

San Cristobal was one of those little shantytowns that grow up on the edges of cities. People moving from the provinces had built shelters of scavenged materials to survive until they found employment in the city and saved enough to escape the hovels. During the hurricane, jagged sheets of tin roofing, secured only by loose rocks, had slipped their anchors and slashed through the streets like rust-edged scimitars. When we entered San Cristobal, it looked like photos of a war zone.

Ships lay beached among the shanties. Wind had stripped foliage from the trees, and the snapped trunks lay like broken matchsticks on the ground. Exposed bodies lay unattended. The elderly showed signs of fast physical deterioration. Children wandered the streets in a daze looking for parents that had been swept away by the four-story tidal wave.

The most unnerving aspect, though, was the sound, or, more precisely, the lack of noise. Although many people were milling about, shock had silenced the buzz of boisterous conversation that always fills Caribbean markets and gatherings. As we moved through the carnage, two sounds emphasized the horror of the scene—the low, raspy wail of children and the constant *chchung, chchung, chchung* of

Matt's camera as it documented the devastation for the rest of the world.

As a father of young children, the distress of the children especially moved me. I wondered, *Where would you start to recover, to pull your life back together, after such devastation? Prayer might give a sense of calmness, but prayer didn't fill a growling stomach or shelter you from the rain.*

Normally, a basic shelter of palm branches and wide banana leaves could be erected in a few hours. The palm and banana fronds, though, had been twisted and shredded into thin streamers that offered no protection from the ever-returning rains.

Some people were tying sheets to poles, fashioning shelters from the searing September sun. No shelter, though, could protect the people from the ravenous hordes of mosquitoes that made life miserable even for Matt and me. The smell of putrid meat frying in rancid oil was nauseating, but children and adults squatted around the cooking pots waiting for a morsel of food.

Many shacks had been built away from the beach and up a hillside. A handful had survived. As I scanned the hillside, I saw people standing on the edge of one roof collecting water in buckets. Curious about the source of the water pouring off the roof, I walked toward the hillside. Matt followed, his camera never pausing in its *chchung* documentation of the scene.

The people had found a stream up the hillside. They had poked a piece of galvanized roofing into the stream and directed the stream down a series of dilapidated roofs to an accessible place. A huge crowd of people, all with buckets, stood waiting their turn for the most basic of all needs—water. The people of San Cristobal were starting over, beginning with the basics—water, food, and shelter.

ROAR RESPONSE 5

WALK IN THE MOMENT. NEVER FEAR WHERE GOD MAY LEAD YOU TOMORROW.

It was the indomitable spirit of the victims of the hurricane in San Cristobal and their ingenious ways of surviving and going on with life that fired a deep determination within me to help people who have been victims of devastating circumstances. As a Christian, I could never again tell hurricane victims, "I wish you well; keep warm and well fed," and do nothing about their physical needs. The sense of personal responsibility began to weigh heavily on me. Was this a call from God to devote my life to first-response ministry following disasters? Sometimes it's hard to separate God's voice from our own emotions, especially in traumatic situations. On that trip to the Dominican Republic, however, I gave no thought to a *call* to relief ministry. I focused on doing the job at hand.

After viewing San Cristobal, Matt and I got back on the road and drove deeper into the countryside. We followed the storm path as it turned north and slightly westward, then bounced along the mountains through a ragged valley. I determined in my mind to return and bring assistance. Haiti was poor, but somewhere in either Haiti or the United States, I would find help for these people. At one remote mountain village, I spoke to a Catholic priest and filmed footage with my little video camera. I couldn't portray the suffering, but I needed something to try to communicate the need to donors.

"I am going to bring help to you," I promised. "I won't forget you and your people."

I left the Dominican Republic with determination to run to the roar—to find a way to help the villagers that I had met. Two events, however, would prevent me from keeping that promise.

ROAR RESPONSE 6
SOMETIMES YOU HAVE TO ACCEPT A CLOSED DOOR.

Matt wanted to do a story on Port-au-Prince, so he came back to Haiti with me and stayed in our home a couple days. During the next two days I assisted Matt, delivered my newscasts at Radio Lumiére, and tried to find donors for relief supplies.

Since Radio Lumiére had no wire services, Matt went to the U.S. embassy to find the latest news. When he came back to our home, he said, "Joe, it doesn't look good. There's another tropical storm following the path of David, and it looks like it's going to turn into a hurricane."

**In his heart a man plans his course, but
the LORD determines his steps.**
—PROVERBS 16:9

Again, I broadcast the warning that a hurricane might be headed
our way. Strangely, *Frederic*, as it came to be called, wasn't following
the rules of meteorology. A high-pressure area usually trails and
dominates an area after a storm passes through. Following David,
however, a low trough remained in place. Now Frederic was barrel-
ing down that track.

As Frederic passed through the Lesser Antilles, the winds eased.
Alternating between a tropical storm with 45-mph winds and a
tropical depression of 30-mph winds, Frederic spent a couple days
off the coast of Hispaniola gorging itself on seawater. Then the
storm rolled up the mountains of the southern peninsula of Haiti
and spewed its water load.

Haiti, shaped like a right hand forming a backward C, has mountains climbing to over eight thousand feet. Using the hand imagery,
the south peninsula has a mountain range that extends from the
base of the hand to the end of the thumb.

When Frederic loped over the peninsula, it dumped nearly twenty
inches of rain. The deluge, starting at the mountain spine, gushed
down the slopes. Unchecked by water management or storm drain-
age ditches, the amassing water flow ripped down the slopes
uprooting crops and the few remaining trees. It swept hovels, goats,
chickens, and people toward the sea. Survivors were left without
food, shelter, or any means of providing for themselves. It would
take many weeks, even months, to grow food for their families.

As the reports of devastation filtered back to Radio Lumiére, the
statistics became a blur to me. I entered a personal storm that almost
took my life. Trying desperately to gather donations and keep on top
of news, I seemed to be fighting the flu. I started vomiting, and I had
diarrhea and a horrendous headache. Then the fever came. This was
unlike any flu, fever, or headache I had ever experienced. The doctor
diagnosed possible cerebral malaria. Life expectancy for sufferers of
cerebral malaria is measured in hours. My temperature rocketed to
106.9 degrees, and I was completely out of my mind, a wild person. In a
desperate move to save my life, medics gave me an eight-week dosage

of Aralen at one time. Cardiac arrest and temporary blindness followed, but the medics revived me, the fever broke, and I survived.

To me, the enormous need in the Dominican Republic was a call
from God to serve those hurricane victims. But God tells us, "My
thoughts are not your thoughts, neither are your ways my ways" (Isa.
55:8). Sometimes God builds a delay into our plans. When Joshua was
a young man, he heard God's call to "possess the land," but the even-
tual fulfillment of that call came after a forty-year wilderness experience. Joshua was ready, but he had to wait until God dealt with the
sins of his compatriots. Joshua could have grown bitter and blamed
others for the delay. Instead he did the task at hand and became an
aide to Moses. God used those years to train Joshua to take Moses'
place.

No matter how strong the call to service, move in the presence
and timing of the Lord. And as you wait, continue to do the work at
hand, knowing that in the lesser obediences God is preparing you to
fulfill the greater call.

ROAR RESPONSE 7

SET ASIDE REGRETS OVER NOT REACHING A
SELECTED GOAL. LISTEN TO THE CRIES ALONGSIDE
YOUR PATH. RESPONSE TO THESE CRIES WILL
PREPARE YOU FOR A GREATER WORK AHEAD.

I came out of the illness with only 114 pounds on my 5 foot 10 inch
frame. I was weak and downright scrawny. My promise to help the
people in the Dominican Republic haunted me, but I saw no possible
way to return. I was simply too weak to attempt the trip. Furthermore, Haiti was suffering. No one would give aid to the Dominicans
when Haitians needed it just as badly.

Two weeks after Frederic came through the Caribbean, a missionary from the southern peninsula, Beth Weaver, met with the
staff of Radio Lumiére. She had just come from the village of Dame
Marie. Their village had been hit hard, but a place beyond them had
been hit harder. All the food, livestock, crops, and homes had been
swept away. Swollen rivers and impassable roads had isolated the
people from assistance.

According to Beth, the mothers had walked to Dame Marie and were begging food for their starving children. Beth and her husband, Jay, had given away their food and had nothing left to offer. Beth had awakened at 3:00 a.m. to the sound of weak scratching at the door. When she stepped outside, she saw bloody fingerprints on the door. Mothers had been scratching on the door, hoping to find food for their little ones.

Beth's story ripped my heart. I cried out to God, "There has to be a way to find some help." I had fifty dollars, but I needed a lot more to buy food for a village.

That evening I attended a crusade in the soccer stadium. A prominent American evangelist had come to Port-au-Prince and booked the stadium for a special service. Since the church that supported my ministry also supported the evangelist, I attended the service and sat on the platform. Nearly fifty thousand people turned out, filling the stadium and the field. As I sat on the platform with the evangelist, though, my mind was more focused on how I could turn fifty dollars into a truckload of food than on the service in progress.

Rather than focusing on salvation, the evangelist preached on "give, and it shall be given unto you" (Luke 6:38, KJV). To a culture that had grown accustomed to handouts, the message on tithing and giving to God didn't seem to apply. He continued, though, telling the Haitians that giving to the Lord would produce a harvest.

Then the evangelist did something unbelievable. He took an offering.

While the offering was being taken, the evangelist turned to me and said, "Have you given your best, Joe?" Although I concurred with his teaching that the Haitian people should tithe and give to support their own ministries, this wasn't the night that I wanted to be an example for the people.

I opened my wallet. All I had was the single fifty-dollar bill. I pulled it out and gave it to him, but I didn't go home feeling blessed. I felt heartbroken that I had nothing with which to buy food for the little mothers beyond Dame Marie.

Back home that night, the phone rang. A caller in California said, "I heard about your mission, and God has spoken to me to give you two thousand dollars. We have wired it to your account. You can write a check on it anytime."

When I had recovered enough to speak, I said, "I know exactly what I'm going to do with the money. I'm buying food for some little mothers who have been praying and trying desperately to get food for their children."

When I had handed the fifty-dollar bill to the evangelist, I had surrendered my means of providing food for the mothers. God's provision of two thousand dollars confirmed that He was the source of my call to service, and He would be the resource for its fulfillment.

Although I was still weak and fighting dysentery symptoms, I set out to deliver food to the mothers. No matter how sincere my promise to help the priest and his people in the Dominican Republic, I knew that I wasn't going to be able to keep that promise. That failure made carrying out this mission even more important.

I bought two thousand dollar's worth of staples—rice, powdered milk, oil, soap, and a few other items. My car could never hold the food or make the trip, so I went to a friend who had a brand-new red Daihatsu dump truck. It had seventy kilometers on the odometer. When I told him I needed it to take food to some starving people, he said, "Sure. Take it." I loaded the food and supplies and my five-year-old son Stephen into the truck, and we took off for Dame Marie. With God's miraculous supply of funds for the food, I felt confident of His continued blessing on my relief ministry.

Little did I know that a pride of ferocious lions lay on the road ahead.

After twenty-six hours of driving on roads and scraps of roads, Stephen and I came to the Grande Anse. Still swollen by the rains, the three-hundred-yard-wide river raged out to sea. Maybe some malaria parasites still clung to my brain, but I decided no flooded river would keep me from making this delivery.

I eased the truck into the water, and as we progressed, the truck began to float downstream toward the ocean. Out of nowhere about fifty people appeared, waded into the river, and stopped the truck from drifting farther. With their assistance, I was able to make the other shore.

The road on the other side of the river climbed out into a rockslide, then a mudslide. Already terrifyingly narrow, the roads were now hardly more than a widened goat trail along the mountainside. Making sure that Stephen was still locked securely into his

seat belt, we slithered, slid, and jolted our way to Dame Marie where
we met Beth's husband, Jay, who would go with us to the isolated
village.

Jay and I bore a "Mutt and Jeff" contrast in appearance. Jay, with
a full beard and strong physique, was a little over six feet tall, and
I, with my 1970s' version of bushy mustache and sideburns, hardly
cast a shadow on a bright afternoon.

When we got to Li Let, a village about seven kilometers from our
destination, we ran out of road. Li Let was a little fishing village
right on the ocean. Dugouts were pulled up on the beach, and nets
and drying fish lay about the beach and on thatched lean-tos. Six-
foot high mounds of faded conch shells littered the beach.

What was once a little stream that flowed to the sea and provided fresh water for the village of Li Let was now a ten-foot-deep
gorge cutting through the road.

Jay and I stopped and got out to look at the deep river gorge and
the silt buildup at the mouth of the stream. In the background,
drums beat softly. Someone was getting ready for the evening
voodoo gathering.

"Joe," Jay said, "I don't think there's any way to keep going." The
banks of the deep gorge were sandy and crumbled, eliminating any
possibility of building a temporary bridge. Deep silt had piled up at
the mouth of the stream and extended into the ocean.

ROAR RESPONSE 8

A "BURNING HEART" CALL WILL EMBOLDEN
YOU TO RUN TO THE ROAR.

There are times when the call—that inexplicable God-given call to
serve—is the driving force that makes us go on. Jeremiah called it "a
fire shut up in my bones" (Jer. 20:9). He wanted to keep quiet, but the
Word of God was burning in his heart, and he got tired of holding
it in. This type of call is an inescapable burden to forge ahead, even
if you have no assurance of success. Yes, you hear the roar clearly.
You are not ignoring it. Maybe you will fail. Maybe your efforts will
appear foolish to others, but the call to follow God in obedience is
louder than the roar of defeat. Paul called it a "Woe-to-me-if-I-don't-
follow-the-roar" call. (See 1 Corinthians 9:16.)

I looked at the gorge and the silt, and I thought of the people in the Dominican Republic and the women's bloody handprints on the door of Beth's house. I was seven kilometers from my destination. I had been through rock slides and mud slides, and I had been washed down two rivers. I might not keep my promise to the people in the Dominican Republic, but I was going to finish this mission. There had to be a way to cross this gorge.

Since few vehicles passed this way, the head of the village came to investigate us. Unlike most Haitian men, the leader of the village was a huge man. Weighing about 200 pounds, his skin was so dark that his features were almost indiscernible. Only his eyes, burning, a fire-engine red, let you know there was a man inside the powerful body. When I looked at his eyes, I saw rattlesnake meanness. A half-dozen men, muscled by rowing and pulling nets, surrounded him, mimicking his nastiness. We had dropped into a nest of bullies.

I walked up the beach from the silt buildup. The sand was blackened by silt, but it seemed solid enough to drive the truck across.

The village head watched me, and when I came back to him, he said, "On one other occasion the river formed a silt buildup like this. A Land Rover backed up and went real fast and went over the silt buildup." I still didn't know a lot of Creole, so I asked Jay to interpret for me to make sure I had heard him right.

One part of my brain said, "This isn't going to work. This is ridiculous." However, the malaria-impaired part of my brain said, "I'm forty hours into this trip and two weeks off my deathbed. I'm scrawny, weak, and stinking, but I've come this far. I'm not letting a gorge stop me now."

I backed that truck up and flew down that beach like a banshee. When we hit the silt buildup, the truck sank until the chassis was beneath the waves and the water was coming in the floor of the new red Daihatsu. We were sunk, sunk, sunk beyond words.

The head of the village sauntered up. He crossed his arms and with a wide grin said, "Give us the food, and we'll get you out." I had the fleeting impression that I had been set up.

By this time nothing was going to stop me from delivering the food to the little mothers. I was a man with a mission. "I would love to give you food," I said, "but I've got to get it to the next village."

"Well, we aren't going to help you."

I pushed on the back of the truck and the front went deeper into the mud. I pushed on the front, and the back went down. The new Daihatsu kept sinking deeper and deeper. When the tide turned, the water would probably submerge the truck.

By now, the whole town had gathered to watch us try to get the truck out. My only hope was the appearance of another vehicle that could pull us out.

"When did the last vehicle come through here?" I asked the leader.

"Oh, couple weeks ago."

Water lapped at the food, so Jay and I unloaded everything on the beach, and Stephen sat on the mound of supplies. I asked the people for planks to put under the wheels, but they ignored our request. "Give us the food, and we'll help you," was their only response.

The afternoon sun had dropped behind the mountains, and, as the shadows lengthened, the drums throbbed louder. I glanced over at Stephen and saw that some of the men who hung with the bully were slapping and punching my son. He was bravely wiping blood from his nose with his arm. I rescued Stephen, kissed him on the forehead, and locked him in the truck with the keys inside.

Stephen had tried to protect the food, but the people had dragged off several 100-pound bags of rice and flour. "This food is for others," I yelled at them.

"We need this food. We're hungry, too," the leader answered.

"I'll bring you food another time." The people in Li Let were no doubt hungry, but they had not been isolated and weren't starving as the people in the next village were.

"We want *this* food," the leader said firmly, as he slapped a big bare foot on one of the bags of rice.

The scene was deteriorating rapidly. At the most, we probably had twenty minutes until the people took all the food.

When I rejoined Jay, he said quietly, "I just heard them talking. They say at sunset they are going to kill us."

I didn't know of any way to get the truck out, but I refused to stop trying. "Sit on the food, Jay," I said. "Try to make sure we have a little to take if we ever get out of here."

Jay sat on the food, and, as the sun set, I kept trying to dislodge the truck from the silt bed.

God often allows us to exhaust our resources and get ourselves in desperate situations so that He can reveal His power to us. When we are giving our best, and suffering and defying the odds and filling our minds with positive affirmations, we don't like to admit that we just can't follow through on some dreams and accomplish all that we desire, much less what God desires. Whether I wanted to face the truth or not, it stared me in the face—we couldn't dislodge the truck, we couldn't hold the food much longer, and we had no means of escape if the crowd turned violent.

The quick tropical darkness fell, and, along with the thumping drums, I heard the growl. Some think that voodoo is a benign religion, but my encounters with it have not been pleasant. Motivated by gods that condone gaining material goods and power over others, a Haitian mob seems to take on a spirit of its own and exhibit a power that is more than the sum of its components. The growl that emanates from one of these violent mobs will convince almost anyone that there is a hell and demons. I heard the growl and looked over at Jay who was about thirty yards away.

I saw Jay stand, and then I saw Jay go down. I thought, *My God, they have just hit him.*

Maybe it was God's power or maybe it was the malaria parasites, but something came over me. I took off, and you could just about hear me tick, tick, tick across the water and mud. I screamed, "Jesus!" at the top of my lungs. They had Jay on the ground and one of the steel-armed fishermen was starting to pound Jay's head into the sand.

All puny 114 pounds of my body came over the top of the food. I came right up under the bully with the palm of my hand and connected with his forehead, all the while screaming, "Jesus!"

The power in that blow lifted the nearly 200 pounds of solid muscle and mean snarling spirit straight into the air and dropped him on the ground so hard that the wind was knocked out of him. He lay paralyzed on the hard sand.

I turned my hand over, looked at it, and said, *Whew!*, but there was no time to figure out how I had stopped the man. Six of his cronies were descending on us. All I had for protection was my hand. I charged them, one by one, connecting the palm of my hand with their heads and yelling "Jesus." Each one dropped to the ground, paralyzed.

Jay got to his feet, and I said, "Interpret for me! I'm gonna preach to these people."

Jay was speechless. "Go on," I said. "First, tell them to get that food back here right now."

"Tout moun toune manje kouyéa," Jay said. To me he said, "Go ahead and preach."

I climbed up on what food was left and said, "Look at me." I smacked the chest of my thin body. "Look at me! Do you think I did that?" I pointed to the seven men still stretched out on the sand. "Who do you think did that?" I asked.

The people gasped, *"Bon Dieu."*

"You're right. God did it." I preached like a crazy man. After about fifteen minutes, the town leader sat up and slowly stood. In the sand was a perfect outline of his body, including the crinkles of his hair. It looked to me like a 400-pound angel had knocked him down and sat on him. One by one, the six others stood up and, like little lambs, listened to me preach. At the end, I told them, "I know that you need food, too. I promise you that I will be back and bring you food, but this food is not for you. It's for that village across the gorge."

We still had to get the truck out before the tide turned. A light seemed to turn on in my tired brain. We had a little hydraulic bottle jack, and I was sure that if we had planks we could get the truck out.

"Bring me some planks and help me get this truck out of here!" I said. I think they tore planks from the sides of their houses because they started toting planks from everywhere. You could hear the boards being dragged through the undergrowth, and I soon had all that I needed.

I went back to the truck but couldn't get inside. Stephen had fallen asleep. I was thankful that God had given him such peace that he had fallen asleep, but I couldn't awaken him. Soon the whole village was yelling, "Stephen! Stephen!" and jostling the truck. They finally shook the cab hard enough to roll him from the seat and awaken him. Sleepily he opened the window and handed me the keys.

Through digging under the wheels, jacking the vehicle to take pressure off the tires, and sliding in planks, Jay and I were able to get the truck out in a short time. When we reloaded the truck it was obvious that a lot of the food was missing.

"Bring the rest of the food back," I told the people.

They brought back every 100-pound bag of flour, every 100-pound sack of beans, every box of macaroni, and even the boxes of candy. They knew God had visited their village and that a miracle had taken place.

After seven more jolting kilometers we rolled into the little village and delivered food to the mothers. I hadn't been able to keep my promise to the people in the Dominican Republic, but I had successfully completed this mission.

◆ ◆ ◆

As I had moved further into lion territory, I had met many lions—lack of funds, lingering malaria symptoms, flooded rivers, blocked roads, and bullying thieves. On the road, the lions had roared and even attacked. The cry of desperate mothers, however, had drowned the lions' voices. As you move deeper into lion territory you will hear both the lion and the call for help. Through Hurricanes David and Frederic, God unstopped my ears and enabled me to hear the cry of disaster victims.

Do you hear the roar?

Impossible! Don't come here! Turn back! It's not your problem.

Do you hear the call to run to the roar?

Help me. I'm spiritually destitute. I'm oppressed. I'm hungry. I hurt. I'm sick. My children are crying. My children are dying.

Which voice is louder? The lion roar or the Macedonian call of "Come over...and help us" (Acts 16:9)? What God-planted desires are you stifling? Could they be cultivated and used to bring hope to those who cry for help? What needs lie along your path today? Start doing the job at hand, and keep your heart and mind open to God's leading.

CHAPTER 3

THE ULTIMATE GUIDE

TRUST YOUR GUIDE TIP 1

MAKE SURE THAT YOU TRAVEL WITH AN EXPERIENCED, RELIABLE GUIDE.

SOMETIMES PEOPLE TAKE a couple of trips into a foreign country and then decide that they have enough guide experience to organize and direct tour groups. These guides can usually attract travelers looking for a bargain tour, and as long as the tour runs smoothly, everyone is happy. If a problem arises, however, the guide's lack of expertise and lack of understanding of the culture can turn the trip into a nightmare. Savvy travelers to the habitats of dangerous wild game will check the credentials of the hired guide. These travelers recognize the inherent danger of the territory and the necessity of having a qualified guide who can handle the unexpected.

In today's multicultural environment, a sincere believer can follow a charismatic guide or in-vogue belief and get into serious spiritual confusion. These budget guides accept all beliefs and philosophies as legal tender. The traveler may enjoy this cheap spirituality for a while, but when they encounter problems, they soon realize they have an incompetent guide.

Christ is the only reliable Guide. He proclaims, "I am the way" (John 14:6). His experiences in lion territory are not based on a couple vacations on Earth and a memorization of Fodor's travel book. Christ lived in lion territory, and He faced the same lions that you will face. His credentials are inked in blood. Furthermore, He triumphed in great warrior style by crushing the head of the Satan-lion.

What does it cost to engage this triumphant Guide? His guidance is a gift. God gave us His Son, but you will soon discover walking with Him isn't a casual saunter down a country lane. This Guide will begin to strip you of hindrances to your walk, and then give you a cross to lug down the path. The romantic, adventure image of lion territory begins to fade as you consider the dangers of lion territory and the cost of engaging the only reliable Guide. The rewards of reaching those who cry for our help, however, far outweigh the personal cost. The apostle Paul said, "I consider everything a loss compared to the surpassing greatness of knowing Christ Jesus my Lord, for whose sake I have lost all things. I consider them rubbish" (Phil. 3:8). Paul, looking at the distant reward rather than the lions, said, "For our light and momentary troubles are achieving for us an eternal glory that far outweighs them all" (2 Cor. 4:17).

On your spiritual trek in Lion Country, make sure that you follow the Guide who has walked the trails and engaged the great Satan-lion and his pride of lesser lions. When you meet the lions, you will be glad you did not engage a discount Guide.

TRUST YOUR GUIDE TIP 2

TRUST THE JUDGMENT AND ACTIONS OF YOUR GUIDE.
HE KNOWS ABOUT DANGERS THAT YOU DON'T SEE.

Following the showing of the *JESUS* film that night in Africa, I discovered the importance of traveling through wild animal country with a seasoned guide. As we left the village, I felt excitement rather than fear of meeting a man-eating lion. After having heard about Maritz's exploits, I believed that our African King David could deal with lions or any other danger that we might encounter that night. According to the accounts we had heard, Maritz had served with the Rhodesian secret police during the struggle for independence. The rebel force had branded Maritz as their number one enemy and had set out to kill him.

Eventually the rebels found out Maritz's travel itinerary and set an ambush to kill him. Maritz, however, had been hospitalized and had sent his father to the rendezvous. His father was murdered; the rebels shot one bullet into the older man for every rebel Maritz reportedly had slain. His father's body was riddled with nearly one hundred holes.

When news of his father's death reached Maritz in the hospital, he went berserk, and medical personnel had to restrain him. Somehow, the Spirit of God cut through the agony, anger, and horror of that experience and touched Maritz's heart. That night Maritz confessed his sins to Christ and surrendered his life to God's authority. He had gone on to become a Christian who was respected by both loyalists and rebels. Wherever we had traveled, everyone had greeted Maritz with affection and appreciation. While Christianity had tempered his fierce warrior nature, he still possessed a champion spirit that defied any man or beast that threatened those left in his care. I figured Maritz could keep us safe that night.

The Land Rover's electrical system seemed on the edge of failure at all times. The headlights, already knocked cockeyed by some charging beast, flickered and dimmed. Although Maritz seldom drove over fifty kilometers an hour, it would be easy to overrun the headlight beams. About thirty minutes away from the village, we were making good time but running a little blind on some turns because of the faulty lights. Since our flickering beams and the stars were the only lights for nearly fifty kilometers, we could spot any approaching vehicle well in advance.

I was beginning to relax a little, and my mind wandered to biblical conjecture. *The sky must have looked this way to Abraham. Surely this black-purple, velvet sky was how God had intended to display the stars. When God promised Abraham that his descendents would be as numerous as the stars, the sky must have sparkled just like this. Too bad man had to…*

Whump!!

We all lunged forward as Maritz yanked the wheel to the right and braked hard. The Land Rover stopped as if it had hit a four-foot-wide oak tree. In our headlights, a Cape buffalo staggered off the road.

We had been in a blind turn and slowed to about thirty kilometers when the buffalo, having heard the sound of our *tap-tapping* engine, had run across the road. Maritz had locked up the brakes and veered to the right, but still had clipped the Cape buffalo with our left front fender. With no time to push in the clutch, the Land Rover engine had died instantly. The impact of the collision had crushed the fender onto the tire; Maritz could not turn the steering wheel back to the left, and the wheel would not roll.

"I don't think he's hurt too badly," one of the pilots said about the buffalo. "Probably has a big bruise. We were only doing about thirty when we hit." Suddenly, several Cape buffaloes came pounding through the darkness and *whooshed* by on both sides of the Land Rover. The wounded animal fell in behind. Dust and bovine odors lingered in the air.

"Did you see those horns?"

"I could smell his breath!"

We were exhilarated by the unexpected close encounter with wild beasts that we had only seen on *National Geographic* programs. We hadn't seen a lion, but the evening was providing a truly African adventure.

Maritz was frantically trying to start the engine. "Come on, baby! Come on, baby!" he was saying to the Land Rover. The engine emitted only a *whomp, whomp, whomp* sound.

Maritz seemed stressed. His frantic efforts to restart the engine surprised us. Maritz, though, knew things about Cape buffaloes that we didn't know. He knew that Cape buffaloes had killed more unsuspecting hunters than lions or other wild African beasts. He also knew that the buffaloes had not really gone away.

"Come on, baby, start!" *Whomp! Whomp! Whomp! Whomp!* The engine, having stopped in an unconventional manner that abruptly halted the transmission, drive shaft, and wheels, now refused to restart.

While we in the back continued with our animated descriptions of the buffaloes, Maritz's voice grew louder and more strident. "Start! Start! Start!" he yelled.

Finally the engine caught. Maritz grabbed the steering wheel, put the Rover in gear, and let out the clutch. Due to the collapsed fender, the wheel was jammed to the right, and he could only move the vehicle in a tight right turn.

"Come on!" Maritz yelled to the Land Rover.

We sat staring at the panicked warrior, big-game safari guide. *Why not get out, hammer out the fender, and go on our way?*

With superhuman strength, Maritz seized the steering wheel and cranked the wheel hard left, pushing the fender out. Gaining a little leeway, he inched forward. The fender, pressing on the wheel, made a screeching, grinding sound, and the steering wheel jerked out of Maritz's hands.

Then we heard the muffled drumming that intensified to the recognizable sound of pounding hoofbeats. It was like a scene from *Jurassic Park*. The earth pulsed, and a galloping rumble filled the air as the returning herd approached.

The Cape buffaloes had reacted just as Maritz knew they would. Galloping off as though in retreat, the nearly one-ton animals had made a wide arc and circled back for the kill. Moving at speeds up to sixty-five kilometers an hour, the solidly built buffaloes would use their bodies as weapons. When they attacked the Land Rover, it would be like a fleet of pickup trucks hitting us.

Maritz, knowing that the buffaloes would gore and batter us to death, was screaming, "Jesus!" to the heavens and "Come on!" to the Land Rover.

We newcomers to Africa looked back to see over fifteen thousand pounds of angry, enraged, killer animals emerge in the starlight. They were on a direct course for the rear of the Land Rover.

Closing in and coming toward me at top speed was a mature Cape buffalo with yard-span horns. I tobogganed my body to the floor, and at the same split second, Maritz raced the engine, popped the clutch, and the Land Rover lurched forward.

The horns of the buffalo passed over the top of the seat I had just left, and I heard the animal's gasping breath as it missed the kill.

Maritz's last-instant lunging start had saved us from their focused charge. Before the buffaloes could regroup and make another pass, Maritz had the squalling Land Rover moving.

Gradually the Land Rover picked up enough speed to outrun any returning buffaloes. When it was apparent that we had escaped, Maritz yelled, "Hallelujah!"

After driving for about a mile, Maritz stopped, got out, and took a tire iron to the fender. A tie rod and the front-end steering assembly had been damaged, but we were able to continue our journey. When we arrived at our hotel at 2:30 a.m., we were still recounting the buffalo encounter.

We escaped harm that night because we had a seasoned guide with us. In your spiritual immaturity and ignorance, you may view some experiences as great opportunities or adventures, while your Guide sees mounting danger that can destroy your spiritual life. You may not sense the danger, but God does, and He will often move to extricate you from the situation and circumstances. You may not understand His methods of delivery, but He knows how to get you to a safe place. When you choose to walk with Christ, you walk with a faithful, trustworthy Guide.

TRUST YOUR GUIDE TIP 3

DON'T PANIC IF YOU CAN'T SEE THE GUIDE OR HE DOESN'T IMMEDIATELY ANSWER YOUR CALL FOR HELP. HE HAS HIS EYES ON YOU. HE WILL NEVER ABANDON YOU.

You may choose to travel through lion country on an air-conditioned safari bus, sipping lemonade and viewing distant lions through binoculars or a camera lens. But *running to the roar* requires action—it requires getting off the bus. Some friends and associates may cheer you on and express admiration for you as you take those first tenuous steps into the unknown, but others will mutter, "Big mistake." Rarely will anyone else step off the bus with you.

When the bus pulls away and your security disappears in a cloud of dust, you will soon realize that you are standing there all alone in dangerous territory. Suddenly all the enthusiasm you felt as you stepped off that bus gives way to increasing doubt and uneasiness about your decision.

Not only does venturing for God involve separation from security, but it also brings a separation from the familiar. Most of us can handle change if our security base remains intact or if we are still in the midst of familiar faces and surroundings. But when we step into unfamiliar lion territory where all the security we were provided in the past is gone, our bravado wavers.

When God calls you out of the bus, it may seem like a great idea—at first. But when the high grasses of the unknown begin to rake over your skin…when you scan the horizon for a scraggly tree to break the intensity of the sun…when the tepid water in your canteen runs low and you are parched and dry, you may start to ask yourself, *Was it really God who called me, or did I just use poor judgment when I left the safety of the familiar?*

Standing there in the middle of those danger-laden grasses, you have no idea how to forge a path to wherever it is God wants you to go. You may even begin to question the reliability of your Guide. Or maybe you wonder if you have what it takes to be able to understand and follow His directions. You thought you heard His clarion call, "Run to the roar," but right now you are filled with terror at the imagined cough of a distant lion. And the enemy of your soul—Satan himself—whispers in your ear, "Ah ha! You made a wrong turn. Now you're mine!" You call out for guidance, but God seems beyond hearing distance. Did you mistake His direction at that last branch in the path? Is He so far away that He will never hear your cry?

> **It is by no means enough to set out cheerfully with your God on any venture of faith. Tear into smallest pieces any itinerary for the journey which your imagination may have drawn up. Nothing will fall out as you expect. Your guide will keep to no beaten paths. he will lead you by a way such as you never dreamed your eyes would look upon. He knows no fear, and He expects you to fear nothing while He is with you.[1]**
> **—STREAMS IN THE DESERT**

In this chapter we are going to consider how to handle one of those first lions that we meet. Moses, a veteran lion fighter, told the Israelites that they would soon face adversaries in the Promised Land. He admonished them, "Be strong and courageous. Do not be afraid or terrified because of them, for the LORD your God goes with you; he will never leave you nor forsake you" (Deut. 31:6).

Getting off the bus will involve some separation. God may move you into a different group of friends and from one lifestyle to a completely different one. Physical distance may separate you from family and friends. However, when you step out of the bus and enter lion territory, you never travel alone—God goes with you.

Abraham left a modern city to travel as a nomad across the Promised Land. David left the pastures to play music in Saul's palace. Following God's rejection of Saul, Samuel anointed David as the next king of Israel (1 Sam. 16). Soon after David's anointing, Saul, tormented by an evil spirit, asked David to come to the palace and play soothing harp music to make him feel better. At first glance, it seemed that David's position as palace musician was a shortcut to the throne. Instead of being crowned, though, David found himself dodging spears. Instead of a shortcut, David came face-to-face with the dangerous lion of Saul's jealousy.

So stepping off the comfort of your safari bus may thrust you face-to-face with a lion. If you fail to remember that your Guide will never abandon you, instead of running to the roar as God has called you to do, you may find yourself cowering in fear as the enemy clears his throat and licks his chops.

◆ ◆ ◆

I have had quite a few opportunities to learn this important principle in my own life as I have learned to follow God's call to run to the roar. One of the first lion encounters came when I got off the safari bus in Haiti. After visiting the country and seeing the immense physical and spiritual needs, I felt God was leading me to minister in that country. I resigned from an executive position that had provided a comfortable middle-income salary, sold my Louisiana home, and took my wife and our three children, ages five years, two and one-half years, and nine months, to Haiti.

I certainly did not go to Haiti to bask in the tropical sun. Our home was in Carrefour, close to the Port-au-Prince Bay and notorious for traffic congestion. The louvered windows and doors in our house were protected by steel security bars. Built to catch the slightest breeze, the louvers were never closed. The din of roaring trucks and blaring horns and the stench of raw sewage drifted through our house day and night. In spite of the unfamiliar living conditions, we were happy. We had the security of a home, a good vehicle, and a developing ministry. I felt that I was following God, and He would care for us and provide for our needs.

One night, though, a rattle at the gate swept away a hunk of my security. I opened the gates to a Haitian police officer who said, "We've come to get the car."

"What?" I had no idea what he meant.

He pointed to the Suburban parked inside the gates and said, "You have Pastor Jean's car, and we have come to take it to him."

"This is my vehicle," I said. "My church in Louisiana bought this for me and shipped it here. This isn't Pastor Jean's."

"We have papers saying that it is Pastor Jean's car." One of the officers extended the title to me and pointed out Pastor Jean's name.

"But we put it in his name to get it through customs easier," I said. "It isn't his. It's mine."

"According to Haitian law, the car belongs to Pastor Jean. Give us the keys, or else we'll have to arrest you."

In a moment of sudden clarity, I realized that the pastor had set me up. The details of the arrangement came rushing back to my mind. I had eagerly accepted the pastor's kind offer to help me get the vehicle into Haiti, but he had been laying the groundwork to seize the vehicle from the start.

Reluctantly, I handed the officer the keys to the Suburban. I knew that I would never see the vehicle again. The pastor had orchestrated a perfectly legal way to get the Suburban.

Since I had no money to buy a car, I had to use public transportation, provided for the most part by *camions,* or *tap-taps.* Riding a tap-tap often meant sharing space with live chickens and goats. I could handle banking and going to the airport to get our mail, but bringing home bottled water and groceries for a family was difficult. An outing with my wife and three small children was simply impossible. The loss of the Suburban also prevented me from continuing my ministry in Haiti. As I struggled to meet the basic needs of my family, I wondered, *If I have no means of ministry, why stay in Haiti?* This path of service was going nowhere. I would be better off back home in Louisiana making money and sending it to Haiti. After stepping off the bus when God called me to Haiti, I had come face-to-face with my first lion.

One day I entered my tiny office, put my head in my hands, and told the Lord, "What have I done? How can I care for my family? We have no transportation to use in ministry or even to go to the market to buy food or water. Lord, I need a car desperately, and I have no money."

I sat with my head in my hands and faced the questions that had been rustling through my mind. *Is this God's place for me and my family? Have I made a mistake?* We had come to Haiti under no particular mission organization, but we had financial and spiritual backing from friends, acquaintances, and some churches. That support, however, did not cover unplanned expenses, and I could not ask them to give again for a vehicle. *Could I have mistaken God's leading to Haiti? Had I made a big mistake in what I considered God's will?*

As I lifted my head, I noticed a white paper on the floor, under the edge of the door. It had been there the day before, but when I had come into the office, I had absent-mindedly kicked it aside. I crossed the room and picked it up. It was an unopened envelope that apparently had blown off my desk and lain on the floor a couple days.

**Even the most devoted Christian, while exercising a
faith which must surely bring an answer from God,
knows what it is to have lurking just around the corner
the question whether perhaps he might be mistaken.**[2]
—**WATCHMAN NEE**

According to the return address, the letter was from Sam, the president of a large publishing house. We had met when I had handled publishing contracts for my former employer. Sam and I had discussed my decision to go to Haiti, and we had kept in contact with each other. I opened the envelope and unfolded the letter inside.

Inside the letter lay a check for $2,000.

That unexpected check paid for a Polski, a cheap little Polish car that met the needs of my family and ministry. To an observer, the check was a piece of paper, money to buy a vehicle. To me, though, it was a note from God saying, "Son, I didn't abandon you. I heard you when you called out to Me. In fact, I heard you before you called out, and I put supplies on your path so that you would find them at just the right time."

Our Guide has promised never to abandon us. He may be out of view, but He is always there. He knows where and when you will reach the end of your resources and often plants a cache of supplies to meet your needs at the exact moment you reach that site of desperation. He will watch over you with great care as you take those first uneasy steps in running to the roar.

Why do we have to face situations like this? Why did God allow my transportation to be taken? God teaches many lessons through these experiences. During these times, He brings us to the realization that we, in ourselves, have insufficient resources to do His work. At the same time, He shows us the vast, unlimited resources He has reserved for our use. With His supply at our disposal, we can attempt projects that are far beyond our resources or capabilities.

TRUST YOUR GUIDE TIP 4

DON'T BE AFRAID TO CALL FOR HELP. YOUR GUIDE HAS A NEVER-FAIL COMMUNICATION SYSTEM THAT CAN INSTANTLY ALERT OTHERS TO YOUR NEEDS.

Not only will you never travel alone when you step off the bus at God's prompting, but you will also discover that He sends provisions and assistance to you at just the right time. When Elijah fled from Jezebel, he found himself standing in the tall grasses of fear and intimidation, pursued by an evil lioness. But God was with him, and He provided food and water to sustain Elijah. (See 1 Kings 19:3–9.)

God also intervened by reminding Elijah that he did not travel alone. Though Elijah felt as if he had been deserted, God reminded him that seven thousand other people had not bowed to Baal, and they were traveling in the same dangerous country as Elijah was. God not only promises that He will stay with us, but He also has troops that He can deploy at any time to help us. Sometimes we catch a glimpse of some of these warriors; others are hidden from view.

> We believe in the providence of God, but we do not believe half enough in it. Remember that Omnipotence has servants everywhere, set in their places at every point of the road.[3]
> —CHARLES SPURGEON

One summer God deployed a couple of His New Mexico ground warriors to face a lion that nearly destroyed me. After speaking at a series of meetings in California, I began the long trek of flying a Cherokee 140 back to the East Coast and then to Haiti. Just before I left the West Coast, the nation had been saddened by a major airline crash of a Boeing 727, Flight 759, near New Orleans that demolished six houses and killed all 145 souls aboard and 8 people on the ground. It would be months before the FAA released an official report, but the probable cause was cited as an encounter with a microburst-induced wind shear, which imposed massive downdrafts on the airliner.

On my return flight across the States, I planned to close one leg of the journey at Albuquerque, New Mexico. Flying east, I picked up the VOR (navigational aid) signal leading into Albuquerque when I was about sixty miles out. The vast western landscape took on the evening hues of gold and rose, and then darkened to purple velvet. In the distance, Albuquerque's lights sparkled like jewels.

Lightning pulsed the cumulonimbus clouds that lay twenty-five or thirty miles beyond my destination. Nevertheless, I radioed Albuquerque approach and flight service for a weather briefing. With their assurance that the weather was clear, I began to set up my approach to land on the north-south runway.

As I set up a long final approach, another pilot landing in front of me radioed that he had encountered turbulence. I glanced at the thunderstorms. They were still well out of range, probably twenty-five miles away, but I went on alert and tightened my grip on the yoke. At that point, the runway was in sight and everything seemed perfectly normal.

Suddenly the plane bucked like a bronco. With the runway just a mile ahead, I focused on keeping the airspeed up and my lunch down. As soon as I crossed the threshold of the runway, I cut back the power in order to descend and land, but an updraft popped the plane higher. Then the plane dropped and rose again, like a bouncing ball.

A blaring emergency transmission warned: "Wind shear on all quadrants!" Terror almost stopped my heart. I was caught in the same weather phenomenon that had brought down Flight 759. Unable to set the plane down on the runway, I shot past the end of the runway and started out over Albuquerque. The minute that I cleared the plateau edge, the plane dropped like a rock. The airspeed indicator went from 160 mph to 0, then back to 160. In the popping, pulsing wind, the plane kept losing altitude. Only the natural descent of the earth from the plateau kept me from hitting the ground.

It was as if the little blue Cherokee were a remote-controlled plane being flown by a child who had found the controls. The plane climbed, dropped, pitched, and bucked. When I was about a hundred feet above the trees, I crossed a residential area. The downtown buildings of Albuquerque loomed. Still unable to gain altitude, I slipped the plane between two tall buildings. Out of the corner of my eye, I could see desks and computers in offices.

Ahead, I saw an interstate highway and decided to land the plane there if necessary. I lined up with the highway and flew toward the airport. To my right, I could see the airport. I told the tower operator,

"I just want to land as quickly as possible."

"The winds favor runway two one," he radioed back. Winds were blowing at 80 knots, and all of a sudden, something clear as a bell inside of me said, *Do not land on that runway!*

I came back to the tower, "What's that other runway?"

"The winds are favoring runway two one."

"I don't care what the winds are favoring; what is that other runway?"

"Two six."

"I'm gonna take two six."

Gaining the necessary altitude, I proceeded another fifty degrees, lined up with runway two six, and set up my approach. "Wind check," I called.

"Two six—eight zero knots."

The winds had completely changed! Had I landed on runway two one, I would have been caught in an angling 80-knot wind. The little blue Cherokee would have probably flipped and landed on its back.

By the time I lined up with runway two six, the winds had stabilized and were blowing at 80 knots in favor of runway two six. The Cherokee made a very slow dragging approach, bucking in the popping winds. The plane climbed, then dropped, then climbed, but the winds blew steadily at a 260 heading. Pouring on the power, I finally crossed the threshold. As soon as I crossed the end of the runway, I eased back the power and touched the runway. Gliding to a stop, I expelled my breath in relief. *I was going to live.*

Suddenly the plane rolled backward! Quickly I jammed the power back in, pushed forward on the yoke, and planted the airplane on the runway. The little blue Cherokee chattered. I was trying to make it stick to the ground, and the winds were trying to lift it. Caught between the opposing forces, the plane was being dribbled on the runway like a basketball.

Suddenly the winds eased, and the Cherokee lunged ahead. I pulled back on the throttle, got on the brakes, and taxied into the Fixed Based Operations (FBO) of the Albuquerque airport. A bewildered lineman walked out of the FBO blinking as if he were stunned. The windows had blown out of the FBO. A twin turboprop Mitsubishi MU2 had been picked up and flipped. Several other planes were damaged.

"Where did you come from?" the lineman asked.

"I just landed."

He stared at me and said slowly, "My God."

"I know." I definitely knew that my God had saved my life and directed me to a safe landing.

The wind shear that had hit the Albuquerque airport no doubt had come from the thunderstorm raging thirty miles east of Albuquerque. Apparently a microburst, or very severe downdraft inside the thunderstorm, had blown out the side of the storm. Like a monstrous power leaf blower held close to the ground, the microburst had driven tornadic winds thirty miles across the plateau to the airport.

Following the flight, I calmly made my usual logbook entry—at least I thought I did it calmly. Weeks later, when I looked at the entry, I realized that it had been written in inch-and-a-half-tall shaky letters. With the logbook updated and the plane secured for the night, I took a cab to a hotel in Albuquerque.

As we passed through downtown Albuquerque, I pointed to a building and asked the driver, "How tall is that building?"

"It's a twenty-two-story building."

"I flew by the twenty-first floor just a little while ago," I told him. "I could see the desks and file cabinets in the offices."

A week later as I was speaking in a church in Slidell, Louisiana, I told the people how God had delivered me from the deadly force. After the service, a man made a beeline to me. "Let me ask you a question about your Albuquerque story," he said. "Was your airplane black and white?"

"Dark blue. It looks black."

"A little airplane, with the wings on the bottom?"

I nodded.

"It was July 11 at about 6:45 in the evening?"

"Yes." By now, the man had my full attention.

"You're not going to believe this," he said. "I don't live here. I'm here visiting relatives. I'm from Albuquerque. On the evening of July 11, my wife and I were at home in Albuquerque, out in the backyard barbecuing. A terrible wind suddenly whipped up and began tossing the trees and everything that wasn't fastened down. We heard an airplane very, very close to us. We immediately looked up. The plane was so low, about a hundred feet above the ground, that we thought it was going to crash into our house. The plane's wings were shaking and wobbling, and it didn't look like the pilot had control of it. My wife and I quickly grabbed hands and began praying that the Lord would protect the pilot and that airplane. The last we saw, the little plane was shaking and wobbling off toward the horizon."

We stood looking at each other, and our eyes began to tear. God had deployed His ground troops to intercede for me on that fateful flight. And on this night in a church in Slidell, Louisiana, God had providentially brought us together so that we would both know how He had answered prayer and exerted His mighty power on my behalf.

◆ ◆ ◆

In Africa, herdsmen build huge bonfires to keep lions from their livestock. Saving a goat or a cow often means staying up later or throwing an extra log on the fire. In the same way, the prayers of God's saints often mean the difference between saving or losing a life or a soul. Too often we get so caught up in our own attempt to stay clear of the lion that we fail to see the lion tormenting a brother or sister. The couple in Albuquerque stopped in the middle of barbecuing dinner to pray for me.

Paul told the Ephesians to put on their armor and to stand their ground. He told them to be alert and stand against the devil's schemes (Eph. 6:11), and to "pray in the Spirit on all occasions with all kinds of prayers and requests" (v. 18).

Stay alert to the dangers on your path and to the Spirit's guidance to pray for those around you. The couple in Albuquerque prayed because they could see the danger I faced. Sometimes the Spirit will direct you to pray, and you won't know why. Take time to respond to those promptings.

The assurance that God is with me has held me steady in many crises. As you step forward to follow God and run to the roar, remember that you do not travel alone. Even when you make mistakes in judgment or when circumstances beyond your control thrust you into the lion's face, remember this—*your Guide will never abandon you*. He has troops that He can activate from any place in the universe.

Take courage, and step out of that safari bus. Answer God's call to run to the roar of a distant, dangerous lion. You may travel to places in lion territory that are far from friends and family. You may get out there in the tall grasses away from vehicle range, out of communication range, and unable to call for human assistance. But you can never travel out of prayer range.

CHAPTER 4

PICK YOUR LION

LION SELECTION TIP 1

YOU CAN'T FIGHT EVERY LION. FOCUS YOUR
ATTENTION ON DEFINITE GOALS. DON'T TRY
TO MINISTER TO ALL THE CRIES YOU HEAR.

WE CAN'T FIGHT all the lions. Some lions aren't worth fighting. Some should be left for others to fight. My family has accused me of always going for the most difficult lion. I confess that I do pick the lion no one else will venture near, the one no one else wants to handle, the one that seems impossible to conquer.

I lived in Haiti in the 1970s and early 1980s when Jean-Claude Duvalier, known as "Baby Doc," governed Haiti. As a dictator, he squelched all opposition. Corruption and greed impoverished the nation. Knowing that a heart change at the top would bring change in all levels of government and society, I wondered, *Why not minister to the president and bring him to Christ?*

Getting to Baby Doc and his wife, Michele, however, was more difficult than I had imagined. An ironclad barrier separated them from the common people. However, Michele's youngest brother, Frantz, was a pilot, and through aviation I established a friendship with Frantz. A handsome, personable, charismatic young man, Frantz spoke perfect English. As the baby of one of the wealthiest families in Haiti, this brilliant pilot had everything going for him.

From the very start, I told Frantz, "I want you to accept the Lord." He joked with me about flying and religion, and I realized that our friendship needed to go beyond the airport if he were to take my message seriously. Associating with Frantz away from the airport, however, presented dangers to my reputation as a Christian and a missionary pilot.

Under a dictatorship, no one dares make a derogatory comment about the first family or the extended first family, but the language of shrugged shoulders, raised eyebrows, and innuendoes spoke clearly. Frantz was a jet-setter and probably a drug runner. Frantz lived in the "pit of sin." As a former resident of the pit, I knew that someone had to go in after him, so I decided to have a banquet and invite Frantz.

Before the banquet, I went to visit E. B. Dane, friend and U.S. consulate general who was known as "Eb."

"Eb, I want you to know that I'm going to have a banquet, and I'm going to invite Frantz Bennett."

"Oh?" Eb said, raising his eyebrows and looking intently at me.

"I want to lead Frantz Bennett to the Lord. I wanted to make sure that you know my only connection to Frantz is one of spiritual concern."

Eb smiled. "I understand," he said. "Thanks for letting me know."

A man's judgment is best when he can forget himself and any reputation he may have acquired and can concentrate wholly on making the right decisions.[1]
—RAYMOND SPRUANCE

I knew that approaching *lions* of this corrupt regime could jeopardize my missionary career and even my life, but my concern was for *neglected people.* Neglected people don't always eat from Dumpsters and sleep near warm sewer grates. Some live behind guarded gates and down long lanes that end on a private beach.

Why do we avoid some neglected groups?

These people appear to have it all. They have wealth, physical beauty, fame, power, worldly wisdom, or a combination of these. Intimidating barriers surround them. The lions that guard their gates roar, "Go away! You have nothing of value to offer these people." You can't go knock on their door and ask, "If you died tonight…?" or hand them the Four Spiritual Laws.

Paul urges us to pray, intercede, and thank God for those who have authority. Daniel and Joseph had close association with leaders of the nations in which they lived. While we do not know of any dramatic conversions among these political leaders, we do see the respect that these leaders held for Daniel and Joseph. Sometimes through business connections or unusual circumstances God will put you on a direct course with those in the upper echelons of society. One such encounter in Haiti gave me an opportunity to witness to members of the elite 5 percent that own all the wealth of Haiti.

LION SELECTION TIP 2

NOTHING LIES OUT OF THE POSSIBILITY RANGE FOR YOUR GUIDE. TO HIM, NO LION SITUATION IS HOPELESS.

A low-pressure system had produced a series of on-again, off-again storms around the island of La Gonâve, located in the Port-au-Prince Bay. Along with three veteran missionaries—Richard, a French Canadian, Don, who served in Cap-Haïtien, and Joel, who had been in Haiti fourteen years—I planned to conduct a three-day *JESUS* film crusade on La Gonâve. Since the island was a short hop from Port-au-Prince, we were able to fly there between intermittent storms. The rains had stopped, but a strong wind still blew, and the seas frothed whitecaps. From the air, I noted extremely rough seas around the Arcadine Islands. Reefs around the tiny islands provided excellent snorkeling, but a sharp-dropping, deep ocean channel, with a strong current moving toward open sea, also made it treacherous. Once, while snorkeling near the islands, I had found myself two hundred yards away from my starting point within a matter of moments. To an unsuspecting swimmer, it could mean, "Next stop—Cuba!"

We landed the Cessna 206 (N1003V) on the salt flats on the north side of the island, and the men with me prepared to set up the film equipment. During our preparations, I noticed strange planes circling the area. One looked like a Haitian military plane, and the other like a light U.S. Navy twin-engine aircraft. I wondered about the planes, but I turned my attention back to preparations for the evening.

We put the speakers on top of the Cessna's blanket-padded wings, set up the projectors under the wing, and draped a tarp from the wing to protect the sensitive film from the sea mist. A steady wind blew so hard that we had to strap down the equipment and use rocks to hold down the tarp. Guy wires, secured by thick steel spikes that could be driven through asphalt and rock, steadied the Da-Lite Fast Fold screen. Team members stood ready to flex the jointed legs and drop the screen if the wind gusted. A howling wind forced us to crank the volume high.

After showing the film the first night, we broke down the equipment and loaded it into the plane for protection and safekeeping. Then we went to our accommodations—a mud and wattle hut with thatched roof—where we put down our air mattresses and fell asleep in a well-ventilated room.

At 2:00 a.m. I awakened. A gale-force wind howled through the thin walls. With visions of the Cessna sliding into the ocean, I got Joel up, and we jogged a mile to the flats to check on the plane. Just before we left the rocky path, we picked up a couple good-sized boulders for additional anchors.

As I had suspected, the Cessna was straining at the lines, raring to fly. Given enough lift, the 206 would fly. The plane didn't care if 30–40 knots of power came from a 300-horsepower engine or from the wind. We strapped and bungeed everything we could and piled boulders in front of boulders to keep the plane from leaving the ground.

Having done all that we could to secure the plane, I stopped a few moments to look across the salt flats. In the moonlight, the high seas breaking over the reefs looked like a vast plain of whitecaps. I was suddenly cold. *Thank You, Lord, that I'm not out there. Thank You for a little mud hut to sleep in tonight.*

The next morning the angry bumblebee sounds of a Cessna 337 aircraft awakened me. The plane usually flew to Jérémie each day, and I couldn't imagine why it would be in the La Gonâve area. When I heard a U.S. Navy twin circling, I knew that something was wrong. None of the mud huts had phones or CNN, so we could only guess at what was happening.

Since we had planned a three-day crusade on the island, we had some free time. Out at sea the waves still ran high, but the reefs broke their fury before they swept ashore. Using an inflatable raft, Don and I paddled to a calm area to go snorkeling while Richard and Joel snorkeled near the beach. Before Don and I could don our masks, a powerful Cigarette powerboat started working its way through the reefs toward us. Frantically, I waved the captain back, and we paddled out to meet him.

A young man called out, "Have you seen any bodies?"

"Bodies?" I said as I reached to grab the side of his boat.

"My father and my uncles were fishing in a 20-foot Mako boat in the Arcadines, and they didn't come home. Boats and planes searched all day yesterday. They couldn't have survived the high seas last night, so the search has been called off. There were six of them, and I'm trying to find their bodies."

"They aren't dead," I said. "They're alive."

"Who are you?" he said with disdain. "Why do *you* say that they are alive?"

"I say, 'They aren't dead! They are alive.'" I couldn't explain why, but I felt that the men were alive and the Lord wanted to do a mighty miracle. "I have a plane," I told him. "I'll go find them. What's the name of your boat?" I asked, pointing to his powerboat.

"*Silou 1.*"

"Do you have a radio?"

"Yeah, I have a radio." Exhausted and distraught, the young man had little patience with my questions or my attitude of hope.

"What frequency do you monitor?" I asked.

"Channel 14."

"*When* I find them, how can I reach you?"

He looked at me as if he would like to smack my face but said, "Ibo Lele hotel has been coordinating the search. You could tell the control tower to call Ibo Lele. Ibo Lele could contact me by radio."

"OK," I said, and Don and I started paddling back to the shore. We paddled so furiously that Richard and Joel thought we had encountered a shark.

On the beach I quickly explained the situation and said, "They've given up the search for these men, but I think God wants to give us a miracle today." We grabbed cameras and sprinted toward the salt flats. Under the wings of the plane we joined hands, and I prayed.

"Lord," I said, "we don't have a clue where these men are. You know exactly where they are. Please show us. Thank You. Amen."

◆ ◆ ◆

Action springs not from thought, but from a readiness for responsibility.[2]
—**DIETRICH BONHOEFFER**

Some lions just have your name written on them. You can't explain why, but deep down, you sense this is a lion God wants you to go after. David had not planned to fight Goliath. He was just delivering some snacks to his brothers when the Philistine giant thundered the challenge. David saw the need and said, "Hey, this is something I need to handle." David went after Goliath, fully expecting God to help him. Sometimes, as in the case of David, we respond out of a sense of "God wants me to do something about this, and He'll be with me." The job could possibly be done by someone else, but we feel confident that with God's help we should just go do it. At other times, we respond out of responsibility. When four kings carried Abram's nephew Lot off to captivity, Abram gathered 318 trained men and went after his nephew. Abram knew that no one else would bother to rescue Lot. Sometimes we are the only one that would bother to pick this lion.

I couldn't give a logical reason to look for the men lost at sea. They weren't my responsibility. I just knew I had to search for them, and I believed God would enable me to find them.

After a quick preflight, we rolled back the boulders, untied the plane, and took off.

Joel said, "What are you gonna do, fly along the coast and look for bodies?"

"Be quiet, Joel," I said.

"But, he was looking for bod—"

"I said to be quiet, Joel. We're not looking for bodies. We're looking for people."

Twenty miles of sea separated La Gonâve from the mainland. Planes and boats had searched along the coast of the mainland, the area around La Gonâve, and southward past the Arcadines.

The minute that I took off, I hit my stopwatch. After leveling off at five hundred feet, I called the Port-au-Prince tower. "This is One Double O Three Victor. I'm joining in the search."

"Oh! Wonderful, One Double O Three Victor." In a less enthusiastic voice he added, *"Bon chance, Monsieur."* Everyone had given up hope of finding the men alive.

I set a course that was 90 degrees away from the search area. Flying the 206 at 120 knots, we headed out to sea, toward Cuba.

Away from land, the wind still blew at near gale force, spuming the sea as if it were in a mammoth blender. As the stopwatch registered the minutes, I calculated the miles. One minute equaled two miles; two minutes equaled four miles; three minutes equaled six miles. At three minutes and thirty seconds, my heart started pounding. At three minutes and forty-five seconds, I sensed my head being turned to the left. I looked down. I strained to see a fleck of difference in the frothing seas.

"There they are!" I screamed. And then they were gone. I snapped the stopwatch on exactly four minutes—eight miles.

"I've lost them," I said, "but they're down there!"

I put the airplane into a 60-degree bank, pulled the power back, rolled back in, and found them again. Below us, we counted six men clinging to the white hull of the overturned boat. Then they vanished again in the whitecaps.

"Port-au-Prince," I yelled into the mike, "this is One Double O Three Victor! I've got the lost men! They are on the 308-degree radial and 32.6 miles from the Port-au-Prince VOR."

"*Béniswa étènèl* [Praise the Lord]!" the Port-au-Prince controller said, and from thirty-five thousand feet above us came the gravely toned voice of an airline pilot who echoed in English, "Praise the Lord!"

"Does it look like anyone is alive?"

"We see six men clinging to the boat," I told the tower. "I can stay until you get a helicopter here to rescue them."

"*Li pa posible. Li pa posible,*" the operator said. "It isn't possible to send a helicopter. The search ended several hours ago. The helicopter has landed, and everyone has gone home. *Li pa posible.*"

"I only have a couple of hours of fuel, and we're eight miles out at sea. You must get a helicopter to rescue these men *now!*"

"One Double O Three Victor, I'm so sorry, but we can't help you."

"Please, Port-au-Prince, please. I've found these men, and I don't know how much longer they can hold onto that boat. Can't you find someone to fly out here?"

There was a pause, then the controller said, "We tried, but since the search was called off, no one answers our calls."

I remembered that the young man in the search boat had told me that Ibo Lele was coordinating the search, but my mind went blank. I could not remember the name of the boat or the channel that the young man monitored. Not knowing what I would say, I opened the mike. And, from some deep recess of my mind, the words came pouring out.

"All right, Port-au-Prince," I said, "there's a rescue boat called the *Silou 1*, and it's working Channel 14 in coordination with the Ibo Lele Hotel. Call the hotel on the landline. Ask them to contact the *Silou* by radio and get back to us."

While we waited and circled the capsized boat, we took pictures of the scene below. The men's upturned faces were clearly visible, and they reflected both exhaustion and hope.

Since the message and reply had to be relayed to Ibo Lele, to the *Silou*, then back to Ibo Lele, and finally the tower, we circled several minutes before the tower responded. Finally, we heard, "One Double O Three Victor, the *Silou* is south of La Gonâve." I waited for more information. La Gonâve was forty miles long. The area separating us constituted hundreds of square miles of sea. From the *Silou's* location, it would be impossible for the young man to locate us.

"Is that all you have?" I asked.

"That's all we have," the tower replied.

I prayed, "Lord, what should I do?" It seemed that the Lord spoke to my heart and said, "I led you to them the first time; don't you think I could lead you to them the second time?"

My earlier insistence that the men were alive, then flying directly to them had stretched my faith. The idea of leaving the men and expecting to find them again bordered on tempting the Lord. Finding the overturned white boat had been like finding a needle in a haystack. Leaving the men now would be like being blindfolded, throwing the needle back into the haystack, and expecting to find it again. If I did not find them the second time, they would surely die, and I would feel responsible for their deaths.

How could God not provide a helicopter when He had led us to the men? We had been giving God the glory and praising Him for His grace and help in finding the men. And now, we were going to have to fly away and hope to find the boat again. I felt like God had given me a gift and then yanked it from my hands.

One of the most testing situations in a person's life is to trust God for a gift, then have the gift taken from you. Abraham faced this trial when he placed Isaac on the sacrificial altar. In our lives, we rejoice with our friends over great victories and give God glory for our success, then suddenly a ministry collapses, a business goes into bankruptcy, a cancer survivor finds the disease has returned. Through the waiting time for a promise, the receiving of the promise, and sometimes the taking away of a promise, always keep in mind, *the promise belongs to God.* We do not possess it. God does.

Why did God have to retest my faith? I had no answer.

In a gut-wrenching decision based simply on faith, I told my passengers, "God gave us one miracle today. He's going to give us another one."

"What do you mean?" they asked.

"We're going to have to find the *Silou* and lead it to the men."

I got down low, on the deck, dropped the flaps, and used all the airplane language that I could to tell the men on the overturned Mako, "We'll be back. We promise. We'll be back." Finding the *Silou,* though, in an area of hundreds of square miles would be like finding a second needle in the haystack.

Setting a straight course, I flew miles over open ocean and through the bay toward the area south of La Gonâve. After flying eighteen miles, I saw the glint of a boat on the water. We had found the *Silou*—the second needle.

Dropping the flaps, I slowed the plane and waved the wings, and the *Silou* followed. Halfway to our destination, the *Silou* ran into debris that had been ejected from the boat when it had overturned. Believing that I had found only debris, the captain chopped power and started perusing the area.

I turned the 206 back around and got right down on the deck, almost skimming the waves. Using airplane language again, I waved the wings and motioned, "Follow me!"

The *Silou* leaped back up to speed and whammed across the waves. In the open sea, waves boosted the boat with its spinning prop into the air, then slammed it back into a trough. The *Silou,* though, never slackened its pace.

Using the stopwatch and the VOR radial, I returned to the location where the boat had been.

The boat was not there.

I groaned. *How could we ever find the white-hulled needle in this haystack of whitecaps? We could be right on it and never see it.*

"Lord," I said, "You promised me…"

"Left. Turn left." Responding to the still voice, I banked left, and there they were.

"Thank You, Jesus!" I cried. I put the plane down on the deck and circled until the *Silou* caught up with us.

The capsized boat, though, was invisible in the troughs of foaming waves, and the *Silou* roared toward the survivors at full throttle.

"My God!" I screamed. "He's going to slice right through their boat!"

The *Silou* crested a wave and in that instant, the captain saw the Mako. He chopped the power, rolled the boat sideways, and slid by the capsized boat.

"Thank You, Jesus. Oh, thank You, Jesus," I gasped.

From the plane we watched the survivors board the *Silou*, and we documented the rescue with our cameras. After the men were aboard the *Silou* and on their way home, I thought of how exciting it would be for us to fly to Port-au-Prince and personally meet the rescued men. I didn't know who they were, but I knew that helicopters, U.S. navy planes, and speedboats would never participate in a search for ordinary Haitians.

Just when I was ready to set a heading for Port-au-Prince, the Lord reminded me, *"Son, you've got a crusade to do."* God had used me to rescue lives, but my greater task was to rescue lost souls. He had entrusted me with His work, and I had a responsibility to do that work. Besides, how could I conscientiously take credit for the rescue? It was God's doing.

After returning to La Gonâve, I did my usual meticulous logging of the flight, numbered it as Haiti Flight 339, then devoted the next two days to the crusade. During the daytime our mission team spoke in services and held seminars, and at night we showed the *JESUS* film. The morning following the last showing of the film, we loaded the plane and started back to Port-au-Prince.

In the air, I radioed the tower. "Port-au-Prince, this is One Double O Three Victor."

"Where have you been?" The controller spoke so loudly that the transmission was distorted.

"Been on La Gonâve, doing a crusade there."

"The whole country has been looking for you. You're a hero."

"I'm no hero. Anyone can fly a straight course for four minutes. God's the hero."

"You need to contact those people," he said. "They want to talk to you."

I still didn't know who the rescued men were, but at the airport I found that planes from Guantánamo Bay had been a part of the search and rescue effort. When I called the phone number that I was given, I received profuse thanks and an invitation to a banquet given in my honor.

"We had cameras on board," I told the caller, "and we have a lot of spectacular shots of the rescue. If you would like, I can put together a slide presentation, and you can invite some of your friends in to see the pictures."

The rescued men lived in multimillion-dollar homes that overlooked the city. They were a part of Haiti's elite, which owned and controlled most of Haiti. In an elegant home with trained servants, Rafael, one of the survivors, told me how the boat had capsized.

"We were fishing off of the Arcadines, and the winds and currents got crazy. We saw a ten-foot renegade wave coming, and the captain fired the twin 150 engines and throttled it. One engine misfired, and we slewed to the side, and the wave hit us broadside. The boat flipped and landed inverted. We clung to the boat. Planes came near us, but they couldn't see the white boat in the waves. We knew that we had little chance of survival in the waves and current."

Rafael continued, "After twenty-four hours, we had drifted about twenty miles from where we had capsized and despaired of anyone finding us. One of the men decided to swim ashore. I grabbed him by the shoulder and said, 'You're not going anywhere.'"

Rafael paused, then said quietly, "I told them, 'We're such fools. We haven't even prayed.'"

Rafael leaned a little closer to me and with a little grin said, "Now, I'm a Catholic, so I held onto the boat with one hand and tried to comb my hair with the other hand, as I wanted to look proper when I prayed. Then I said, 'O God! Save us!' As soon as I said that, I heard your plane. Everyone else said, 'It will circle over us just like the others,' but I said, 'No! This one has our number.'"

The slides, showing the white-hulled boat in the frothing seas, emphasized the miracle of the rescue. Had I simply found the men and a helicopter had immediately rescued them, they could have considered the rescue *luck*. But to find the men in the waves, leave them, find the *Silou*, then find them again in the sea, gave credence to my insistence that God helped me. In a way beyond my wildest dreams, God received glory among the spiritually neglected elite of Haiti.

◆ ◆ ◆

I continued to solidify a friendship with Frantz Bennett through contact at the airport. In an effort to lead Frantz to Christ, I organized a banquet and invited him. Frantz accepted my invitation, and I determined to speak boldly to him about Christ at the banquet.

On Thursday, the day before the banquet, I saw Frantz at the general aviation airport.

"I can't make that dinner tomorrow," he said.

"Frantz, I don't know what you are doing, but you need to make that dinner."

"I really can't make it."

"It would be good if you came," I urged. I had put a lot of work into arranging the banquet and didn't want to lose this opportunity to witness to Frantz.

He shook his head. "Sorry, Joe. I have another appointment that I have to keep."

On Saturday, Frantz's father called. "Frantz is in prison in Puerto Rico," Ernest said. "Is there anything you can do?"

"Let me try to go to Puerto Rico and see him," I said.

I called Eb at home and told him of Frantz's arrest. "Eb," I said, "I want to go see him. Can you get me clearance into the prison?"

"Absolutely," he said.

Eb's contacts got me right into the maximum-security area of the prison, and I entered Frantz's cell within twenty-four hours of his incarceration.

"Frantz, you should have had dinner with me," I told him.

"Is there anything you can do to get me out of here?"

"Frantz, I don't think so. All I can say to you is, 'This holds the key to your freedom.'" I handed him Bibles in French and English. Before I left, I prayed with him.

After I returned to Haiti, I found Ernest Bennett in his enormous coffee export depot in Port-au-Prince. I spoke to him about how Frantz had planned to attend my banquet but had backed out at the last minute. While I was sorry for his arrest, I had no power or contacts that could get him released.

As we spoke, the door opened, and Frantz's mother entered the depot with purposeful strides. According to the language of innuendoes and shrugs, she was a powerful woman. She approached me with eyes firing daggers. Stopping inches from my face, she stared in unadulterated hatred and then spat on my feet.

God, in that moment, gave me a sense of peace and understanding. I knew she was angry, and I also knew she was suffering deeply. Frantz, the baby of the family, had been a source of delight and pride. Now, her dreams for him were going up in smoke, and I was the only person she knew to blame.

As she spun on her high heels and walked away, I said, "Ernest, I had nothing to do with this. If anything, by the Spirit of God, I did everything I could to keep him out of it."

Ernest looked at me as if a spotlight had just focused on me.

"Think about it!" I said. "Why would I be trying to urge him to have dinner with me if I knew he was flying cocaine? If I had been part of the sting, I would have done everything I could to promote his flight. I would not have tried to get him to stay home."

He started backing away from me, and I yelled, "Ernest, I didn't know anything about anything!"

I left the coffee depot knowing that I had upset a very powerful family, but I walked away in peace. The Bennetts might not understand, but God knew that I had gone into the pit, risking my reputation and now possibly my life in an attempt to pull Frantz to safety.

No planning or forethought had gone into rescuing the men at sea, whereas I had planned for months to rescue Frantz. The quality of your intentions or the depth of your planning will not always determine acceptance or success when you run to the roar. You may encounter an opportunity that offers little time to plan, and you meet with unexpected success. At other times your best efforts will yield no apparent spiritual harvest.

LION SELECTION TIP 3

DON'T BE AFRAID TO APPROACH A DIFFICULT LION.

If it's easy, everyone is doing it. Choose the lion—the contract, the client, the project, the ministry—that others stop short of engaging. I've flown many reporters to disaster sites and found that some gravitate toward easy places. They headquarter in a capital that provides comfortable accommodations and dependable communications; they pull information from other reports and negotiate for footage. Other reporters go close to the edge and plunge into the epicenter of disaster. Individually and collectively, we tend to focus on the easy lions. We pray for family, friends, neighbors, church members, and those who once attended our church. This is good, but while we focus on those who have heard so many times, others never have the opportunity to hear about Christ for the first time.

You don't have to travel far to meet a difficult lion. What about the neighbor who files a complaint against you with the homeowners' association? The teacher who scoffs at your spiritual and family values? The teens who skateboard on your freshly painted railing? The complaining employee? Whom do you know that irritates everyone, including you?

Going against these difficult lions doesn't mean that you battle these people. It means that you oppose the Satan lion that rules their lives. As you face these people, ask yourself, *Has anyone ever lifted this person in prayer? What can I do to show this person God's love?* Confrontation may be inevitable, but keep in mind that defeating the lions that rule their lives is more important than protecting your rights.

Look around. Make friends with and start praying for that difficult person who repels everyone. *Don't be afraid to choose a difficult lion!*

CHAPTER 5

WEAPON OF CHOICE

WEAPON SELECTION TIP 1

"TAKE...THE SWORD OF THE SPIRIT, WHICH
IS THE WORD OF GOD" (EPH. 6:17).

EARLY IN MY work in Haiti, I recognized the need for a plane, but a plane was far beyond my financial means. While praying and reading my Bible in late March of 1981, I asked God to supply a plane during the next year. I wrote the prayer and the date in my Bible.

Nearly a year later, a veterinarian from Orlando spoke to me in Haiti. Our conversation was short, probably about seven minutes. As he turned to go, he said, "I can see you need an airplane. I'll get you some little puddle jumper."

"That would be great," I said. I hadn't been in Haiti long, but I had been there long enough to know that people's emotions ran high on the mission field and that they made many, many promises. When they got home, they usually forgot their promises. Knowing the failure of well-meaning people to follow through on promises, I gave his parting statement little thought.

In March of 1982, while in Orlando, I met the veterinarian again. He made no mention of the plane, but somehow we ended up at the Executive Airport at almost eleven o'clock that night.

"Let's take a look at that plane," he said, motioning to a dark blue Cherokee 140.

As I walked up on the wing to peer inside the cockpit, he handed me a set of keys and said, "How do you like your little airplane, Joe?"

When I finally had my emotions under control, I told him, "About a year ago, I prayed that God would supply a plane during the next year. This is an answer to prayer."

In my room that night I opened my Bible to the written request for a plane. God had provided the plane on the 365th day following my request. Although God eventually supplied larger airplanes, the little Cherokee always held a special place in my heart.

The Cherokee was not a weapon, but rather an instrument of ministry. As you run to the roar, ask God to help you see what instruments would equip you better. When you have the mind of God on what He wants you to do, you can boldly ask Him to supply the need.

God puts many instruments of ministry in our hands, but He gives us only one weapon. Old Testament characters fought visible enemies with swords, rocks, the jawbone of an ass, a nail, and even lights. In the New Testament Paul tells us that "our struggle is not against flesh and blood, but against the rulers, against the authorities, against the powers of this dark world and against the spiritual forces of evil in the heavenly realms" (Eph. 6:12). We fight invisible forces. Our weapon is the Word of God.

◆ ◆ ◆

During the first years of my ministry in Haiti, I had worked with several mission organizations. I had conducted seminars, done radio broadcasts, flown medical supplies, and assisted on many other projects. On Good Friday of 1982, in Jérémie, I discovered our choice weapon—the Word of God—sheathed in a different scabbard. This discovery would forever change my ministry.

Jérémie is located near the southwestern tip of Haiti. Isolated near land's end by flooding rivers, mudslides, and bone-rattling roads carved into mountainsides, the town has a reputation for weirdness, wildness, and violence. Signs of voodoo abound in the area. Naked, demonic-crazed people attract little attention on the streets of Jérémie.

On Good Friday, fellow-missionary Jeff Givens and I rolled into the middle of Jérémie in a Land Cruiser. Jeff immediately proceeded to turn his Land Cruiser into a crusade machine from which we would show the *JESUS* film. I had heard good things about the *JESUS* film but never had viewed it. In my opinion, films fell short of truly presenting the gospel. I did have a special interest in seeing the Creole version of the film, though, because I had played a small part in getting it translated into the language of the Haitian people. Through contacts in the U.S. consulate, I had helped Gaudin Charles, a Haitian radio announcer, get a visa to go to California. There, Gaudin had done the voice of Jesus in the Haitian Creole version of the film.

Jeff jacked up the Land Cruiser and put a platform on top of it that extended from the headlights to the taillights. We were almost ten feet off the ground. I hoped that no sudden wind gusts would come through Jérémie that night. After arranging the film and sound equipment on the platform, we hung a white sheet from a tall building to serve as a screen. From our perch high above the audience, we started the film rolling as soon as darkness fell.

Some of the people had seen French or French-dubbed films, but since few people in Jérémie were fluent in French, their understanding of film plots had been limited to the visible action. When the opening narration of the *JESUS* film began in Creole, the audience gasped with astonishment. As each scene unfolded, the people pointed out objects of interest, *oohed* and *aahed* at touching scenes, made fun of some characters, and hissed at Roman soldiers.

I immediately recognized that the *JESUS* film differed from other religious films. Besides being in the language of the people, the script was pure Gospel, taken from the writings of St. Luke. The simplicity and power of the gospel captured my attention so fully that I didn't immediately hear the low, booming, single notes from the bamboo *base-vaccine*, a musical instrument. At first it was hard to differentiate the distant sounds from the action on the screen and the chatter of the crowd. However, Jeff and I both soon realized that the deep throbbing rumble did not emanate from the audio speakers or the viewers. We stood and looked far up the street. A half-mile away we saw the dim flicker of candles. A *rara* band was coming.

During Lent, bands of voodoo celebrants, called *rara* bands, dance and play instruments in the streets. Originating as a celebration of Judas's victory over Christ on Good Friday, this vibrant street festival is a blend of music and voodoo. To many it is simply a reason to dress in gaudy clothes and dance in the streets; for others it is an intense association with voodoo spirits.

In a *rara* celebration, whistles shrill, whips snap, and food-tin trumpets blare as dancers cavort down the streets. The predominant musical sound, though, is the enormous *base-vaccine*. Made from bamboo about five inches in diameter and more than four feet long, the instrument gives off a single, deep, rib-rattling note.

Rara bands start out small and grow in size as they travel. Celebrants, emboldened by their numbers and charged with homemade rum, sometimes meld into an unruly mob intent on *dechouke*, or destruction.

Dechouke actually carries a deeper connotation than the English word for destruction. *Dechouke* is such a taking apart that the destroyed object is seldom identifiable. Using only their fingers, the people can dismantle a vehicle until the make is unknown. As a mob moves into a *dechouke* mode, the air is often filled with a low growl that seems to rise from hell itself. On Good Friday the *rara* bands are bigger, wilder, and more violent than at any other time.

The approaching band had already taken on the voice of menace, and our crusade machine, our equipment, and the crowd that had gathered in the center of town lay in the path of the dancing, booming, and chanting throng. Jeff and I knew that our position on the elevated platform made us vulnerable to attack. If the mob started jostling the cruiser, we and all the equipment would tumble into a mass of arms and hands ready to strip us of equipment, personal possessions, and maybe our lives. The audience, though conscious of the approaching *rara* band, was staying to see the baptism of Christ. We couldn't stop the film and run if the viewers were willing to stay.

Up to this point, the face of the adult Christ had not appeared on the screen. Now Christ was walking through a crowd along the Jordan River. With His back to the camera, He stepped into the water. The *rara* band thundered to within fifty yards of the crowd and kept coming. I looked at Jeff to see if he was preparing to jump and run. He appeared calm.

The camera focused on the feet of Christ wading into the Jordan River. As Christ continued His walk toward John the Baptist, the booming *base-vaccine* and whistles drowned the soft music score and the voice of John.

Then the camera focused on the face of Christ. His eyes, full of kindness, looked down from the screen hung on the front of the tall building in the center of Jérémie, and the *rara* band stopped as if hitting a brick wall. In the film Christ did not speak, but simply gazed intently. In the silence of His penetrating gaze, the members of the *rara* band lowered their instruments and quietly merged with the audience.

When I witnessed how the *JESUS* film had stopped the *rara* band dead in its tracks, I began to cry. The voodoo celebrants, intent on revelry and possibly mischief, were now reverently listening to the words of Jesus. The more that I witnessed the response of the audience to the words of Christ, the more I cried. My tears were more than misty-eyed emotion. I was sobbing. *God was speaking to me.*

That evening the Lord revealed to me the power of the *JESUS* film, and I felt that He commissioned me to take the *JESUS* film around the world. From that night on, showing the *JESUS* film was the most important part of my ministry.

WEAPON SELECTION TIP 2
TAKE CARE THAT YOU DO NOT DULL THE SWORD.

The power of the *JESUS* film lay in its pure presentation of the Word of God. When Paul gives a description of the full armor we need to protect ourselves from the devil's schemes, he adds the sword, which is the Word of God. (See Ephesians 6:10–18.) The Word of God serves as both a defensive and an offensive weapon.

We have a tendency to dull its edge in order to make living the Christian life easier for the next generation. You have a responsibility to present the sword to those around you, and to those of the next generation, in pristine condition. Protect it from the corrosion of tradition, cultural changes, or easy faith interpretations.

> **A thousand times over, the death knell of the Bible has been sounded, the funeral procession formed, the inscription cut on the tombstone, and committal read. But somehow the corpse never stays put.**[1]
> —BERNARD RAMM

Treat the Word of God with care. It is not an outdated, inert weapon. The writer of Hebrews said, "The word of God is living and active. Sharper than a double-edged sword, it penetrates even to dividing soul and spirit, joints and marrow; it judges the thoughts and attitudes of the heart" (Heb. 4:12).

Battles emerge among lion fighters in regard to appropriate

weaponry. Generational and cultural changes in worship styles, music, drama, church attire, moral values, and social issues create conflict among those fighting evil. The handle of the sword or the scabbard may change, but the blade cannot be replaced. God's Word remains the weapon of choice for those who run to the roar.

CHAPTER 6

TRAINING FOR TRACKERS

TRACKING LESSON 1

HAVE A TEACHABLE SPIRIT. GOD WILL ALWAYS HAVE MANY LESSONS TO TEACH YOU (PS. 25:4).

IN AFRICA, QUALIFIED lion trackers teach trekkers how to read evidence of lions on the trail and spot small wildlife. They explain the medicinal use of plants, folklore, and culture and draw attention to the beauty of nature. These guides also provide information on staying safe in wild-game country.

As you travel through lion territory, your Guide wants to do more than just lead you to a lion encounter. He wants to teach you many lessons so that you can grow in knowledge of Him. Along the way, He points out assurances to eliminate worry, comfort to heal wounds, and psalms for encouragement. He'll teach you to distinguish between truth and tradition and how to avoid deception.

No matter how long you travel with the Guide, He will have more to teach you. And He doesn't teach us all the same lessons at the same time in life. Some learn patience and long-suffering early in their walk, but struggle with moral purity. Others give of their time and resources, but gossip or create dissension. Eventually, if we respond in obedience, we will meet every issue—but it is the Guide who decides the order of these encounters. Refrain from pride in what you have learned. Bear with those who have not learned the same lessons that you have.

◆ ◆ ◆

No matter how far you travel on the trail, you will encounter situations that reveal your weaknesses and teach you to rely on God's strength. I dashed off to handle a lion in Haiti and quickly found that I was not as prepared as I thought I was.

64

By the time I had moved to Haiti, I was a licensed pilot with hundreds of hours of experience in several types of aircraft. I felt confident of my flying ability, but I knew nothing of quick-building afternoon storms in the tropics. In Haiti, I occasionally rented a Piper Tomahawk—a dreadful little plane that pilots dubbed the *Traumahawk*. With a hi-T tail, it flew terribly with mushy, bad, stall characteristics.

When an author of a poignant anti-Castro book describing Christianity in Cuba came to Haiti, I arranged a 3:00 p.m. radio interview for him in Cap-Haïtien and offered to fly the author to the interview. Instead of a two-day road trip, we could be back home by 5:00 p.m. Our departure time—2:00 p.m.—rang no warning bells in my mind. We flew to northern Haiti, and the author did a powerful anti-Castro interview that would reach much of the Caribbean, including Cuba.

At 4:30 p.m., right on schedule, we left Cap-Haïtien in the little Tomahawk. As soon as we lifted off, the airport attendant rolled tires on the runway, closing the airport to all traffic. As we climbed, I noticed distant massive, roiling thunderstorms stacked forty- to fifty-thousand-feet high.

The towering storms blocked the mountain route to Port-au-Prince.

I set a westerly course along the coast, then turning southwest, flew the ten-mile wide corridor between the north coast of Haiti and Cuban airspace. Fast-moving, billowing clouds rose like walls on both sides of the plane.

Surrounded by storms, I considered an emergency landing in Cuba, but then I remembered my passenger. He had just told Cuba what he thought of Castro, and his opinion was clearly stated in about fifty books stacked in the back of the plane. I might find a way to toss out the books, but I still had a passenger whose passport would reveal his identity. In a choice between thunderstorms and Castro, the storms seemed a better choice.

Lightning sparked and bounced through the clouds, showering the sea with sporadic light. Miraculously, a ten-mile-wide corridor of clear air stayed open before me, and like Moses passing through the Red Sea, I flew between the towering walls of violence to safety.

**"Because of the Lord's great love we are not consumed,
for his compassions never fail. They are new every
morning; great is your faithfulness" (Lam. 3:22–23).**

Now, as a pilot with over six thousand logged hours, I shudder when I recall the experience. God truly extended abounding grace and compassion to me that day.

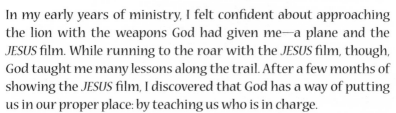

Tracking Lesson 2

Don't carry unnecessary weight.

In my early years of ministry, I felt confident about approaching the lion with the weapons God had given me—a plane and the *JESUS* film. While running to the roar with the *JESUS* film, though, God taught me many lessons along the trail. After a few months of showing the *JESUS* film, I discovered that God has a way of putting us in our proper place: by teaching us who is in charge.

Just as I logged each flight, I numbered and logged each *JESUS* film crusade. Major mission organizations commissioned me to show the film at their churches scattered across Haiti. I conducted crusades for pastors who would make follow-up contact with those who attended the film. The *JESUS* film ministry had a spectacular start, with requests coming from all over Haiti. On the way to Montrouis one day, I stopped at a scenic pullover where the bay edged the road. Here, fifty miles northwest of polluted Port-au-Prince, the bay gave credence to the now defunct Haitian travel slogan, "Haiti, Pearl of the Antilles." Under a brilliant sky, the bay lapped colors of blue that made you want to grab a camera.

I got out of the car feeling like Billy "Joe" Graham. I had set a goal to see ten thousand people respond to the *JESUS* film, and according to my crusade log, about twenty-five hundred people had come forward to commit their lives to Christ.

When I glanced back to the haze of Port-au-Prince, though, the reality of the needs of Haiti cast a shadow on my accomplishments. In downtown Port-au-Prince, I daily shouldered my way through market crowds and nosed the little Polski car between people-laden tap-taps. With every takeoff and landing at the airport, I crossed the squalid pit of desperation—Cite Simone.* Millions in Haiti lived without hope in this life or the next. The people's needs lay heavily on my heart.

While my puny harvest of twenty-five hundred might impress North American supporters, I knew that my efforts were like a Midwestern farmer trying to reap a wheat field with nail clippers.

"You must pour out more blessing!" I said. I walked the beach, kicking sand and insisting that God bless the ministry more. With a plane and such a powerful ministry tool as the *JESUS* film, I had a responsibility to reach the people. I could be conducting mammoth crusades and seeing thousands come to Christ if only God would cooperate.

The natural beauty of the bay expressed God's creative power and made me cry out for His supernatural power that would enable me to reach the multitudes. I was doing all that I could, but I knew God could do more.

"You've got to help me save these people, Lord!" I kicked a piece of broken coral across the sand and told God again, "These people are so needy; You must help me save them."

His answer came as a rebuke: "Son, you have this all wrong. You don't save anyone. I save them. Just keep preaching the gospel. And by the way, I'm saving people that you don't even know about."

> **Just as the rod of God is emblematic of the Word of God, so the staff of God is symbolic of the Spirit of God. In Christ's dealings with us as individuals there is the essence of sweetness, the comfort and consolation, the gentle correction brought about by the work of His gracious Spirit.[1]**
> —PHILLIP KELLER

◆ ◆ ◆

We look for visible results of our work: completion, an established work, hope that what we have begun will continue beyond our lives. When we plant seeds, we want to harvest the crop. When we lay the foundation to a house, we want to set the walls, put on the roof, and put on the house numbers.

---

* Cite Simone, named for Simone Duvalier mother of Baby Doc; renamed Cite Soleil after Duvaliers fled in 1986.

In God's work, you are just one member of a mighty, eternal work-force. You won't do it all, and you won't complete the work. God's work has gone on for millennia, and it will continue until He says it's done. God only asks that you do the task at hand. He will take care of the end result. God alone starts and completes a project.

The faith chapter, Hebrews 11, closes by telling us of people who pleased God with their great faith *but never saw the promise.* As far as we know, Abraham, heir of Canaan, died in possession of one piece of land—a burial plot. If you don't see visible results, you may be tempted to question God's leading. You may wonder, *Is God making the best use of my life?* When no *visible* signs of success exist, people of *great faith* trust that God has not wasted their talents or lives.

Some quote, "If it's to be, it's up to me." *It isn't up to you* to make God's plan work. If it's important to Him, *He will make it work.* All He asks is that you follow closely, learn from Him, and obey His commands. Don't carry the unnecessary weight of trying to make God's plan succeed.

Although a plane could get me to the general location of a cru-sade, many areas required additional travel by vehicle, animal, or foot. I usually rendezvoused near a grass-strip airport with a pastor or missionary, and we traveled on together. Going as a team pro-vided companionship and spiritual support as we entered areas of strong voodoo influence and spiritual darkness.

Due to poor communications, though, I occasionally missed a ren-dezvous. On one such occasion, I traveled by vehicle from Les Cayes to an isolated area. Alone, I endured six hard hours of back-wrenching lurching over rutted roads, along trails, and down streambeds.

When I arrived at my destination, the commandant of the vil-lage gave me permission to set up the film in front of the huge Cath-olic church that dominated the center of town. The church was in a pitiful state of disrepair.

I parked about 150 feet from the steps of the church and started setting up the screen. From the first moments, I was ready to turn around and go back home. I was hot and tired and beat from the trip, and the gathering crowd was very brash and disrespectful.

Having no one to help further aggravated the situation. Unassisted, I had to handle dual generators and dual projectors. I dared not ask for help because my equipment would vanish. As I set up the film amid the growing banter and taunts, all I could think of was, *I've been away from my family, and I want to go home.* I wondered, *Why did I even come here?*

When the sun had set, I started the movie. I had always insisted on using quality sound and projection equipment to run the four half-hour reels, but quality was wasted on this crowd. This was nothing more than a carnival, with me being the central draw. A woman had set up a charcoal cooking stand right beside my equipment, and grease boiled and popped as she fried food.

I'm losing them, I thought as someone starting a *ding, ding, ding* banging on a kettle. They clearly had no interest in anything above base animal instincts.

Halfway through the first reel I was ready to shut down the film, pack it up, and leave. The only people who seemed to be paying attention were in a small group of cascading ages—an older man, three women, a young man, and a couple kids who had brought stools and were sitting by the projector.

As I debated whether to continue, I sensed the presence of Jesus. It seemed that He put His arm around my shoulder and said, "Let Me speak to you a minute." I walked to the back of the crowd and a little beyond to a couple of rocks. Sitting on one of the rocks, I let go of my turbulent thoughts and listened to the Lord.

"Do you see this unruly crowd?" He said. "*This* is rabble. I had rabble. Let Me show you something."

I felt impressed to walk back through the crowd to the projector and the group of cascading ages—the old man, the young man, the three women, and the two kids. "Son," He impressed on me, "*this* is why you came here."

Stepping back from the audience, I began praying for those that I had been sent to reach. And the evening of frustration turned into a time of rich fellowship with Christ and of truly understanding what it meant to share in His sufferings. My suffering—dealing with rabble—enabled me to know Jesus better.

Suffering is a two-way street. We like the verse telling us that since Jesus "suffered when he was tempted, he is able to help those who are being tempted" (Heb. 2:18). It's easy to accept the idea that Jesus better understands us because He shared in human suffering.

How do you feel about suffering in order to understand Jesus better? Any time you share suffering with another individual—loss of a loved one, hurricane, earthquake, war, illness, or even a mission trip—you form bonds with that person as you trade stories of frustration and methods of coping. You will even find yourself laughing at absurd accounts of suffering that would appall others who have not had similar experiences. On the path to the roar, you won't enjoy learning by suffering, rejection, or disappointments, but it is often God's method of training us on the trail. Paul, no stranger to beatings, lashing, stoning, bandits, and shipwreck, said, "I want to know Christ and the power of his resurrection and the fellowship of sharing in his sufferings" (Phil. 3:10). In church services, we celebrate what we know about Christ, but we learn what we celebrate through suffering.

As you go through difficulties, STOP and realize that Jesus went through similar experiences. Jesus faced rejection from family, church, and even His disciples. He hungered, He hurt, and He was pressured by people wanting something from Him or trying to get Him to conform to their ideas. LOOK at how He coped with the situation. Through all that Jesus experienced and suffered, He continued to focus on doing the will of His Father.

LISTEN to how one traveler made it through the Valley of Baca, a place symbolic of weeping:

> Blessed are those whose strength is in you,
>   who have set their hearts on pilgrimage.
> As they pass through the Valley of Baca,
>   they make it a place of springs…
> They go from strength to strength,
>   till each appears before God in Zion.
>   —PSALM 84:5–7

TRACKING LESSON 3

DON'T REFUSE OR CASUALLY DISMISS ADVICE
FROM OTHERS ON THE TRAIL. PRAYERFULLY
CONSIDER THEIR SUGGESTIONS. THEY MIGHT
HAVE A VALUABLE LESSON TO TEACH YOU.

As in any profession or work, I experienced a gamut of emotions ranging from exhilaration to boredom as I continued in the *JESUS* film ministry. There were times when I just plain didn't want to leave home and go out, but out of obedience to the call of God, I would go. No matter how enthusiastic or spiritless I felt, the Word of God went out as a living, active force that changed people and communities.

Experience and advice from others enriched my *JESUS* film ministry and increased its effectiveness. On one crusade, a French Canadian missionary from Cap-Haïtien suggested that I stop the film before it finished and talk to the people.

After having shown the film hundreds of times, I must admit it was hard to take advice from someone else on how to improve the ministry. In my mind, no one should tamper with the film's pure presentation of Scripture. My only concession to change had come at the close of the film. The producers had added an invitation to receive Christ, and I had substituted my own invitation to come forward and pray for salvation.

"I don't touch it," I said. "The film speaks for itself."

"I believe," Richard said, "that if you stop the movie when the crucifixion starts and say a few words, your audience will be more attentive during the last part of the film."

I brushed aside his advice, but memories of recent showings made me think about his proposal. About 40 percent of the audience had been leaving before the film ended. To people unused to fast-moving visuals and sound effects, the film overloaded their senses. Also, they were unfamiliar with the teachings of Christ and had difficulty processing so much new information. By the end of almost two hours, the people appeared to be drained, mentally and emotionally. Furthermore, when the first spike went into Christ's hand, those who were familiar with films realized the hero wasn't going to escape, and they left believing the film was ending.

I had felt like a fisherman dropping the corner of a full net and watching the fish swim away, and I hadn't known how to keep the net in place.

Since we were doing a three-day crusade, I decided to humor Richard. Following his instructions, I stopped the film at the point where a Roman soldier placed a steel spike in the hand of Christ and struck it with a mallet.

"There's nothing wrong with the film," I told the audience, "but before we see the rest of the story, let's take a few minutes to stop and catch our breath and consider what Christ has done for us."

Referring to what they had just viewed, I told them that Christ was sinless, but He had willingly suffered the beating and being nailed to a cross for their sins.

Then I said, "At the end of the film, we are going to give you an opportunity to come forward for prayer." I pointed to the rest of the mission team and said, "Whatever your need, we will be here to pray with you."

Instead of drifting away, the people intently watched the remainder of the film, and when I invited them to come forward for prayer, many more responded than had in the past. From that day on, I not only stopped the film after the first stake was driven into Christ's hand, but I also trained others to do the same when they showed the *JESUS* film. That simple change dramatically increased the effectiveness of my *JESUS* film ministry.

TRACKING LESSON 4

SOME SECTIONS OF THE TRAIL ARE TEDIOUS AND BORING. YOU'LL FIND YOURSELF SAYING, "I WOULD RATHER BE..." YOUR GUIDE, NOT YOUR EMOTIONS, MUST DETERMINE THE STARTS, PAUSES, RESTS, AND STOPS ON THE TRAIL.

Along with lessons in humility and willingness to learn from others and from God, I learned that when I got weary and discouraged on the trail, God had other resources to tap to get the job done. Had it been up to me, one group of people deep in the heart of one remote cane field might have never heard the gospel. God, though, had a fresh substitute ready to step in when my faith was weak.

In the tropics, weather usually follows a pattern—morning sea showers, clear skies until about 2:00 p.m., gathering storm clouds over land, showers in late afternoon and early evening, and clear night skies. Since the film had to be shown in darkness, services had to be scheduled in early evening, close to the time of the daily showers.

After watching storms repeatedly lope to the edge of a viewing place and stop as if encountering an invisible shield, I had great faith that God would hold back the rains.

Boxley, another missionary, accompanied me on many crusades in Haiti and the Dominican Republic. Gangly, with features so sharp that they looked as if they should be sanded, Boxley had a sense of humor that enabled him to turn our most trying experiences into hilarious adventures.

Boxley was from an ultraconservative group of Baptists that wasn't given to a wildly charismatic embracing of miracles. He was just a steady, wonderfully solid person that didn't plunge over into the deep faith realm. On our first trip together he had said, "We can go, but we may get rained out."

"Don't say that again," I told him. "The power of God can hold back the rain."

Boxley looked at me like a West Texas toad in a sandstorm.

"I'm not joking," I said. "The rains come right up to the edge and stop." I knew that he thought I was exaggerating. "We can pray, and God will hold back the rains," I insisted.

After Boxley had accompanied me on several crusades and had seen the storms stop short of our viewing area several times, he too developed great faith in God's staying hand when storms threatened.

On one occasion, his faith was stronger than mine. Boxley had scheduled a showing of the film in a little nothing village buried in the sugarcane fields on the Central Plateau of Haiti. About two hundred people had settled in a place so obscure that only those who stumbled into it knew of its existence.

After loading Boxley's Subaru with four hundred pounds of generators, projectors, and lighting equipment, I asked him, "Are you sure the Subaru will make it?" The car squatted near the ground, looking like a toy.

"It has four-wheel drive," Boxley said. "I take it out there all the time. We'll just pray that it doesn't rain." He grinned when he said "rain" as if it were a joke. Up to this point, I had shown the film more than three hundred times and had been rained out once. Boxley never had been rained out.

Confident that we would make it, Boxley took a paved road and then a gravel road. After the gravel road, he took a one-lane road used by sugarcane wagons. The wheels of sugarcane wagons are as tall as an adult, and they gouge ruts deep enough to tip a car on its side. Carefully, Boxley positioned the Subaru so that it straddled the ruts. A slip of eight to twelve inches either way could put the Subaru on its side with the wheels completely off the ground.

"It wouldn't take much rain…" I said. I didn't need to finish the sentence. The ruts held three to four feet of dried mud. We both knew that a downpour could turn the road into an impassable quagmire that would strand us for days.

"It won't rain," Boxley assured me.

We moved deeper and deeper through the cane fields until we were about fourteen kilometers off the gravel road. "If it rains," I said, "we'll be stuck here in a sea of mud."

"It'll be OK," Boxley assured me. "God will hold back the rains."

"You're sounding like a charismatic now," I ribbed him.

"Well, I've seen those rains stop enough times to believe God will stop them again," he replied.

Changes in the clouds, though, made me uneasy. In undeveloped countries such as Haiti, missionary pilots develop a honed weather sense. There is no flight service to call for a weather update. You are your own controller, meteorologist, weather briefer, radar, maintenance—you are everything. If you get into trouble, there is no one to call. So, being a pilot in Haiti, I was tuned to the weather in a way that Boxley was not.

Above the rippling cane fields I noticed clouds rolling toward us from the west. After having flown aircraft with color radar, I could look at clouds and gauge fairly well whether they contained precipitation or not. The buildup in the west held precipitation. We were traveling toward it, and it was moving toward us.

"Box, this doesn't look good."

"We're almost there," he said. "Let's keep going. Besides, there isn't any place to turn around here."

I did a perimeter scan. Clouds were building behind us, to the north of us, and to the south. It was one of those all-quadrant rain systems common to the plateau that produced lush crops and foliage.

All I could think of was getting stuck away from my waiting family. In spite of limiting long-range (three-day) crusades to two or three times a month, my family needed to see more of me. I had been on a very serious regimen of making sure that I was home each night. If it rained on this road, I could be stuck out here three or four days.

I leaned over and put my hand on Boxley's shoulder. "Box," I said, "I don't like the weather. I think we should try to turn around. It's gonna rain, and we're gonna be stuck here."

"God will stop it," he said.

"Box, I'm a pilot. We've got towering cumulonimbi on all four quadrants. Listen, man, this is stretching even my faith. I think we should go back."

"The people are waiting for us. It could be months before we get back to show the film. We might never get back."

"Boxley, I have to get back for my family tonight. I can't be stuck out here. You've seen the ruts in the last fifteen kilometers. Just a little bit of rain, man, and we're stuck out here for three days."

"OK, Joe, listen! They're expecting us. We only have another two and a half or three kilometers to go. Let's go into the village and tell them we can't stay. We'll work on rescheduling and then go back. Is that all right?"

"OK, but we need to get in and get out quick. This stuff is coming right now. I can feel it in the air." Lightning zipped through the distant sky. The air seemed cooler and a bit clammy.

The little village was a rubber stamp of hundreds I'd seen before. Mud and wattle houses with thatched roofs, chickens scratching in the dirt, naked children peeping from behind their mothers' skirts, and the local pastor approaching in his three-piece polyester suit, tie, and sneakers.

Quick, I thought, *let's reschedule and get out of here!*

Boxley, in his slow gentle manner, greeted the people as they gathered. Before we could tell them that we were leaving, they led us to a field where they had placed split-log benches.

"We have everything ready," they said. "You can show the film here."

I wanted to say, "That's nice. Someday, I'll come back in my four-wheel drive vehicle that has a winch. Right now, we've got to go. We'll see you later."

When Boxley and I mentioned rescheduling the film, they said, "But…but…but…we want you to show the film now. Everyone has been waiting."

Boxley looked at me and said, "Joe, let's pray about this."

I knew where this was going. If we prayed, we would probably stay, and I didn't want to stay. Everything inside of me was saying, *Flee!* Boxley might have faith that the rains would stop before reaching us, but I had enough weather sense to know that these clouds were going to unite in a torrential downpour. After this rain, only a helicopter would be able to get us out. Not only did we not have access to a helicopter, but we also had no phone, no radio, or any other means of communication. We wouldn't even be able to let our families know why we hadn't come home.

Twelve or fourteen of the church members gathered in the field, and we joined hands in a circle to pray. The second that we touched hands, I heard in my spirit one word—*Stay!* The Spirit of God spoke to my heart in a firm, and not very gentle, manner, and I knew that I had to stay.

This is going to be a long week, I thought. I glanced around wondering which of the bedbug-infested huts I would be spending the next two or three nights in.

As soon as the last *Amen* died away, I said, "Come on, Box, let's set it up."

We set up the film and ran it as the rains moved to about a half-mile beyond the field. Moisture, like dew, filled the air and dampened the equipment, but the rains just hung there on the edge of the village as if they were chinning themselves on some invisible barrier.

Since I was familiar with the film, I gave the altar call and asked those who would like Jesus to save them from their sins to come forward. As I went through the invitation that I had given hundreds of times, my eyes were on the clouds, and my thoughts were on my family. On a deep inner level, I was thinking, *Come on. Let's hurry this up.* During the altar call I mentally packed the Subaru and calculated how much time it would take to get out before the rains moved.

A steady stream of people came forward for prayer. As the Spirit of God began moving, my thoughts finally shifted from my concerns to the reality of the scene. Out of the corner of my eye, I detected some very slight movement. As I began to pray with people who had come forward, I again noticed movement to my side, but in the darkness and with the harsh platform lights, I couldn't distinguish the person. Nearly ten minutes passed before a shriveled, elderly woman, about four feet tall, emerged from the shadows. Bent by age and probably arthritic, she shuffled a half-inch at a time toward the platform.

When I saw her, I went to her, and leaning over I said, "*Ki sa ou vlé Bondyé fè pou ou, manman? Ki sa ou vlé?* [What do you want God to do for you?]"

I had to lean close to hear the quavery weak voice. "*M vlé Jézi sové mwen.*"

"I want Jesus to save me," she had said. Breaking into tears, I threw my arms around her and embraced her. We prayed together, she accepted the Lord as her Savior, and the Holy Spirit whispered to me, "This is why I wanted you to *stay* tonight."

What started out to be just another night of ministry and another village turned out to be so much more. Had we returned at a later date, the little woman who appeared to be in her nineties might not have been living. This was clearly God's appointed time for her salvation.

In a way, I felt badly that I had entered the service with so little enthusiasm, but I knew that faith and enthusiasm for God's work doesn't soar all the time. No matter how high our faith rises, at times it sags under the weight of daily concerns. This was a night when my faith was down, but God had given me a companion in Boxley, and his faith had soared that night. We packed up the equipment and drove out of the cane fields on a miraculously dry road. And the rain fell behind us, dropping like a curtain at the end of a stage show.

TRACKING LESSON 5

TAKE DELIGHT IN THE JOURNEY. DON'T GET SO FOCUSED ON THE LIONS THAT YOU MISS LITTLE BLESSINGS. GOD DELIGHTS IN GIVING YOU SURPRISES ON THE JOURNEY.

Jesus didn't spend all of His time hanging around the temple, teaching in synagogues, or praying in solitude. We see Him at a wedding, out on a boat with the disciples, sitting by Lake Galilee, and having lunch in the home of Mary, Martha, and Lazarus. When you leave the safety of the bus—family, friends, co-workers, and all that is familiar—you will find more joyful surprises than you ever imagined. The journey isn't all blazing sun, briars, and mosquitoes. God has wonderful gifts along the way that exceed our expectations.

On the morning of July 4 in 1982, God set one of those incredible gifts right on my flight path.

> **Certainty is the mark of the common-sense life:
> gracious uncertainty is the mark of the spiritual
> life….We do not know what a day may bring
> forth….We are uncertain of the next step, but
> we are certain of God. Immediately we abandon
> to God, and do the duty that lies nearest, he
> packs our life with surprises all the time.[2]**
> —OSWALD CHAMBERS

On July 4, 1982, the space shuttle *Columbia* landed at Edwards Air Force Base in California. That day I was flying the Cherokee 140 toward Los Angeles, where I was slated to speak at a Full Gospel Business Men's Fellowship meeting. Flying the Cherokee from Haiti to Florida, and then across the United States, required days of flying. The Cherokee 140 was originally a two-seat trainer with a small baggage area. You could put a couple cushions in the back and call them *backseats*, but you wouldn't want to fly any heavyweight passengers. When I pushed the throttle forward, instead of being thrust backward in the seat, I fell forward. The Cherokee had little power and little payload capability, but slowly and surely it got me to my destinations. In order to break the boredom on the long cross-country flights, I sometimes conversed with air controllers.

On that Fourth of July in 1982, when I flew west out of Houston air control and into Albuquerque air control, I identified myself to the Albuquerque air controller and gave my altitude and intentions, "Eight Two One Three Charlie. Passing through eight point seven (8,700 feet) for ten five (10,500 feet)."

"Roger," the controller answered. "Eight Two One Three Charlie…squawk ident."

I pressed the transponder button, which transmitted my location to his radar screen, and then asked, "How did they get you working on the Fourth?"

"It's seniority. I get double time, so it takes a little of the sting out of it."

"Did the *Columbia* land OK?"

"Beautiful landing. We watched it on TV," the controller said. "President Reagan was there to greet the astronauts. We also got to see *NASA One* take off with the *Challenger* on its back. The 747 is ferrying the *Challenger* to the Kennedy Space Center for the shuttle's maiden flight."

He hesitated a minute then said, "One Three Charlie, where are you going?"

"Ultimately, Los Angeles."

"What's your routing?"

"Flying to Flagstaff."

"Stand by a moment."

"Sure," I said. I had all the time in the world.

When the controller returned, he said, "One Three Charlie, how would you like to see the 747 with the *Challenger*?"

"What! What are you talking about?"

"*NASA One* is going to be flying close to your route. If you would like to see it, I can change your route, and you can see it in the air."

"Sure!" I said. "Just tell me where to go."

He gave me a different intersection to fly to and then asked, "How high can you get that Cherokee?"

"I don't know. Twelve, thirteen thousand feet."

"That ought to be close enough. Think you could get it to fourteen thousand five?"

"On a good day," I said.

"Their routing is pretty direct, and they fly at one five thousand and at about two five zero knots. How's your fuel?"

"Stopping in the next hour."

"OK. Find a place to land. Be quick. Soon as you take off, start climbing, contact us, and we'll vector you."

I made a quick landing in Cochise, Arizona, grabbed a burger while the plane was being refueled, and then took off. At about five thousand feet, I called Albuquerque Center.

"Squawk ident," the controller said.

After I pressed the transponder, he said, "Perfect time, One Three Charlie." He gave me a heading change, and I started climbing to try to get to 14,500 feet. While the Cherokee wheezed through 10,000 feet and kept going, the controller kept me updated on the position of *NASA One*.

At 12,700 feet, I looked up, and directly above my head was a cloud layer at 14,000 feet. It was thin, smooth, and flat, but thick enough that you couldn't see through it.

"Albuquerque," I said, "you're not going to believe this, but there is a solid layer at one four thousand."

"Say your altitude."

"Passing through twelve eight (12,800 feet)."

"Oh, man! This is terrible. We've been working on this for three hours."

"I know," I said. "I wanted to see that shuttle. I was gonna take a picture of that thing and send it to you."

We had been broadcasting right over the main frequency for Albuquerque Center, and some of the pilots who had been listening to the exchange, broke in with "Sorry, it didn't work out for you" comments. Then the airwaves were quiet. Everyone was disappointed.

Suddenly the radio crackled. A deep professional voice said, "Albuquerque Center, NASA One requesting lower. One three thousand (13,000 feet) ought to do." The pilot of NASA One had been among the pilots monitoring the conversation.

Albuquerque Center responded, "Roger, NASA One. You're cleared to one three thousand."

The controller had maintained his emotionless controller tone while talking to NASA One, but when he called me, I could tell he was excited. "One Three Charlie, get down to one twelve five (12,500 feet). He's coming down so you can take a look at him."

"That's neat, NASA One," said a pilot who had heard the exchange. Other pilots opened their mikes and added their comments. Disappointment in the air had changed to excitement.

After I dropped to 12,500 feet, Center directed me to turn a couple degrees to the right. "Be looking. Be looking," the controller said. "He'll be at about 12:15, just slightly to your right. Be looking. Be looking."

All of a sudden, like a white ghost, NASA One with the Challenger on its back popped out three or four miles ahead of me.

"I've got it! I've got it! It's right where you said it would be."

"Begin a standard right turn," the controller said. "Make it slow. Keep him in sight. Space yourself. I want you to parallel his course."

I began a very slow right turn while keeping the 747 in my sight. By the time I had completed a 180-degree course reversal, NASA One and the Challenger were flying beside me and at about 500 feet above me. I felt like I was on Interstate 95 in a golf cart, running alongside a semi pulling two trailers.

I think the pilot slowed the big 747, because the big plane did not flash past. It slipped by, right outside my left window, allowing me plenty of time to take photos.

The airwaves really came to life then. Everyone, including the air controller, asked, "One Three Charlie, what did it look like?"

"It was absolutely spectacular, guys. I'd give anything in the world for you to see this."

I snapped pictures, but without a zoom lens, none of the photos could come close to portraying what I saw with my eyes and felt in my heart. In my wildest dreams, I would have never imagined that *NASA One* would descend to fly alongside a little Cherokee 140.

◆ ◆ ◆

As you move on the trail, you will encounter many blessings that you would have missed had you stayed on the bus. Jesus said:

> No one who has left home or brothers or sisters or mother or father or children or fields for me and the gospel will fail to receive a hundred times as much in this present age (homes, brothers, sisters, mothers, children and fields—and with them, persecutions) and in the age to come, eternal life.
> —MARK 10:29–30

Yes, you travel in persecution territory. But you also travel in a blessed territory. Those who have left the bus to travel away from the familiar usually have a network of friends that cover the world. They don't live in "the good old times," but they eagerly look forward to the next adventure with God.

Yes, you hear the roar, and you face suffering on the trail, but keep your eyes on the ever-faithful Guide who has perfected a safe faith-trail through lion territory. Your Guide has endured the worst that lion territory could give, but He kept going because of the joy set before Him (Heb. 12:2). Keep your eyes on Him, and look for the joy in the journey.

CHAPTER 7

PERSEVERANCE PASSAGE

PERSEVERANCE POINTER 1

DETERMINE YOUR GOAL.

YOU ENCOUNTER SOME lions in sudden, unexpected, intense meetings that last a few hours. Accidents, sudden illnesses, natural disasters, and other situations require an urgent, bulldog tenacity in confronting the lion.

One hot afternoon, as Abraham was sitting at the entrance to his tent, he looked up and saw three men standing nearby. He invited them to lunch, and later one of them—the Lord—told Abraham that He was going to check out Sodom to see if the evil reports were true. (See Genesis 18.) Since Abraham knew that the reports probably fell short of detailing the wickedness that existed in Sodom, and the Lord would probably strike the people dead on the spot, Abraham immediately started interceding in a roundabout way to save his nephew Lot who lived in Sodom.

"Would you spare the city if fifty righteous people lived there?" Abraham asked. When God agreed, Abraham reduced the number to forty-five. From there, Abraham knew he was stretching the mercy and kindness of the Lord, but he pleaded for the city if forty, then thirty, then twenty, then ten righteous people could be found. Abraham's persevering request for mercy probably spanned an hour or less.

Those short, intense runs to the roar often spring on you through a phone call, a knock on the door, or an e-mail.

◆ ◆ ◆

One evening in Haiti, I was lost in the sixth book of *The Chronicles of Narnia* when the phone rang. Peter's courage and boldness had captivated my attention. Reluctantly, I picked up the receiver. It would probably be a wrong number and an argument would ensue over whether the caller had the right number.

Getting a call through in Haiti required discipline to dial the phone in a very slow and timed method. A single call could take ten to fifteen tries before connecting, and in spite of dialing a correct number, you often reached a wrong number.

Holding my place in the book, I answered. The call was from Tim Dodge, pastor of the English-speaking church that we attended in Port-au-Prince. "Joe," Tim said, "we have a missionary, Dorothy Erdman, whose kidneys have completely failed. We were told that if she doesn't get on a kidney dialysis machine within twenty-four hours she will die. It's already been close to twenty-four hours, and we're afraid we're going to lose her. Can you help us arrange an emergency flight to a dialysis machine? We heard that there's a dialysis machine at the U.S. base in Guantánamo Bay, Cuba, but we can't verify it."

Just as Peter in *The Chronicles of Narnia* rose to the occasion, I felt God was calling me to meet the challenge of saving this missionary's life. "Give me wisdom, Lord," I prayed, as I agreed to help.

Transporting Dorothy would require a plane that had oxygen and could accommodate a stretcher. I knew of only one such plane in Haiti, a Turbo Cessna 207. I placed a call, and, miraculously, the call went through without delay.

"Frantz," I said, "we need a plane. We have a missionary dying of kidney failure, and we need to get her to a dialysis machine. Can you help us?"

"Of course," Bennett replied. "Call Christian, and he'll fly you and the passenger."

I called Christian, who was co-owner of the Cessna, and we began discussing our options. First, we had to locate a dialysis machine. I started the process of contacting Guantánamo in Cuba. The phone connected to the American embassy in Haiti on the first try, and an officer contacted Guantánamo, inquiring about a dialysis machine. The reply came immediately. "Not available."

In the flurry of phone calls to find a dialysis machine and emergency transportation, Tim called to say that Dorothy was slipping into a coma. As the clock ticked beyond the twenty-four-hour survival time, our options dwindled. Medical resources in the neighboring Dominican Republic were almost as limited as in Haiti, and so a search there would probably be futile. Dorothy probably couldn't survive a flight to Miami. Furthermore, the Cessna could not fly to Florida without refueling. Since airports in the Caribbean closed at sunset, we would have no place to refuel.

Finally, Christian said, "If this lady is going to be saved, we're just going to have to make an effort to fly her to San Juan, Puerto Rico." He hesitated and then said, "It will cost about $1,200 to cover the flight."

PERSEVERANCE POINTER 2

FACE REALITY IN THE PURSUIT OF A GOAL.

I focused on getting Dorothy to a dialysis machine, but reality required that I accept that none was available in Guantánamo Bay, Haiti, or the Dominican Republic. Some people have faith in faith. The faith of a Christian is grounded in reality. We may not be able to see what we have faith in, but it does exist. I had faith that God would help me, but that faith was grounded in the reality that no dialysis machine was available in the surrounding countries. The end of my goal clearly lay in San Juan, Puerto Rico.

The courage of Peter, high king of *The Chronicles of Narnia*, came to mind. "I'll be responsible for her bill," I told Christian. I had no idea how I would pay for the flight, but I went to a phone and called Tim.

"Bring Dorothy to the airport," I said. "We're going to take her to San Juan for medical treatment."

By the time we had pulled the back seats out of the plane to make room for the stretcher and fueled the plane, the sun had set. Flying after sunset required filing of an IFR (Instrument Flight Rules) flight plan, but we didn't want to file the flight plan until we knew that the mission was a *go*.

Haiti has few ambulances, but Dorothy's friends managed to bring her to the plane in an ambulance. When they pulled the stretcher from the ambulance, I stifled a gasp and nausea. Erdman, now in a coma, had extremely yellow skin, and her body emitted the stench of death. Dorothy Erdman was in the process of dying.

Dorothy's husband, Jim, crawled into the back corner of the plane, and we placed Dorothy, with dripping IV, behind the pilot and copilot seats.

"Let's go," I said to Christian. "She doesn't have much time. We'll file the flight plan after we're in the air." I was not willing to compromise her life in order to dot every FAA (Federal Aviation Administration) i and cross every t.

With little hope of saving her life, Christian pushed the throttle of the Cessna forward, and we rolled down the runway. As we climbed and flew between mountains of eight thousand and ten thousand feet, we encountered clouds.

Christian looked at me and said, "I'm afraid to take her any higher without oxygen." The oxygen tank in the plane had not been filled.

I turned in the copilot's seat and placed my hand on Dorothy's forehead. It was cold and clammy. *Was this a hopeless flight?*

Jim sat hunched up in the corner, crying.

About an hour into the flight, Dorothy began to convulse.

"She's dying!" Jim screamed.

Dorothy let out a terrible cough, exhaling all air from her body, then lay completely still.

**Against all hope, Abraham
in hope believed (Rom. 4:18).**

"No! No!" I yelled. "She will not die. Pray, Jim."

Jim huddled in the corner sobbing, "My Dorothy. My Dorothy. My Dorothy is gone."

"In the name of Jesus," I cried, "come back to life!"

I reached into the back of the plane and grabbed Jim. "Pray!" I screamed at him through my own tears. "Pray, Jim. Believe God for your wife."

Jim, now in a fetal position, moaned, "My Dorothy. My Dorothy. My Dorothy is gone."

Again I cried, "Jesus, don't let her die!" But she lay motionless with no life signs.

Except for the drone of the engine and Jim's soft sobbing, the plane was silent. We flew on through a vast darkness broken only by the plane's strobe lights and distant thunderstorms that intermittently fired the sea. The cabin air, at nine thousand feet, was chilly. I reached back to touch Dorothy's forehead again. There was no warmth. I avoided taking a deep breath. The lion had marked Dorothy Erdman's bloated body with the distinctive scent of death. It *was* a hopeless flight.

◆ ◆ ◆

Hope falls into two categories—hope for things we desire and hope for things God has planted in our hearts. Hope based on what you would like to happen differs from hope based on God's Word. How can you know when to hold on to hope as Abraham did and when to accept a hopeless outcome as God's will?

Sometimes we base our hope on *our* ideas of God's plans. When God's path turns out to be "not quite what we had in mind," we question God. Often, though, when we take a close look at what we considered God's leading, we realize that we got an idea from God and then ran with it. Abraham based his hope on God's promise of "I will make you into a great nation" (Gen. 12:2). Abraham also ran with his own plan to fulfill that promise when he had a child by Hagar.

When hope vanishes, look at the scriptures God impressed on your mind. What did the scriptures really say? What did you hope that they would say? Sometimes, especially when you hope for something a long time, it is hard to face the reality of what God has promised and what He has not promised.

Sometimes there is no way that you can make "what you hoped for" happen. You must accept the reality of what God has really promised and go on. When your hope, however, is based on scriptures that the Lord has directed you to and that He has repeatedly and firmly impressed on your heart, you can snap your safety belt to hope and hang on for dear life.

My effort to save Dorothy Erdman's life had been a response to a Davidic type call—there is a lion. With God's help, I can defeat this lion. In spite of my best efforts and belief that God would assist me, this lion still roared in my face. *Had I assumed God was going with me to fight this lion, when God had no interest in engaging it?*

PERSEVERANCE POINTER 3

WHEN HOPE VANISHES, DON'T TURN AND RUN BACK. STAND YOUR GROUND.

Since takeoff, Christian had been trying to file an IFR flight plan and get clearance to land in San Juan. So far, his attempts had been rejected. Even after explaining, "We have a medical emergency onboard, and we need to get our passenger to a hospital," clearance to land had been denied. We could declare a flight emergency, but a false report could result in possible seizure of the plane and the pulling of both of our pilots' licenses.

Should we turn and go back home with Dorothy Erdman's body?

I couldn't believe that God had brought us this far to let her die. The phone call to me had come at a moment when *The Chronicles of Narnia* had inspired me to rise to the challenge of saving Dorothy's life. Only God could have gotten the Haitian phone system to operate as perfectly as it had this evening. Finding an ambulance was a miracle in itself. And the supply of the plane…who would believe that the president of Haiti's brother-in-law would help us with a plane? Furthermore, Dorothy had lived far beyond the twenty-four-hour survival time.

No! The hand of God had been evident throughout the whole evening. *It couldn't end like this!*

Remembering *The Chronicles of Narnia*, I turned to Dorothy and cried out one last time, "O Jesus! Bring Dorothy back!"

Dorothy coughed and began breathing again.

"Jim! Jim! She's alive," I yelled.

Jim continued sobbing. I reached into the back of the plane and shook him. "Jim! Your wife is alive!" Finally, Jim comprehended that Dorothy, though still unconscious, was indeed breathing. Although Dorothy had started breathing, she still had to endure two more hours in the harsh, dehydrating environment of high altitude.

While I had been focusing on Dorothy's life signs, Christian had been fighting with San Juan over permission to land and clear customs. Puerto Rico, with its stringent flying regulations, required one-hour advance notification to customs before landing. Failure to notify at the proper time could result in a $10,000 fine. Instead of granting permission for an IFR flight and notifying customs, the controller was hassling Christian about the nature of the flight and the legality of the flight. "Tell them it's an emergency flight," I told Christian. "Tell them we have a very ill person aboard."

Christian relayed the message, and when I heard hesitation in the controller's voice, I took over the microphone. In a firm and authoritative voice I said, "This is a mercy flight. We have a dying woman aboard. Have an ambulance waiting for us."

Grudgingly, they agreed to call an ambulance. We landed in San Juan and, following ground control's complicated instructions, taxied rapidly past 747s, 707s, and other large airliners to a designated parking spot. An ambulance stood waiting.

"Secure the plane, Christian," I said. "I'll get Dorothy to a hospital."

"There's a Holiday Inn next to the airport," Christian said, "I'll be there. Let's plan to leave at 6:00 in the morning to go back to Port." I nodded agreement and got into the ambulance with the Erdmans.

PERSEVERANCE POINTER 4

PERSEVERE WHEN OTHERS VIEW YOUR DREAM OR GOAL A LOST CAUSE.

Since Jim had been a United States war veteran, we headed to the veteran's hospital. "I'm a veteran," he explained to the admitting staff, "and my wife is dying. We need to get her on a dialysis machine."

"We only take veterans," the clerk said. "You'll have to take her to the public hospital."

Saving Dorothy's life seemed hopeless. By this time, she was far past the twenty-four-hour time limit of living with failed kidneys. When we pulled up to the emergency room of the next hospital, her uremic-poisoned body was an even more pronounced yellow.

In the emergency room, the young admitting person, yelled, "Who brought this woman here?"

His intensely negative reaction stunned me. "I did," I answered. "I'm the pilot that flew her here." I glanced at Jim, expecting him to claim some responsibility for her being there, but Jim provided no help at all. He was seated in a corner, doubled over mumbling, "Dorothy is gone. My Dorothy is gone."

"Why did you even bring her here?" the admitting person yelled. "Why did you wait so long? I've never seen anything like this in my life!"

"Just get her on a dialysis machine," I yelled back.

"You should have left her alone. You should have let her die," he said. "If she ever comes out of this coma, every organ in her body will be destroyed. I have never seen anything like this before."

Dorothy's bloated, grossly yellowed body reeked of organ decay.

"You get this woman on a dialysis machine," I demanded. Angrily, the triage unit transferred her from the stretcher to a hospital bed.

Having done all that I could to save Dorothy's life, I went to the Holiday Inn where I got about three hours of sleep. The next morning Christian and I flew back to Port-au-Prince, but the story didn't end. While Jim sat by the bedside of his comatose wife for twelve days, Christian battled with the FAA over the unauthorized flight. Rather than commending Christian for a bold, successful flight that saved a woman's life, they wanted to fine him. While Christian worked to resolve issues with the FAA, I faced the impossibility of raising $1,200 to cover the cost of the flight. I could and would donate part of the money, but there was no way that I could cover the entire bill. Tim Dodge, the pastor who initially contacted me about Dorothy, presented the need to the church, and in one evening the people donated enough to cover the flight costs.

In Puerto Rico, Jim stayed by Dorothy's side for twelve days, praying that God would heal and restore his wife. On the twelfth or thirteenth day, she awakened from the coma. All of her organs functioned normally, and during the next month of hospital recovery, doctors came and went marveling at her miraculous recovery. Dorothy went on to live a normal life for sixteen more years. When Dorothy did pass away in 1996, Jim sent me a tape of the eulogy in which he described the night that God brought Dorothy back to life.

The run to save Dorothy's life was extremely intense but lasted less than twelve hours. That short passage through lion territory had several U-turn options. I could have made a U-turn at—no dialysis machine in Guantánamo; a $1,200 flight cost; an air controller's refusal of landing permission; no admittance to the veteran's hospital; or at the public hospital's preference to "let her die." I kept my eye on one goal—get Dorothy Erdman connected to a dialysis machine. I had no idea what the outcome would be, but I refused to veer from the goal.

◆ ◆ ◆

Often, these sprints to the roar mean life or death to someone, and you may be the only one in a position to make a difference. If you can make a difference, step up and step forward and run to the roar. In these situations, always know what the ultimate goal is—keep your sights on the goal—work within the realms of reality. When hope vanishes, don't quickly turn back. Keep going, and trust God for the outcome.

Don't expect applause. Sometimes your good intentions may even create problems. Christian still had to deal with the FAA, and I still had to raise $1,200. Persevere in spite of the problems. In the end, you will know that you accomplished a worthy goal.

On some runs to the roar, you will encounter intense conflict that demands dogged, stubborn perseverance. At other times, running to the roar will require a plodding, putting-one-foot-in front-of-the-other trek.

Nehemiah's reconstruction of the walls around Jerusalem required a fifty-two-day run through ridicule, insults, intimidation, and death threats. The men worked from first light of dawn until the stars came out, and they slept with their clothes on in case they were called to defend the wall. In Jerusalem, Nehemiah persevered for nearly two months and never stopped running until the doors were set in the gates and gatekeepers and guards were posted.

Noah provides the best example of long-term perseverance. Board after board, caulking after caulking, year after year, Noah ran through the roar of mockery to condemn the lion, build the ark, and become an heir of righteousness (Heb. 11:7).

Some long, persistent runs to the roar begin as intense encounters, then seem never to end. They include rehabilitation after an accident or illness. Many long, persistent runs are preparation for God's ultimate use of our lives. Others are simply the journey of our life—rearing a family, being a caregiver, establishing a ministry, meeting a social need, or developing a business or career. Just as Noah constructed the ark, board by board, day in and day out, keep at a seemingly unending task until the goal is reached. Achievements that require lengthy perseverance will usually give you more pleasure than a sudden overnight success or windfall.

No matter the length of perseverance, some pointers remain the same:

1. Know your goal.
2. Make sure your faith is grounded in reality.
3. Avoid U-turns. Try a different way, but don't go back.
4. Let the Guide, not people, mark the stops on the trail.

◆ ◆ ◆

One of my God-given goals was to take the gospel to Cuba. On the long and arduous passage to take the gospel to Cuba, I had to repeatedly put the perseverance pointers into use and even add a few new ones. Many Caribbean flights took me close to Cuba. When I flew near the island, I often prayed for the people of Cuba and prayed for a way to take the *JESUS* film to them. In 1990, the president of Christian Television Network (CTN), Bob D'Andrea, asked if I would fly him to an appointment in Alabama. On the flight he said, "Joe, the Lord has really put it in my heart to go into Cuba."

I told the copilot to take over, and I slid my seat back in order to converse with Bob.

"Bob, I believe this is of God. The Lord has spoken to me, too. Many of my trips have taken me within a few miles of Cuban airspace. I've often wondered what would happen to that communist nation if they had a good revival. Let's do it!"

"Some U.S. ministries are slipping in the back door through Mexico," Bob said.

"I'm not sneaking in," I said. "Do you remember reading about Brother Andrew in the book *God's Smuggler?*"

"Yes," Bob said.

"On one trip he was carrying a whole carload of Bibles and got backed into a corner with no escape. When the guard asked about his intentions, Brother Andrew said, 'I'm taking Bibles in,' and the guard let him through. I refuse to sneak into Cuba and whisper Jesus' name in some dark corner. I'm going to Washington DC and find a way to legally enter Cuba."

"If you can get in," Bob said, "I want to go with you."

I flew to Washington DC and went to the Office of Foreign Assets Control (OFAC) of the U.S. Department of the Treasury. OFAC was the branch of government that enforced the economic and trade sanctions against Cuba.

At OFAC, I met Marcella, a congenial African American woman. In spite of her warm personality, she had a professional bureaucratic manner that sent a clear message: "We play by the rules here. We dot every i, and we cross every t. Don't even think of trying to fast-talk your way past me."

"Marcella," I said, "I want to go to Cuba."

"You can't go to Cuba," she said.

"Oh, come on, Marcella," I said. "You know there are loopholes."

She pulled off her reading glasses and looked across the desk at me. "Why do you want to go to Cuba?"

"I want to see Christianity dominate Cuba. When Christianity dominates, oppression ends. People respect the rights of others."

"You can't go to Cuba," she said.

"Marcella, I know that loopholes exist. I've worked with the FAA long enough to know that there are ways to get around some of these regulations. Show me how to get there."

She frowned and shook her head. It wasn't as much a negative reaction as an "I can't believe that you are saying this" reaction.

"Listen, Marcella, I want to go to Cuba and show the *JESUS* film. If there is a strong move for God in Havana, and the people get a taste of spiritual freedom, they will live their lives differently. Even government officials will want justice and freedom in their country."

"That's interesting," she said. She looked at me with a you-are-wasting-my-time expression. When she saw that I was serious and that I wasn't going to go away, she rolled her chair back to a file cabinet and pulled out some papers. Handing the papers to me, she said, "Here are the exemptions." She motioned to a table and said, "Sit over there and see what you can find."

As I stood, she motioned for me to hand back the papers. "I will point out a few things," she said, and casually pointed to a couple paragraphs with her pen. "You might want to look at those."

"Research?" I said. "I like that. How about a documentary? The president of a Christian television network wants to collaborate with me. I think we could go to Cuba and make a television documentary on Christianity. Would that fit the bill?"

"That would do it," she said slowly.

After filling out forms signifying my intentions to go to Cuba to do a documentary, I left Marcella's office, saying, "Thank You, Jesus, for opening the door to Cuba!" I had no idea how small that opening was and how difficult squeezing through it would be.

PERSEVERANCE POINTER 5

PERSEVERE WHEN THE WORK REQUIRES TEDIOUS,
REPEATED, SEEMINGLY UNNECESSARY ACTIVITIES.

With clearance from OFAC, I then turned to the Cubans for permission to enter their country. The Cubans had no embassy in the United States, but they did have a Cuban Interests Section in the Czechoslovakian embassy. The Cubans' initial response to my request was *no*. I prayed, and persisted, and finally obtained permission.

Then, my U.S. clearance was canceled.

I returned to Marcella's office. "What's going on?" I asked her. "I get clearance, and now it's pulled!"

"How did you ever get permission from the Cubans?" Marcella asked

"Marcella!" I said. "Give me a break! I got permission because I was persistent. I don't have any hidden agenda."

"Well," she said, "we really can't let you go." She had several legitimate reasons for canceling my clearance. I wondered if OFAC had given me initial clearance because it was an easy way to get rid of me. They, no doubt, had thought the Cubans would refuse my request and I would never return to the Treasury Department.

By now, though, Marcella was beginning to realize that I didn't give up easily. She sat, turning her pen end to end, and then finally said, "Let me see what I can do, Joe." Thus began the tug-of-war between two countries. One country would reinstate my clearance, and the other one would cancel it.

Knowing the risks of losing my plane, my freedom, and even my life, I meticulously logged every conversation, every contact, and every communication. Fax machines were just coming into wide use, and I either called Marcella or faxed details of every move I made. I not only sent details to Marcella at OFAC, but I also sent details of my activities to the Cuban Interests Section, the U.S. Treasury Department, and the Cuban Affairs in the State Department. Similar communications went to the Ministry of Tourism in Cuba. Although I ultimately hoped to fly my own plane to Cuba, I first concentrated on entering Cuba on a commercial airline. After nearly three thousand communications—personal appearances, letters, phone calls, and faxes—I received final clearance to fly to Cuba on a diplomatic charter.

On that first flight, the pilot allowed me to sit on the flight deck of the 727, and we discussed planes and flying. To my surprise, during the landing in Havana, the pilot grunted and struggled with the plane as he held the nose of the plane in the air and appeared to do a wheelie down the runway.

Aghast, I sputtered, "What are you doing?"

"Waiting for the railroad track!"

The rear wheels went *clunk! clunk!* as they struck something on the runway.

"There's a railroad track about six thousand feet down the runway," the captain explained.

On that first trip and on future trips, most of my twenty-four-hour time allotment was spent in tedious back-and-forth trips between bureaucratic offices. I had assumed that, after the first trip, getting into Cuba would be easier, but every trip involved several clearance changes and two thousand to three thousand communications.

◆ ◆ ◆

Running to the roar isn't all excitement. Stephen passed out food to the poor, and Paul sat in prison during much of his ministry. You will have many boring, plodding days. Never give up during the plodding stage. "So do not throw away your confidence; it will be richly rewarded. You need to persevere so that when you have done the will of God, you will receive what he has promised" (Heb. 10:35–36). As you run to the roar, keep your goal in mind, and be willing to do the necessary drudgery work to complete a task.

Month after month I plodded through faxes and phone calls. Eventually, after months of tedious, repetitive work, I was able to get clearance for three or four other Christians to accompany me. While I laid the groundwork to do the documentary and worked on clearance to fly my own plane to Cuba, others on the team worked on obtaining permission to show the *JESUS* film in theaters.

PERSEVERANCE POINTER 6

SOME EVENTS, CIRCUMSTANCES, AND SITUATIONS WILL
NEVER MAKE SENSE. DON'T TRY TO REASON THEM OUT
OR TRY TO FIGURE WHERE THEY FIT IN GOD'S PLAN.
KEEP WALKING, AND TRUST THAT YOU ARE MAKING
PROGRESS TOWARD GOD'S GOAL FOR YOUR LIFE.

Armando, a South American leader of Campus Crusade, was scheduled to accompany me on one flight. Armando would both interpret and help me make contacts with Cuban Christians. Just before I left for Cuba, officers in the Treasury Department said, "Joe, if you go in this time and something happens, don't expect our help. We can't do anything to help you. You are on your own." I thought it a strange warning, but I hadn't expected their help anyway, so I proceeded with my plans.

My final contact with Cuban Interests was equally ominous. "Joe," the liaison said, "if you make this flight to Cuba, we can't guarantee your safety." I hadn't expected protection from either my own government or the Cuban government, but their dual warnings made me wonder if something was up that I didn't know about.

The trip, though, had potential to open doors to the underground church, so I went ahead with my plans. On this trip, along with working on the documentary and trying to get flight clearance, Armando was going to introduce me to Javier, a prominent underground pastor.

Armando and I met at a coffee shop in MIA (Miami International Airport) an hour before check-in time. We both ordered demitasse cups of rich, sweet Cuban coffee and took seats at a round table in the corner.

"Joe," Armando said, "I can't go. My overseer from Campus Crusade has just flown in, and I have to meet with him."

"You have to go!"

"You will have to do this trip alone."

"Armando! I can't communicate with this pastor in Spanish. You could put all the Spanish I know in that cup," I said, pointing to my demitasse cup.

"You can handle it. Just call him on the phone, and he will come and get you. Javier speaks some English."

Armando pulled his napkin from under the demitasse cup and started writing on it. All the while he was writing, I was muttering, "You have to go with me. I can't do this by myself." In the back of my mind were the warnings, "If you get into trouble, we aren't going to help you. You are on your own." I desperately needed Armando to accompany me on this trip.

"When you get to the Riviera Hotel," Armando said, "call this number. Javier speaks English, but the person who answers the phone probably won't speak English. I have written down what you need to say." He shoved the napkin across the table and said, "Here, read what it says. Say it for me."

I kept my arms folded on the table. I didn't want to touch the napkin. I wanted Armando to go with me.

"Joe," he said, shoving the napkin under my hand, "You need to say this. Now say it for me."

All I could think of was, *Do I really want to make this trip?* The warnings bothered me. Was this God closing the door or Satan attempting to block an important meeting with the underground church? I didn't know, and I didn't have much time to make a decision.

"Oh, man, Joe," Armando said glancing at his wristwatch, "your plane leaves in forty-five minutes. We have to work on this. Now say after me…come on, Joe, say it to me."

With one finger, I turned the napkin so that I could see the words, then tried to pronounce the unfamiliar phrases.

"No! No!" Armando said, "This is not French! This is Spanish. You must pronounce each syllable. I'm going to pronounce the words. Say them after me."

He worked with me on the pronunciation until it was time to check in. "OK, OK," he finally said. "That will do. Practice it on the plane."

I stood in the check-in line, thinking, *Do I really want to go? This is crazy. What am I? Nuts? I've been warned, and now I'm going into Cuba with no interpreter and trying to make contact with the underground church. Do I go through with this mission or not? Should I abort this mission?*

There were about forty people in line—all diplomats with assurance that their government would stand behind them. As I moved forward, I alternately referred to the napkin and wrestled with the decision to turn around and go home. When I was about fifteen people from the counter, the ticket agent leaned out and crooked his finger to call me to the head of the line.

"Mr. Hurston," he said, "you will be flying first class tonight." There was no explanation. Mystified, I took the ticket and thanked the agent.

I had flown my own plane to Miami International Airport (MIA) and was dressed in the pilot attire of dark slacks, white shirt, and tie. Since my stay in Cuba was always restricted to twenty-four hours, I carried only a regular pilot's flight case. I boarded with my flight case and took my seat in first class. They had given me the first seat by the exit door.

> **Take a lesson from the mosquito. She never waits for an opening—she makes one.**[1]
> —**Kirk Kirkpatrick**

When we landed in Havana, and the cabin door opened, and the stairs started down, I saw a host of military approaching the plane. One officer carried a clipboard. This had not happened on previous flights. Paranoia gripped me.

I had no intention of hanging around to be interrogated, especially without a trustworthy interpreter. I straightened my tie, squared my shoulders, and as soon as the stairs touched ground, I walked out the door, down the steps, and briskly across the tarmac. I passed the military and gave them a sharp salute. They, thinking I was one of the pilots of the aircraft, returned the salute.

When I walked into the terminal, the building was crammed full of people, and every line through immigration was long. If the military intended to question me, they would catch me here. Off to the right, though, an agent motioned to me. Believing me to be a pilot of an incoming plane, he stamped my passport, and I was out the door in less than a minute.

I'm sure that it was only paranoia breathing down my neck that day, but to me it seemed that I felt the breath of the lion as I stepped out the door. Perhaps I would have been questioned on the plane. Perhaps someone, somewhere sensed I needed help and prayed for me. I don't know, but I do know that God has innovative methods to deliver us, and He seems never to work the same way twice. I think that if we stay open to Him, rather than fretfully try to deliver ourselves,

He can quicken our minds to see escape routes that might go unnoticed. David escaped by putting a decoy in his bed; Paul went out a window in a basket; Jesus slipped through a crowd that intended to toss Him off a Nazareth cliff.

You may not need a unique escape route, but always be open to innovative methods to accomplish your work. Look at how God handled closed doors. He never operated in the same way. He parted the Red Sea with a raised staff, took down the walls of Jericho with trumpets and a shout, loosened the lug nuts on Egyptian chariot wheels, dropped hailstones to rout armies, and sent hornets to evict residents. As you continue on God's trail, keep your eyes on the Guide and not fear. Remember, God has ways that have never entered your mind to sneak you past lions.

PERSEVERANCE POINTER 7

DISCOVER WHERE AND HOW THE HOLY SPIRIT IS MOVING, AND WATCH FOR WAYS TO ADAPT YOUR MINISTRY TO THIS MOVEMENT.

Although I operated in an open and direct manner and documented every step I took in Cuba, one thought continually lurked in the shadows of my mind: a communist regime does not operate by democratic rules. While a communist government could block my entry to Cuba, it could never block God's entry to the country. No country can close its borders to God. As Christians, it is important to watch where God is working in a country, a community, a church, or even in an individual's life. Listen to people around you. Where is God moving in their lives? What burdens concern them? Listen to Christian brothers and sisters. How is the Lord answering prayer? What doors is God opening? I went into Cuba with a plan, but my mind was open to where the Spirit of God was moving.

In spite of the harrowing start to the Cuba trip without Armando, I made contact with the underground pastor, and he took me to the office of Cuban Civil Aviation in Havana, where I met Mr. Suárez. Mr. Suárez was a dark Cuban gentleman with bright eyes. He had grown up in New York, so he spoke very good English.

After introducing myself and exchanging pleasantries with Mr. Suárez, I said, "I'm a missionary pilot. I would like to start making missionary flights to Cuba." My request to fly into Cuba as a missionary was about as absurd as Moses' initial request to let the Israelite slaves leave Egypt.

"And what does your Treasury Department have to say about this?" Mr. Suárez asked.

"After great, great effort they have given me the opportunity to come in and do research on the history of the church in Cuba."

Mr. Suárez looked puzzled and perplexed. He shook his head and said, "Mr. Hurston."

"Just call me Joe or Jose," I said.

"Joe, it will not be easy. Neither your government nor my government really would want you to do this."

"So what's new, Mr. Suárez? What's easy? Do you have anything easy in your life? Nothing's easy."

He chuckled and shook his head.

"After I leave you," I said, "I'm going to your Ministry of Foreign Affairs." The Ministry of Foreign Affairs was the Cuban State Department.

"*You* are going to the Ministry of Foreign Affairs?" Mr. Suárez said. I could tell from his expression that he thought, *This man doesn't have a clue about how our government works.*

"Yes," I said. "I want to talk to them and see their response to my request."

"Get back with me after you see them," Mr. Suárez said, as he started shuffling papers on his desk. I knew that he was pushing me out the door just as Marcella had. He didn't expect to see me again.

After jumping through all the Treasury hoops and all the Cuban hoops, Mr. Suárez gave me clearance to fly the Aztec into José Martí International Airport on a Saturday in late July of 1991. When I neared Cuba on Saturday, however, the tower informed me that I did not have authorization to land. I returned to Miami and immediately began working on authorization to enter Cuba the way I had in the past, on a commercial flight. To my astonishment, by Wednesday, just four days later, I was able to get clearance to fly in on the regular diplomatic charter.

When I landed in Havana, I immediately went to the Department of Civil Aviation.

"Mr. Suárez," I said, "why was I turned back?"

He muttered a few words as if he couldn't explain in English. He never did give me a reason, but he did finally give me full authorization to fly my plane in the next week.

Before leaving Cuba, I met a Christian doctor. When the time came for me to fly back home, he drove me to José Martí International Airport in his Lada station wagon. "I know all about this car," I said. "I had one similar to this one in Haiti. It was called a Polski. Have you figured out all the lights yet?"

"I know it has a lot of lights," he said.

"Lights go on when you move the seats," I said.

"And each gear has a different light."

"It's like boarding a rocket ship," I said. "Must have fourteen lights."

We were laughing about the lights, and then he got serious. He leaned over and lowered his voice. "Joe, can you get me the *JESUS* film?"

I knew that Campus Crusade would supply the film, but I immediately questioned how I could get such a revolutionary film through customs. Our request to show it in the theaters had been denied. Besides presenting the gospel, the movie had a tendency to draw crowds. In a country where more than six people on a street corner could be considered an unapproved public gathering, the *JESUS* film could be considered subversive.

"I can handle getting the film through customs," the doctor assured me. "You get it here, and I'll take care of the rest."

I asked no questions. He apparently had connections that I was better off not knowing about. While I absolutely refused to pay bribes to anyone, I wasn't going to ask how he planned to get the film through customs.

"Here's my flight authorization," I said, waving the authorization papers. "Be at the airport at 10:00 on Wednesday morning. I'll bring the *JESUS* film and the equipment to show it."

As we entered the terminal, the doctor pointed out automatic doors exiting customs. "I'll be right there," he said, and pointed to the right side of the doors. "Those doors don't open from the outside. When you arrive, go to the door and let me in, and I'll handle the rest."

"I'll be dressed like this," I said, pointing to my dark slacks, white shirt, and tie. "On Wednesday, though, I'll have the epaulets and stripes on my shoulder."

"Be sure to come right at 10:00. If I hang around the doors too long, the guards at the door will notice."

"I'll be here at 10:00," I said. Since I was flying my own plane, I felt comfortable with giving him a firm arrival time. "You make sure you are here! I could never get that film through customs."

"If you aren't here by 11:00," the doctor said, "I'll know that they turned you back again."

Perseverance was paying off. In a few days I would reach my goal to take the *JESUS* film to Cuba.

That's a valiant flea that dare eat his breakfast on the lip of a lion.²
—WILLIAM SHAKESPEARE

When I spoke to Campus Crusade about taking the *JESUS* film to Cuba, they donated a full package for showing the film—screen, projector, generator, film, and sound system. On Wednesday morning, I loaded all the equipment in the Aztec and left for Miami, allowing more than adequate time to handle last-minute details. Three other passengers also had clearance to fly with me that day—a copilot, a TV producer, and an interpreter. The interpreter's father had been a wealthy plantation owner in Cuba who, before escaping to Florida, had been tortured by Castro's men. Under extreme duress, the older man's hair had changed from jet black to white in a short time.

PERSEVERANCE POINTER 8

PERSEVERANCE INVOLVES BOTH RESTRAINED WAITING AND BOLD VENTURING.

We can cope with weariness, boredom, discouragement, misunderstanding, and even defeat, but repeated delays prove the real depth of our faith and commitment to persevere. Noah spent 120 years waiting on God. David waited, hiding in caves, to take the throne. Just when Paul would get a good church going, a prison trip would halt his ministry.

Small delays in daily schedules can produce frustration. Many delays can exhaust patience. That first flight to Cuba on the Aztec, I encountered a series of unexpected delays that not only tested my patience but also threatened to jeopardize my life and the lives of the mission team.

When flying to Cuba, all private flights from the United States must be pre-cleared out of Miami International Airport (MIA). Unlike other flights that require customs clearance on inbound flights only, Cuba flights also require customs clearance on out-bound flights. Although I had allowed three hours to handle this clearance, every imaginable delay took place. A customs official did not show up. A paper had not yet cleared an office. Delay after delay kept pushing me closer to takeoff time.

I looked at my watch. Almost 9:00 a.m. The doctor would be at the airport in Havana at 10:00 a.m. If I didn't show at the appointed time, he would leave. I could do nothing to speed up our departure. Finally, clearance came to proceed to Cuba, and we quickly boarded the Aztec.

MIA is a huge airport with long taxiways and runways. The Aztec is a little airplane. I taxied so fast I was almost breaking ground and flying. Soon, I found myself in a stack of about seven airliners. My little Aztec was stuck right in there, and I was waiting and mutter-ing under my breath, "Come on, come on!"

I glanced at the August sun. It was high in the sky. We were late, late, late. Sweat trickled down my face and streaked my aviator sunglasses. I couldn't remember ever being so anxious about a take-off. Right now I should have Havana in view, and I hadn't even left Miami. The doctor wasn't going to hang around the airport long and arouse suspicion.

Finally, I was next to go. I waited, and after being sequenced as number one to go, I said to the tower, "Five Nine Yankee, ready to go."

"Hold short, Five Nine Yankee!" the tower said. "November Three Eight Bravo, you're cleared for takeoff."

"Wait a minute tower!" I yelled. "Five Nine Yankee's next!"

"Hold short, Five Nine Yankee. Three Eight Bravo, you're cleared for takeoff."

I watched slack-jawed as a Cessna 402 came from behind me and took off.

I cussed.

I didn't know what my passengers thought about their mis-sionary pilot, but I cussed. Airport authorities had delayed me and delayed me, and the air controller had detained me with an unheard-of action. At this point, my schedule wasn't slightly off. It was completely blown.

I didn't know what was happening. Airliners don't jump lines. In all my flying days, nothing like this had happened before. Controllers do not sequence you into a takeoff position and then change their minds. We would surely miss our appointment with the doctor. If we were caught carrying the *JESUS* film, we could all end up in prison. All I could do was hope my passengers were praying. I certainly wasn't in a praying mood.

"Five Nine Yankee, you're cleared to take off now," the tower said.

"Thank you very much!"

I did a close imitation of revving my motor and peeling rubber as I took off. My passengers sat in silence, apparently surprised at my actions and the carnal comments coming out of my mouth.

In the air, the Cessna 402 flew ahead of me. My little Aztec was almost keeping up with it. I was furious with the pilot, but I knew I must keep alert for the turn to Havana. At a certain point, at an invisible intersection in the sky, flights to Havana make a turn. No one turns at that intersection unless they are going to Havana. I prepared to announce my intentions to enter the intersection when the pilot of the 402 announced he was entering the intersection.

In my seven or eight flights to Havana, I had never seen a plane, other than our diplomatic charter, make that turn. "He's going to Cuba!" I said, spitting the words. I tried to calm down for the sake of my passengers, but I was steamed. *That guy jumped line on me; I'm late; the doctor isn't going to be there. I've got all this stuff in the airplane, and they're going to seize my plane and throw us in one of Castro's prisons.*

I announced my intentions to enter the intersection to Cuba and checked air traffic around me. Another 402, like the one ahead of me, had been behind me and was staying there. I made my turn toward Havana and flew about six miles behind the leading 402. Now two planes were going to Havana at the same time—a 402 and my Aztec.

Then the Cessna 402 behind me announced a turn toward Havana. *This is weird,* I thought. *Is this a Cuban escort?*

The three of us flew together for the next half hour and entered the traffic pattern at José Martí International Airport. As the Cessna 402 ahead of me approached the landing, I wondered if he knew about the railway tracks that crossed the runway. No pilot wishes disaster on another pilot, but I felt no Christian charity toward a pilot that cut line during takeoff. I hoped those railroad tracks rattled his teeth.

I landed a few minutes later, and the trailing 402 landed two minutes behind me. Three planes were now on the ground—a 402, my Aztec, and another 402. On previous flights, the passengers had deplaned and had taken their baggage inside the terminal. This day, the military, armed with AK47s, immediately surrounded all three planes and began yanking open cargo doors. When I tried to reach for some of the sensitive film equipment, they pushed me out of the way. I tried again to stop them, and they glared at me. I backed off. I didn't have much choice. They had AK47s, and the clips were in them. When I started to protest, I felt that the Lord hushed me with a stern "Peace!" It didn't do much to still the storm in me, but I kept silent.

My passengers were directed into the terminal, and I stayed with the plane while the military unloaded the film, screen, generator, speakers, and other equipment. As a pilot I felt responsible for both passengers and cargo and was ready to fight to preserve both. However, when I again started to protest about the handling of the equipment, I again felt the "Shush! Hold your peace!" from the Lord.

Silently, I watched the soldiers take the equipment off the plane, put it in the back of a military truck, and rattle off. A guard came to me, poked his AK47 in my side, and told me to reposition the airplane. He boarded the plane with me, placed the AK47 across his lap with the barrel jammed between two of my ribs, and directed me to a tie-down quite a distance from the terminal. After securing the plane, a minibus picked me up and transferred me back to the main terminal.

PERSEVERANCE POINTER 9

NEVER ALLOW FEAR TO REDIRECT YOUR STEPS. KEEP YOUR EYES ON THE GUIDE AND THE GOAL.

When I finally walked into the main terminal, I saw my passengers. After making sure they had not been harassed, I started scanning the room. A Russian jumbo jet had just landed, and more than three hundred people were gathering luggage and heading to the customs lines.

Off to the side, I saw the *JESUS* film in a little black box with straps on it. I pointed to more of our equipment and said to the fellows with me, "There's our stuff. Let's get it. There's the film. Over there is the generator. Look for the speakers."

There is a point at which everything becomes simple and there is no longer any question of choice, because all you have staked will be lost if you look back.[3]
—Dag Hammarskjöl

While they gathered everything and heaped it onto pushcarts, I went to get the doctor. Since I wore the standard pilot uniform with epaulets and bars and carried general declaration forms, I had no problem moving around in customs. I stepped outside the door of customs, passed between the guards, and looked to both sides of the door.

The doctor was not there.

Thinking that he had taken a walk in order to avoid detection by the guards, I walked the perimeter of the building where civilians were allowed. The doctor simply was not there. We had missed the appointment, and the doctor had gone. Now I had two cartloads of seditious material on my hands.

I knocked on the door to customs, and someone let me back inside. My passengers were watching a melee that looked like a shark-feeding frenzy. The customs agents were acting like crazy people. They were opening everything, plowing through suitcases, and tossing items in disarray that would leave passengers cursing and struggling to repack. If they treated passengers from a communist country like this, what would they do to us Americans?

I broke out in a sweat that was not caused by the humid tropical air. There was no way we could ever get the film and our equipment past these agents. Furthermore, they could detain and possibly imprison us if they examined the film. I had little fear for myself, but I felt totally responsible for the welfare of my passengers. If they connected the interpreter to his exiled father, he could be in grave danger.

With a sick feeling in my throat, I called my passengers close so that they could hear above the din of hundreds of people. "The doctor isn't here," I told them. "We have all this film equipment, and we could be thrown in jail. I'm just going to tell the customs official the truth. Stay with the equipment and pray."

I looked over the customs area and found the head of customs. He had epaulets and bars all over his shirt and sat in an open, elevated platform overseeing the pandemonium. *Brother Andrew*, I thought, *I know openness and honesty worked for you. I sure hope it works for me.* At this moment, I knew only one thing for certain. Whatever lay ahead, God would be with me. He would not forsake me.

"Señor," I said politely, "I was supposed to meet someone here, and he isn't here. I have all this film equipment for him."

"You have the film equipment?" he asked.

"Yes, I was supposed to meet someone here, and he is not here."

"Show me the film equipment."

I pointed to the film equipment piled on the carts. "It's all right there," I said.

"That is the film equipment?"

"Yes, that is the film equipment."

"That is the film equipment." This time he said it as a statement rather than a question. He waved toward the exit and said, "You may go."

I smiled and gave him my best ingratiating, "Gracias." Under my breath and through clenched teeth, I muttered to the team, "Get going! Get going! Get the stuff out the doors!" My eyes and body language communicated, "Run!" They had enough sense to react without questions. We shoved the carts through the doors and hailed two taxis.

After hurriedly stuffing the equipment and ourselves in the taxis, we made a dash into Havana. The Cuban pastor knew where the equipment was to be delivered and directed us to the church.

All the while we were traveling through Havana, I kept thinking soldiers would block the road and search our taxis, but no one stopped us. We drove down into the basement of a church and unloaded the equipment. Still watching over our shoulders and expecting to be stopped at any moment, we then hurried to our rooms at the Riviera Hotel.

Only when we reached our rooms, did we relax. The *JESUS* film had been delivered, and we had been delivered, but the events of the day made no sense to us at all. We sat in our twelfth-floor hotel room and tried to understand. *Why were we escorted? Why did the military seize our baggage? Why did the customs official let us through without as much as an inspection?*

Unknown to us, God had arranged our flight schedule that day. Even the unprecedented incident of line jumping by the pilot of the 402 had been a part of God's plan. Piece by piece, and with information from the doctor who later called us, we discovered an explanation for the day's events.

The Pan American games were to begin on August 2 in Havana and Santiago. The planes that escorted us were media planes that had clearance to cover the Pan American games. They were loaded with cameras and all types of film equipment.

While I was ranting, raving, and acting carnal about the delays, the Lord was at work slipping the Aztec in between two media planes. When we landed, the Cuban military had assumed we were part of the media team and had transferred our cargo to customs. There, as members of the supposed media teams, the customs officials had given us immediate clearance.

Later, the doctor who was to have met us at the airport said, "I went there. I waited and God spoke to me and told me to leave, so I left. Had I been there to help you, we never would have gotten the film through customs."

God's timing and method of delivering the JESUS film had been flawless. Years later, Cuban Christians still tell the story of how the JESUS film came to Cuba. When I was complaining the most, accusing God of abandoning me, God was doing His best work for me.

Perseverance is an essential element in running to the roar. Peter failed the perseverance test when Jesus was arrested. He denied that he even knew Christ. Years later, Peter tells us that people who do not have faith, goodness, knowledge, self-control, *perseverance*, godliness, brotherly kindness, and love are nearsighted and blind. Peter not only admonishes us to possess these qualities, but he also says that if we want to have an effective and productive knowledge of Christ, we must develop them more fully. (See 2 Peter 1:2–9.)

So how do we develop perseverance more fully?

Suffering.

Here we go again. Suffering. No one really wants to suffer, but Paul says to rejoice in sufferings. What do you have to rejoice about

in suffering? Paul says, "Suffering produces perseverance; perseverance, character; and character, hope" (Rom. 5:3–4).

As you consider the importance of perseverance in running to
the roar, look at how earlier lessons have prepared you to persevere.
You have faced the reality of danger in lion territory, you have gone
through difficult separations, you have placed your faith in Christ
as your Guide, and you are going through training exercises that
require perseverance. Many lessons have been mastered through
suffering. Do you regret the training so far?

Well, I think you will have to admit, the training hasn't been
pleasant, and you wouldn't want to go through it again. But on the
other hand, you are beginning to see benefits, signs of a future harvest of righteousness and peace (Heb. 12:11).

The longer that you walk with the Guide, and the better that you
come to know Him, the more you will understand that His way is
not some dusty path with ankle-wrenching rocks, but a highway
paved by interlocking scriptures that give you firm footing. Read
again the verses in Hebrews 12:1–3, and note the ways in which the
writer encourages you to focus on the goal and run to the roar.

> Therefore, since we are surrounded by such a great cloud
> of witnesses, let us throw off everything that hinders and
> the sin that so easily entangles, and let us run with perse-
> verance the race marked out for us. Let us fix our eyes on
> Jesus, the author and perfecter of our faith, who for the joy
> set before him endured the cross, scorning its shame, and
> sat down at the right hand of the throne of God. Consider
> him who endured such opposition from sinful men, so that
> you will not grow weary and lose heart.
> —HEBREWS 12:1–3

See how it all fits together. The farther you continue toward the
roar, the more you will realize that every step, every heartache,
every joy, every disappointment, every lesson, every accomplishment, every failure, and every triumph have been instruments to
firm the path and prepare solid footing for your next steps.

CHAPTER 8

THE LION'S LAIR

LAIR REALITY 1

PEOPLE SEEM HAPPY IN THE LAIR.
SHOULD WE BOTHER THEM?

WHAT MOTIVATES PEOPLE to run to the roar? Is it a vision of great accomplishment...a desire to rescue others...a sense of responsibility to help less fortunate people...or a concern for social justice? All of these commendable reasons can be handled to some degree without calling on God or referring to the Word of God for guidance. What differentiates those who run to the roar by their own strength from those who go with Christ and use the Scriptures as a guide?

Those who run with Christ not only see the lion and hear the roar, but they also run with a vision of the lair in mind. These people have been former residents of the lair and lived under the lion's paw. Along with alleviating suffering, they long to lead others out of the lair to safety.

Sometimes, especially for very dear friends, you might wish you could launch an intervention and drag them to their senses, but few who leave the lair under pressure stay out long. They must leave the lair with no desire to return. How then can you coax them from the darkness of the lair to the light where they can see the rich and abundant life that lies beyond the lair? It is, once again, doing the job at hand, relying on the Spirit to direct you as you interact daily with people.

For twenty-one years I romped and played in the lair, not realizing that Satan was toying with my life—as a cat with a mouse. I did not know that true freedom and life lay beyond the lion's paw. Rather than running to the roar in opposition to the lion, I lounged in the lion's lair. I disdained those who opposed the lion, called warnings to me, or tried to coax me from the den. Each time that God would reach into the lair to pull me out of sin, the lion would slap a paw on my life and hold me more tightly.

LAIR REALITY 2

EVERY INTELLIGENT THINKING PERSON HAS QUESTIONS ABOUT THE GUIDE AND THE TRAIL. TREAT QUESTIONS WITH CARE.

During my childhood, I hungered to know God. I attended a Catholic elementary school, and many mornings I would get up early, press my clothes, and attend a 6:00 a.m. Latin mass before classes. At funerals and during other stressful times, I consoled members of my extended family. Because I had a tender heart and reached out to others who were suffering, my family jokingly called me "Father Joe."

By the time I reached eighth grade, however, I had questions about my Catholic faith. While discussing these questions with friends, a mother came at me yelling, "How dare you! How dare you talk like this to these children?" In her anger, she dumped the contents of an ashtray on my head.

A few days later the monsignor called me into his office. My questions had offended one of the wealthiest and staunchest supporters of the church. "What do you mean by questioning our faith?" he demanded.

"I'm just trying to find answers," I replied. "I really have questions, and I'm really searching for answers."

By the time the monsignor had finished his reprimand and had outlined his disciplinary action, I had decided that I had had enough of "church." Years would pass before I attended church again. I, as so many others have done, judged all churches by the actions of a couple people.

Some people say, "Never ask God *why.*" God doesn't mind questions if you ask in the right attitude. God probably won't give you a reason *why,* but He isn't distressed by a frustrated question. Since He knows your thoughts, you may as well discuss your questions and doubts with Him.

Perhaps our greatest deterrent in taking questions to God is accepting His answers. He seldom replies immediately, but if you write down your questions and check for answers months or years later, you will find He was listening to you. Answers to your questions will most likely fall into two categories—you have found or are in the process of discovering the answer, or the question isn't that important anymore.

You will often find answers to some questions as God deals with a deeper issue in your life. You may have been asking God, "Why did You place me under this supervisor?" Months later, you may realize "this supervisor" taught you to endure under pressure.

Just as you have had questions about your faith, other people have legitimate questions about God. Keep the apostle Paul's advice in mind when dealing with questions that others may ask. Paul told Timothy:

> Don't have anything to do with foolish and stupid arguments, because you know they produce quarrels…be kind to everyone…gently instruct, in the hope that God will grant them repentance leading them to a knowledge of the truth, and that they will *come to their senses and escape from the trap* of the devil, who has taken them captive to do his will.
> —2 TIMOTHY 2:23–26, EMPHASIS ADDED

Some people will want to quarrel with you and with God. Avoid arguments and a defensive attitude. You don't have to defend God or His actions. Never be afraid to say, "I don't know," or "I'll have to think about that." Use gentleness, and you will be able to lead others to the knowledge of truth and help them escape the lair.

LAIR REALITY 3

AT EVERY AGE WE WIELD INFLUENCE, AND AT EVERY AGE WE ARE SUSCEPTIBLE TO INFLUENCE.

During my childhood, one person emerged as a strong role model. I followed his footsteps, oblivious to the danger that lay on that path. The path started at the Baton Rouge downtown airport. By age eight, I spent every moment that I wasn't in school at the airport. The pilots at the airport were my heroes, but none generated the awe I felt around Barry Seal.

Barry Seal was the biggest thing going at the downtown Baton

Rouge airport. He accomplished feats that others never dreamed of, both in flying and in business. At age eighteen he formed Seal Sky Service, and by age nineteen, he had three planes. Along with flying banners, he had a super-powered airplane equipped with megaphones on the wings.

Example has more followers than reason. We unconsciously imitate what pleases us, and approximate to the characters we most admire.[1]
—CHRISTIAN NESTELL BOVEE

Politicians, especially Senator Russell Long, hired Barry to advertise for them. In those days, before America beautified itself by passing litter laws, Barry would fly low over Baton Rouge dropping leaflets and booming a political message through the megaphones. Everyone in Baton Rouge knew Barry Seal, and everyone wondered how the son of a man who drove a candy truck could have money for three planes.

It would be a while before the people of Baton Rouge realized that Barry's fortunes had taken a turn for the better after he flew weapons for the CIA. As an eight-year-old, I didn't question the source of Barry's funding. I just knew that he was my hero and that everyone recognized him as a gifted pilot.

Mike, my ten-year-old next-door neighbor, hung around the airport, too. An electronics wizard, Mike had just built a Tesla coil. Basically wrapping a cardboard roll with thousands of tiny wires, Mike generated harmless, low-current volts that did strange and wonderful things. Barry had recognized Mike's genius and had hired him. Mike, in turn, had brought me to Barry.

"This is the kid I was telling you about," Mike told Barry. "He flies the old Bamboo Bomber."

"You want to come work for me?" Barry asked.

"Heck, yeah!" I said. For a kid fascinated by flying more than words could describe, working for Barry was a dream come true.

Later I brought in Chris, who as an adult would become an FAA operations supervisor. Along with sharing a love of flying, we, like Barry, came from homes where our fathers were alcoholics. Just as we didn't realize the depth of some of Barry's business dealings when we were children, we did not realize the subtle training we were receiving.

Barry put me to work building banners and doing odd jobs around the hangers. When I was about eleven years old, Barry entered the military and served in Special Forces. When he came out, he began buying planes, and he leapfrogged up the seniority ladder at Trans World Airlines (TWA) until, by age twenty-four, he was the youngest 707 pilot. By age thirty-two, he was the youngest captain of a 747. At the same time, he owned and operated several businesses.

From age eight through my teen years, I worked off and on for Barry in Seal Sky Service, Aerial Advertising Associates, Seal's Texaco, Helicopter Airways, and National Search Lights Associates. Working for Barry and his younger brother Ben involved gut-wrenching labor. Barry set up work schedules that were impossible, but as I met Barry's demands, he gave me increasing responsibility. Under Barry's relentless demands, I built a big ticker tape sign with light bulbs. Barry had hoped to fly the sign under a plane, but we finally modified it to fly under his helicopter. The sign never did quite come up to Barry's expectations, so he abandoned it. The empty control box for the sign lay in the back of a hanger.

Barry drove us to accomplish tasks far beyond our abilities. Along with driving us to excel, he had a genius ability to develop new ideas, and he could handle unexpected problems with instant improvisation. He was like a cat that always landed on its feet. Suave, eloquent, and charismatic, Barry knew how to prepare and direct others to achieve his goals.

No one will ever know Barry's true motive in employing us boys at the airport. In retrospect and due to later developments, it appears that our work for Barry was more than cheap labor. As a tough sergeant, he would curse and threaten us and test our endurance levels. He taught us to go without sleep and to ignore fear. We accomplished feats we never could have done without his threatening, driving force. Why did we stay? We were flying, and nothing else mattered. Barry knew how to use our passion for flying to keep us working and, no doubt, to shape us for future assignments.

Barry and his pilots continually made flights, and often the pilots took one of us boys along. We fought to see who got to fly with Barry. Even when we were so young and short that stretching to reach the rudder pedals almost put us in a reclining position, Barry freely allowed us to take the controls of the planes. A month's resentment of the military-type verbal abuse and horrendous work disappeared when Barry complimented us on a smooth aerial maneuver. We would get out of the plane so high that, for a week, his yelling would be sweet music reminding us of a special time in the air. During the formative years of my life Barry Seal influenced me more than any other person.

◆ ◆ ◆

At every age, we wield influence, and at every age we are susceptible to influence. A child will quickly pick up a playmate's accent; an octogenarian will pick up the critical attitude of a caretaker. The Old Testament chronicles how evil kings influenced nations to disobey God. Jesus compared good influence to salt, to light, and to stars in the universe. The way that you live your daily life will influence those who live in the lair. Your life either accuses or excuses people for sinning. "For we are to God the aroma of Christ among those who are being saved and those who are perishing. To the one we are the smell of death; to the other, the fragrance of life" (2 Cor. 2:15–16).

> **I fled Him, down the nights and down the days;**
> **I fled Him, down the arches of the years;**
> **I fled Him, down the labyrinthine ways**
> **Of my own mind; and in the mist of tears**
> **I hid from Him, and under running laughter**
> **Up vistaed hopes I sped.[2]**
> —FRANCIS THOMPSON, "THE HOUND OF HEAVEN"

When you think of those who influenced you, what did those people say? You probably can't remember any certain speech or advice. You connected with the essence of who they were. Their bawdiness may have intrigued you and attracted you to sample their lifestyle. A sense of God's presence on an individual may have prompted you to go to your room and call out to God in repentance. Neither person said a word, but their influence affected some of your choices. In your efforts to rescue others from the lair, remember that the unspoken message—your influence—is always touching lives.

◆ ◆ ◆

Barry was more than a role model and employer. At eleven years my senior, he was also like a big brother who looked out for me. As a TWA pilot in training, Barry spent a lot of time in Kansas City, where he stayed in the Hotel New Yorker. "Son," he told me, "if you get into any trouble at all, you call Captain A. B. Seal at the Hotel New Yorker. The phone number is Victor 29711. You got that?" I got it. Almost forty years later, the number is still in my head.

Often during my teen years, Barry introduced me to people who came to his offices or that we met after flying to a distant city. He would tell me that they wanted to spend some time with me. These strangers would talk at length, asking me all kinds of questions. After their departure, Barry would say, "That's an important person. He works in the governor's office (or some other influential place). He really liked you." Blindly, I walked deeper into the world of international intrigue.

LAIR REALITY 4

PEOPLE DON'T PLAN TO TRAVEL INTO SPIRITUAL DARKNESS. THEY FOCUS ON ENJOYING LIFE, AND SIN JUST HAPPENS ALONG THE WAY.

I had one close friend during my teen years who was not a pilot. The son of an upper middle-class family, Joe Polozola drove a 1966 Chevelle SS 396. His mother and father had simply given him the gold Chevelle. Joe had such handsome, pure Italian features that he probably could have landed a modeling or acting contract if he had chosen to pursue that career. He represented everything that I worked for in Barry's sweatshop, and I set out to beat him at everything. In spite of the insane competition, we were friends.

One night we started doing push-ups. Neither of us would quit. I'm not sure who reached 137, but one of us did while the other one collapsed on 136. The next day both of us wondered if we had done permanent damage to ourselves. We were absolutely paralyzed. That was the kind of mindless, insane determination we had to beat each other. Joe was rich and spoiled, but he also had more determination than anyone I knew. Polozola was my absolute competition in life; my goal in life was to beat Joe, and his goal was to beat me.

When we were about eighteen, we made a bet about who would make a million dollars before we were twenty-one. The loser would have to pay the other one a million. I'm not sure how that would have worked, but we set out to beat each other making a million.

Polozola was drafted into the armed forces, and I married a local girl and left for California to start work on my first million. Before I left for California, I copied the dimensions of the lighted sign that Barry had abandoned, and I "borrowed" the control box that had been lying in the back of the hanger.

I left home in Louisiana determined to overcome all obstacles that blocked the path to my personal goals of wealth and pleasure. Neither God nor sin was an issue in my life. Ignorantly I chose a bright path that steadily grew dimmer without my noticing the change. Blinded by arrogant self-confidence, I stepped into a dangerous snare.

In California, I met a Mafia-type fellow who looked for investments with high returns. "I can take your money and make a lot with it," I told him. I convinced him that with $50,000 I could make an advertising sign that would fly beneath a helicopter. After building a lighted ticker tape sign thirty-five feet long and six feet wide, I approached the FAA for approval to fly it.

"Son," they said, "this sign will never fly."

"You don't understand," I said. "This sign has to fly!"

Several FAA agents personally guaranteed me that the sign would not get approval. To them, the idea of a nineteen-year-old flying a lighted sign under a helicopter over San Francisco was absurd. "You don't understand," I told them. "The sign has to fly." My investor would not accept failure when $50,000 of his money was at stake.

Sixteen FAA agents, an unheard of number to review and rule on an application, gathered to keep the sign from flying. Although the agents were intent on taking me and my sign apart, in the end they could find no reason to reject my application. "The Sign," as I dubbed it for my business, was cleared to fly.

The Sign advertised the Broadway musical *Hair* and Proposition 13, which was one of the first California tax revolt propositions. It also advertised performances of the Smothers Brothers. The

Smothers Brothers used to love to go to Sausalito, a quaint cove across the Golden Gate Bridge. One night while they were eating in the Trident restaurant, I hovered right outside the window where they were seated and ran the lighted sign.

With success in San Francisco, I planned to build and fly signs in New Orleans, Houston, Kansas City, and New York City. Income from additional signs would not only pay off my $50,000 debt, it would put me on the way to making a million dollars before Joe Polozola did.

And then Barry came to San Francisco.

I had been flying The Sign and hacking away at my debt when Barry called. "Joe, I'm flying into SFO (San Francisco International Airport) at five this evening. Pick me up."

After picking Barry up at the airport, I drove him to see my sign. "What have you done?" he yelled. "You built the sign!"

"Barry, it's not the same sign. I changed the dimensions."

He was cussing me out, but it was a proud kind of cussing. "You did that? Is that what happened to the control box?"

"The control box was empty. It just had cutouts. Nothing else was in it."

"You built the sign," he said shaking his head in wonder.

"Yes."

"You got it approved by the FAA?"

"Sixteen agents came to take it apart, but they gave me approval. I'm making good money with it." His unspoken but apparent pride in my accomplishment meant as much as the FAA approval.

In retrospect, I have wondered if Barry requested a change in flight routing, because after that meeting, he flew the New York-San Francisco route on a steady basis. The calls to pick Barry up at the airport came often.

LAIR REALITY 5

GOD USES MANY AGENTS TO ACHIEVE HIS PURPOSES.

God often uses a variety of agents to catch people's attention and remind them that another life exists outside the lair. Sometimes you will have a brief encounter with someone and sense that God is dealing with the person. Never treat that whisper of the Spirit lightly. You never know who is praying for the individual and how the right words from you could have an impact on them. Keep your heart and spirit open to God's direction. Your influence counts, but sometimes He will prompt you to speak a word of wisdom or warning to someone. In California I surrounded myself with ungodly influences, but God began to use His agents to call me to Him. He spoke through some very unlikely people.

One of the perks of a friendship with Barry was being introduced to airline stewardesses. In the late sixties, TWA employment criteria for stewardesses resulted in a bevy of very attractive young women. My marriage was over, and Barry often introduced me to stewardesses when I picked him up or dropped him off at SFO.

While a passenger on a flight from Baton Rouge to San Francisco, I met one of the beautiful stewardesses that Barry had previously introduced to me. She invited me to the back of the plane where she gave me personal passionate attention. She was phenomenal, and I could hardly wait for her to return to San Francisco. A few months passed, though, before she called.

When she called, I was more than ready to see her. "I'm flying into SFO," she said. "I need to talk to you."

"Of course," I said. "I'll pick you up."

Life could not be better. Dressed in a tweed coat with leather patches on the elbows and a black turtleneck sweater, I pulled up to the airport in my Mercedes coupe to pick up the gorgeous airline stewardess. I glanced around to see how many people were watching us. Heads turned as the shapely stewardess folded her long legs into the car.

My heart hammered. "My apartment is close by," I said, anticipating where the evening was going.

"We have to talk," she said in a husky voice. "Let's go for a drive."

We drove past my place to the Golden Gate Bridge. I suggested pulling over for a while at a viewing area, but she didn't want to stop. I listened attentively as she talked about all kinds of stuff that held no interest to me.

We drove by Sausalito, and then we drove all the way back around until we came to Oakland. She still talked, and the conversation seemed more weird with every passing mile. By the time we got to the Oakland Bridge, I was totally, absolutely bewildered by this girl. I had one thing on my mind, and the conversation hadn't moved anywhere near my interests.

I tried everything. I stopped at a scenic place that overlooked San Francisco and reached for her hand. She pulled her hand away. This didn't make sense to me. What had happened to the phenomenally passionate stewardess on the flight?

This wasn't going where I wanted it to go. Maybe if we had a romantic meal with candlelight and wine, her amorous personality would return. We left the overlook and started across the Bay Bridge. Just before we reached the military base in the middle of the bridge, she looked at me and said, "You know, you really have to forgive your father."

At that point, I was so disappointed. She had not only trashed my perfect evening, but she had also hit a sore spot that overwhelmed me emotionally. I yanked the car off the bridge onto a parking space on Treasure Island, switched off the key and dropped my head, letting it hit the steering wheel.

"I can never forgive him," I said tersely. "I can never forgive him." I lifted my head, looked at her, and said fiercely, "What do you care? Why do you care whether I forgive him or not?"

At that point, she told me why she had really called me. She had committed her life to Christ, and she wanted to tell me how God could help me forgive others and how God could change my life.

A Jesus freak! I thought. *She has totally changed! She's turned into a Jesus freak.* It was obvious that what I had planned for the evening wasn't going to happen. I started the car and drove her straight to her hotel.

I had no desire for change in my life. She might consider my lifestyle sinful, but I loved it, and I didn't need God to change me so that I could love my father. She could go down that dark lonely road of "faith in Jesus," but the path ahead of me blazed with opportunities for success and pleasure. I certainly wasn't going to let Jesus dim my future.

Barry's visits became more frequent. "How's The Sign doing?" he would ask. "How much do you owe on it?"

The sign business was doing well, but my lifestyle, which included an apartment near the ocean, left me with little money to apply to the loan. Until I could get signs running in other cities, it would take a long time to pay off the mafioso who had financed the sign. The man was not noted for patience, especially when it came to loan repayment.

One day Barry asked again, "How much do you owe on your loan?"
"About $40,000."

"How would you like to make $50,000 in one weekend?"

"Man, could I kill a lot of birds with that one stone," I said. "What do I need to do?"

"Well, it's just a mission," Barry said. "You're gonna work real hard. You're gonna work for your money. You'll need to move back to Baton Rouge."

"I can't walk out on my sign business," I said. "I owe $40,000 on this loan."

"I need you, Joe, for this mission. I'll take care of you. This mission will pay off your loan, and I'll help you get your signs going in other big cities."

Since Barry promised a surefire way to clear my debts and establish my business, I agreed to work with him and began planning to move back to Baton Rouge for a while. Just before I left San Francisco, Joe Polozola called. He was home on leave from the military and wanted to talk to me about something. "It's big," Polozola said. "It's bigger than anything you can imagine. You'll be interested in this."

"I'm into some pretty big things, too," I told him. "It would have to be *big* to be bigger than what I'm doing. Go ahead and tell me what you're into."

"I can't, man," Polozola said. "It's so big that I can't talk to you about it on the phone. Let me know when you get back to Baton Rouge."

Whatever the "something big" was, if it were bigger than my mission with Barry and The Sign, I would find a way to beat Polozola at his own game.

After I returned to Baton Rouge, Polozola and his wife, Diane, came to see me. I acted nonchalant as I said, "OK. What's this big thing?"

"It is so big, Joe!" he said. I had never seen Polozola so animated. Both Joe and Diane sparkled with excitement, which made me know they had truly discovered something big.

"Tell me, man," I said. "What is it?"

"It's God. We have found God, and He's bigger than you can imagine. Joe, you've got to give your life to Jesus." They began to tell me how their lives had been transformed since they had met Christ, and they told me that God could change my life for the better.

I tried to listen but finally said, "I can't believe it. I can't believe that you have sold out and turned into…Jesus freaks! Maybe you'd just better leave."

As Polozola and his wife went out the door, he said, "I'll pray for you, Joe."

Cursing him, I muttered, "Don't waste your breath!"

The stewardess had disappointed me with her changed life, but Polozola devastated me.

Polozola was my absolute competition in life. We had been good for each other. The competition drove us to accomplish more than we dreamed. Joe's change of life direction crushed me. It was like training for the Olympics, striving to beat the very top competition, then having the one who drives you to incredible heights suddenly stop trying. I felt outrage. I wanted to scream at Joe, "You can't drop out of the race. I want to beat you!"

When Joe Polozola walked out of my house that day, I figured I had angered him so much and he despised me so much, that he would have no further interest in my life or our friendship.

I figured wrong.

Unknown to me, Joe Polozola made a vow to fast until I found God. As an active member of the military, he had to eat to keep up his strength, so he vowed to eat regularly but to drink only water until I gave my life to Christ. For a man who loved coffee, this was no small sacrifice.

LAIR REALITY 6

IT TAKES MORE THAN REASONING, INFLUENCE, AND WORDS TO REACH THOSE WHO LIVE DEEP IN THE LAIR.

People can brush aside your answers, influence, and warnings, and they can even break off a friendship, but they cannot move beyond the power of your prayers. Few Christians today understand intercessory prayer. Intercession requires more than mentioning a person's name to God, presenting their needs, and asking God's help. Intercessory prayer comes as the Spirit of God moves on your heart to pray. To respond to that prompting, you may need to turn off the TV, lay a book aside, find a quiet place, or even rouse yourself from sleep to pray.

In those moments, look to God for guidance on how to pray. Do not pray for what you feel the person needs, but be sensitive to how God guides your prayers. Often He uses Scriptures to direct your prayers. Intercessory prayer combats spiritual forces that keep people from hearing God's call to leave the lair. In retrospect, I realize that when Joe Polozola began to fast and intercede for me, God began to move in my life in a stronger way. I'm convinced that Polozola's prayers shielded me from strong spiritual forces that could have wrecked my life.

I went back to work for Barry in Baton Rouge and often traveled on his planes. Barry and his pilots transported a variety of materials and people. On one occasion, a fellow passenger, a forthright, salty-talking preacher, started talking to me about the dangers of neglecting my spiritual life.

I cut him off sharply. "Don't talk to me about that stuff. I'm not interested."

"Well, Joe," he said, "you can just go to hell."

I had no comeback.

Unaware that the Hound of Heaven was on my trail, and unaware of the dangers ahead, I plunged into preparation for Barry's mission.

During the next seven months, Barry Seal's mission began to take on huge dimensions. Recruitment had apparently been started a year before the mission, and Barry gave each of us only tidbits of information. He supplied to each of us only the information needed to carry out our part of the mission. As the mission developed, I saw signs of government involvement. I knew that it would involve flying, but I didn't know where, why, or what our mission would accomplish. Parts of the logistical planning troubled me. But more than that, I had a sinking feeling in my gut that this mission was in trouble. I knew nothing about the way God works to answer prayers, but later on I would realize that my unexplainable uneasiness was due to Polozola's prayers and God's stirring of my heart.

Still with unhurrying chase,
And unperturbed pace,
Deliberate speed, majestic instancy,
Came on the following Feet… [3]
—FRANCIS THOMPSON, "THE HOUND OF HEAVEN"

As the mission execution time grew closer, I struggled with the decision of whether to go through with it. I desperately needed money to pay off the loan. As I said earlier, my creditor was not a patient man. This operation, though, was cloaked in secrecy. I had only bits and pieces of the operation—not enough to fully know what we were going to do. In all my business dealings with Barry, he had never asked me to do anything illegal, except drive fast. I wondered if we could be arrested if this mission failed. Some of the planning reminded me of *The Gang That Couldn't Shoot Straight*, a comedy I had seen about some klutzy mafiosi. While I wasn't too concerned with the morality of the mission, I had no desire to participate in a bungled operation.

LAIR REALITY 7

THE REALITY OF THE LAIR—THE OFFAL, THE BONES, THE SCRAPS OF FUR AND DRIED SKIN, THE BLOOD-SALIVA DROOL OF THE LION—CAN ONLY BE SEEN IN THE LIGHT OF THE WAY THAT SHINES THROUGH THE ENTRY.

On a hot July day in 1972, Barry drove to my mother's house in a new yellow Oldsmobile Cutlass that had a black vinyl top. He had come to pick me up for a final briefing before the long-planned mission started. I walked slowly down the sidewalk, but my mind raced. As someone plucking a daisy, I said to myself, I will go. I will not go.

With each step, my confusion increased. *I need the money. Something is wrong with this mission.*

Barry had no patience with me. He reached across the car, opened the door to the passenger's side, and roared, "Come on! Get a move on! We're late already!"

The mafioso wants his money. This mission is going to fail.

I placed my hand on the open door and said, "I'm not going."

"You what!"

"I'm not going to do it."

"You can't do that!"

"Watch me!" I said.

"You can't back out now. I spent months training you for this."

"Barry, through the years you've promised me many things, and you've come short on so many of them. You owe me more than words can say. You take the money that you put in training me, and you take it off the bill that you owe me."

"You don't understand," Barry said enunciating each word. "You can't back out now."

At that point I said, "You guys are so bad you'll probably shoot your foot off." It was one of the classic lines from *The Gang That Couldn't Shoot Straight*. "Barry," I said, "there's something wrong with this deal. It's not good."

"You are dead!" Barry said with a tone that carried threat. He grabbed the door, yanked it shut, and squealed out, spurting road-side gravel.

Two mornings later I sat down at the breakfast table with a cup of coffee in hand, and my mother shoved the front page of the newspaper over to me. She looked at me and said quietly, "Son, you're going to kill me. You're going to give me a heart attack." Banner headlines trumpeted the arrest of Barry Seal.

By nature, my mother was a worrier. She worried about my flying and the way I lived my life. She had witnessed my association with Barry and knew that I had been working closely with him on an intense secretive project. Today's headline news verified that her fears had been grounded in reality.

In a thwarted plot to supply explosives to anti-Castro rebels, Barry and five other men had been arrested. Before Barry could take off for the rendezvous, twenty-six federal agents had swarmed the Shreveport Regional Airport and seized almost seven tons of plastic C-4 explosives in a DC-4 transport plane. From what I had observed, the "mission" indicated government involvement. Barry's mission, sanctioned by one agency, had inadvertently been quashed by another government agency.

All that day two notable things played repeatedly through my mind. How could I, at age twenty-one, have messed up my life so badly? Besides delving in alcohol, drugs, and sex, I had messed up a marriage, owed a hoodlum a boatload of money, and had just missed making national headlines for involvement in an interna-tional arms-smuggling operation. I kept thinking too of how I was worrying my mother to death. I really, really loved my mother. She was my friend, and she was crying out, "Please, son, please change."

I felt so badly that I took refuge in the little room I was staying in at my mother's house.

After a while, I picked up the phone and called Joe Polozola's mother.

"Mrs. Polozola, where is that boy of yours?"

"Oh, you didn't hear? He's out of the army." Polozola had been discharged and had gone to work for a local plumber. She gave me Joe's address and phone number.

I called Polozola's wife, Diane, and asked when Joe would be home. She told me and said that Joe would love to see me. She acted as though she didn't remember that I had asked them to leave me alone seven months previously.

When Polozola came home from work at 3:30 p.m., I was waiting under a shade tree, seated on my Yamaha motorcycle.

"Good to see you, Joe," he said. His greeting seemed sincere.

I grumbled a short, "Yeah," and followed him into the house.

As soon as we entered the house, I shoved him against the wall, got in his face, and cussed him. "You had better not have been lying to me."

"What are you talking about?" he said.

I was almost crying because my life was so out of control, and I felt so ugly. I swore at him again. "You had better not be lying to me about Jesus. If everything you told me about Jesus is true, I would be a raving maniac not to ask Him to save me."

"Joe," he said quietly, "it's all true."

At 3:45 that afternoon, he sat down with me and fielded the questions that I threw at him. Some of my questions were hackneyed eighth-grade level questions about aliens and halos, some were from a distorted media view of God, some grew out of the confusion and distress I was feeling, and some grew out of the deep hunger I had to truly know about God.

Polozola didn't have all the answers, but he treated each question as an important issue. He never once said, "How dare you ask a question about God or faith?" At the table, I drank coffee and Polozola drank water as he pointed out scriptures that answered some of my questions. He listened and preached to me until about 2:15 in the morning.

At 2:15 a.m. I stood and said, "Man, I'm overloaded right now. I can't take anymore."

"See you tomorrow?" he asked.

"Yeah, I'll be here."

Although Joe had spent hours explaining how we are born into the kingdom of heaven, it still didn't make any sense to me. Maybe tomorrow I would understand it better. I went home and went to my little room. At about 2:45 in the morning I got down on my knees, but it seemed that a solid stone wall loomed in front of me. I was on one side, and God was on the other side of the wall. There were no portholes, no breaks. Just a solid wall.

"Just reach your hand through the wall," God seemed to say. I looked at the wall. It represented unbelief, doubt, and every thing that would turn me away from God.

"Reach your hand through the wall." This time the voice was audible to me.

I lifted my hand and cautiously reached toward the wall. In a split second, I sensed the hand of Jesus on my hand, and, like a fast-rising wind out of nowhere, I sensed that eternal life was filling my being. Still on my knees, I whispered in awe, "Lord, I love You. Lord, I will die for You."

As I lingered on my knees, it came to me, "Joe, you have been born again." I needed no more explanation. I knew that I had new life in me. My salvation was the most dramatic event in my entire life. Nothing before or since has affected me as much as that early morning encounter with Jesus.

The next day, I was at Polozola's house when he arrived home from work. We went to the kitchen where Joe, Diane, and I sat at the table. After working in the Louisiana summer heat all day, Polozola was guzzling water.

"Joe," I said, "last night after I left you, at 2:45 a.m., I gave my heart to the Lord."

Without a word, Polozola stood and turned toward the refrigerator. He caught his foot on the table leg and fell to the floor. Without bothering to get to his feet, he scurried sideways like a crab to the refrigerator, gripped the door at the bottom, and yanked it open. Grabbing a quart bottle of Dad's Root Beer, he unscrewed the cap and gulped soda until it squirted out his nose.

I looked at him and thought, *Maybe I didn't make the right decision. This is weird.* "What's going on?" I asked. "What's the deal?"

"You'd never believe me," Polozola said. Three weeks later he told me of his seven-month beverage fast.

Satan had lured me deep into his lair. I was dead in transgressions and sins. I gratified the cravings of my sinful nature and followed its desires and thoughts. I was an object of wrath because I could never measure up to God's righteousness.

BUT GOD, because of His great love for me, opened my eyes and gave me clear vision of my surroundings in the lair. He made me alive with Christ even when I was dead in transgressions. By grace I have been saved through faith—and this was not of myself. I cannot boast. God did not rescue me because of any work I did. My deliverance from the lion's lair was an undeserved gift of God. (See Ephesians 2:1-5.)

CHAPTER 9

DEVOURED

FACT OF THE LAIR 1

IN THE DARKNESS OF THE LAIR A MIRACULOUS
INTERVENTION USUALLY PROVIDES ONLY
A FLASH OF GOD-CONSCIOUSNESS.

THE FIRST PERSON I wanted to see after talking with Joe Polozola
and his wife was Adler Berriman Seal. Barry, charged with con-
spiracy and arms smuggling, had immediately gotten out of jail
on bail. In spite of his departing threat to kill me, I went to Barry,
threw my arms around him, and said, "Barry, I've given my heart to
the Lord."

Barry seemed genuinely happy that I had become a Christian. He
wondered, though, what I had known that had made me back out
of the mission.

"What did you know? How did you know?" he asked.

"God's grace and mercy delivered me," I said. "I had no convictions about this. As I walked to your car it was, 'Maybe I will. Maybe
I won't.' It could have gone either way. God just spared me from the
wrong decision."

I was sure that in time, I could bring Barry to Christ just as Joe
Polozola had led me to Christ, but Barry was firmly ensconced in
the lion's lair. For years I trailed Barry, pleading with him to turn
and escape. The journey took me through moments of hope, anger,
despair, and grief, but I never stopped pursuing Barry or being his
friend. When doors of hope and redemption opened to Barry, I
wept as he rushed past them to a distant promise of adventure and
material success.

When you go deep into the lair to rescue others, you will face spiritual danger. The danger does not lie in temptation to join friends
in sin, but rather in acceptance of God's way of dealing with people.

God is patient, long-suffering, and gentle, but He never takes away the power of choice. Every person chooses his or her destiny. To avoid falling prey to the lion yourself, you must face the realities of the deep part of the lair.

Some want to live within the sound of church or chapel bell. I want to run a rescue shop within a yard of hell.[1]
—C. T. STUDD

◆ ◆ ◆

Barry was no stranger to God's workings. The Hound of Heaven had pursued him, too. The salty-talking preacher who warned me that I was going to hell had been warning Barry for years about the danger of rejecting God. Eleven years before I came to Christ, the preacher had said to Barry, "If you don't get your life straightened out, God is going to kick your…" ending with an expletive.

Not long after that warning, Barry put together a New Year's Eve publicity stunt in Hammond, Louisiana. Barry and his brother Ben planned to parachute from a plane and be free-falling through the air at the stroke of midnight. On that crisply cold New Year's Eve, television crews were on hand to film the stunt. In a rare cold weather snap, snow covered the ground, and stars sparkled in the cloudless sky. The plane circled at ten thousand feet. The first parachutist jumped, and then the second one jumped. We cheered and watched them free-fall toward earth as the clock struck midnight, ringing in the new year.

Ben's chute opened, and he floated to earth.

Barry kept falling. There was no sign of an opening chute. Barry had a habit of milking drama from every event, so we didn't immediately think he was in trouble.

Barry, however, had grabbed his D-ring and pulled his chute, but nothing had happened. The unit had frozen, and he was left holding the D-ring with nothing attached. Barry had then brought in his arms and gotten into his belly pack chute. He pulled the ripcord on it, and it too failed to open.

As we watched and the cameras rolled, Barry plummeted to the field at 120 mph. Terrified by what we would see, we ran to the place where he had fallen. When we reached Barry, he was crawling out of a snow bank yelling, "I'm in heaven! I'm in heaven!"

According to Barry, he knew the end was coming and decided, "If I'm gonna die, I'm not going in face first." He had pulled in an arm, rolled over on his back, and watched trees fly by.

"Then," he said, "it was like the hand of God reached out, plucked me, held me, then dropped me to the ground."

I hadn't seen a big hand come out of the sky, but considering that Barry was unharmed after a fall from ten thousand feet, his story sounded believable.

The next day Barry came into the hanger where I was working.

"Let me show you something, kid," he said.

Barry always wore a jumpsuit, and he proceeded to unzip it. I hesitated.

"Come here," he said again. "Let me show you something."

He pulled down his jumpsuit to expose his rear end. His butt was as black as pitch.

I yelled, "Whoa!"

Barry pulled his jumpsuit back up and said, "God kicked me where the old preacher told me he would."

I don't know how God saved Barry's life, but Barry should have been dead. Sometimes the Lord works in miraculous ways to keep people alive. For one brief moment, they acknowledge that "the man upstairs" was looking out for them, but then quickly brush aside all other thoughts of God.

As one who has escaped the lair, you will view escapes such as Barry's as the long-suffering of God. You will want to thrust a Bible into a survivor's hands and tell him to read, "He is patient with you, not wanting anyone to perish, but everyone to come to repentance" (2 Pet. 3:9). When you see a person treat a second chance lightly, you may feel anger at the person for being so blind and feel anger at God for not revealing Himself more fully. In moments like these guard your heart against bitterness. Accept the very difficult reality that God will not violate the will of a person and enter without an invitation.

FACT OF THE LAIR 2

IN THE LAIR, WHAT SEEMS RIGHT IS RIGHT.

After I gave my life to Christ, I spoke often to Barry about spiritual matters. I didn't know if Barry knew anything about salvation or how to give his life to Christ, but I proceeded to fill in the blanks for him. There was not only an absence of rejection on his part, but also a fascination and attraction to what I told him. He seemed to have a "give me more" attitude. He was like someone with an empty plate walking through a multi-table smorgasbord. He kept looking, admitting that it all looked good, but he could never bring himself to put anything on his plate.

I continued working for Barry, building and wiring lighted signs that were carried on trailers. It was a legitimate and very profitable business, but it wasn't going to pay off the loan on The Sign in San Francisco. In desperation, I went to the mobster's wife. She was known as Rock because of her hard-heartedness. First, I told her that I had given my life to Christ.

She began to cry.

"I don't even feel like crying," she said, "but I'm crying, and I can't stop. This is real." With the Rock's support, I worked out an agreement with the mobster about the loan and then returned to Baton Rouge where I continued working for Barry.

Two years passed before Barry went to trial on the explosives smuggling charges. On the day before the final hearing, we flew to Tampa and back in a Beech 18 Volpar that had the nose gear conversion and two big engines. Previously owned by *Life* magazine, the plush cabin was designed for executives and had a big picture window, comfortable couch, club seating, a table, and a bar. A mahogany door separated the pilot and copilot's seats from the cabin.

Barry was very tired. As we flew, I could see him drifting. Finally, he said, "Fly. I need to sleep. When you get abeam Gulfport, wake me up." Barry stepped back through the cockpit door and lay down on a couch with his head near the door.

I was a competent VFR (Visual Flight Regulations) pilot, but I had little experience in flying in instrument conditions. The weather was clear, however, and the flight was simple: fly ADF (Automatic Direction Finder) from Tampa to New Orleans using WWL-AM (50,000-watt radio station in New Orleans). When I got abeam Gulfport, I would awaken Barry, and we would turn and go into Baton Rouge. We were flying directly into the setting sun, and I often had to divert my gaze from the blinding rays. I was glad when the sun finally slipped into the sea.

When the sun is up over water, a clear demarcation line divides sky from sea. As the sun sets, the orange-pink and blue-gray sky gradually turns to all blue-gray, erasing that sharp horizon line. On this evening, a faint haze smeared the last vestiges of a horizon. I didn't notice the subtle change in the horizon as the sky darkened.

Unknown to me, the gyro in my brain began an insidious tilt, and I began to experience spatial disorientation, or vertigo. I compensated, flying the Beech according to the orientation of my mind. The plane began to lose altitude. When I corrected the pitch of the plane according to what seemed right to me, we began plummeting at a 35–40 degree bank. Quickly, the altimeter unwound, from 10,000 to 9,000 to 8,000 to 7,000 to 6,000 feet. Still trying to correct according to my inner gyro, I struggled to pull out of the dive.

The plane's 200-knot speed pegged the red line. We were flying into the ocean. I had lost control of the plane! Frantically, I leaned behind me, shoved open the door, and yelled, "Barry! Get up here now!"

"No," he said quietly.

My scream had not caught him by surprise. He had already awakened and knew what was happening. Getting up, he leaned through the cockpit door, put his hand on my shoulder, and calmly said, "Joe, you have somewhere between ten and fifteen seconds before the right wing is going to be torn off the airplane. Fly the plane."

"Get up here now!" I screamed.

"No. Look at the little airplane on the instrument panel. Don't look outside the airplane. Look at the plane on the instrument panel."

I looked at the artificial horizon, and there before me was the little dot and line that represented the plane. The right wing was way down.

"Pick up the wing slowly," he said.

I made a grunting noise, like, "Get up here."

"No, just fly the airplane," Barry said.

I wrestled to control the Beech and slowly brought up the right wing. In a matter of seconds I had control of the airplane.

◆ ◆ ◆

How could my thinking and actions seem so right and be so deadly wrong? While I had felt safe in the familiar environment of the cockpit, the plane in which I traveled had changed altitude and attitude. I had neglected to keep my eye on the unchanging horizon and had lost control of the airplane.

My pilot error that day mirrored the mistake that many people make in the way they live. They live according to what seems right in their own minds. If their lives line up with the lives of surrounding friends and the culture, then it must be right. If it feels right, it must be right. No matter how right your choices and lifestyle may seem, if they run contrary to God's Word, they will lead to eternal destruction. "There is a way that seems right to a man, but in the end it leads to death" (Prov. 14:12). The experience of losing control of the plane indelibly marked on my thinking the importance of focusing on the true horizon in both the natural world and the spiritual world.

FACT OF THE LAIR 3

SORROW IS COMMON IN THE LAIR, BUT IT HAS LITTLE VALUE UNLESS IT LEADS TO REPENTANCE.

Barry left me alone and let me fly for a while; then he came up to sit with me in the cockpit.

"I'm going for a final hearing tomorrow," Barry said. "The attorney says it doesn't look good. If I'm sent up, will you take care of Debbie?"

I looked at Barry, my childhood hero, an ace 747 pilot, and an astute businessman. Barry was going to prison for trying to smuggle a planeload of C-4 explosives and was asking me to take care of his wife.

"Barry," I answered, "of course I'll take care of Debbie."

"I don't know how it's all going to end," Barry said. "I've lost everything."

"You should praise God that you got busted," I said.

"Praise God!" Barry said. "Why should I thank God? I've lost my job with TWA, I've lost my reputation, and I'll probably be thrown in prison tomorrow. Why should I praise God?"

"Think of it, Barry. Think of what would have happened if we had pulled that mission off. Do you know what 13,500 pounds of C-4 would have done? Think of how many eyeballs would have been blown out. Think of how many widows we would have made. Think of how many orphans we would have created and how many people we would have crippled. Think of what would have happened if we had been successful. Barry, we need to thank God that the mission failed."

Barry began to sob. His sudden understanding of how heinous the mission would have been was greater than my enumeration of the suffering we could have inflicted. The Spirit of God was laying bare the intents and purposes of Barry's heart. As he kept weeping, I said, "Barry, you have dodged a bullet half the size of a house. You've got to serve the Lord. You've got to serve the Lord!"

With the exception of a few people, everyone was shocked when Barry was exonerated of all charges the next day. The judge declared a mistrial, and Barry went free with all charges cleared from his record. I believe Barry was genuinely sorry for his part in the C-4 smuggling operation, but that seemed to be as far as Barry's repentance went.

Many people feel sorry about the way they've harmed others with their destructive lifestyle, but like Barry, their sorrow only covers troublesome areas of their lives. Godly sorrow requires repentance, a turning from *all* sin to follow God. In the lair, you will encounter many people who weep over their wasted lives and the way their decisions have hurt others. You will rejoice that they have finally come to their senses, but then your hopes will often fade as you see them continue walking in darkness. Your natural reaction will be to write them off your prayer list, but when God burdens you for the salvation of another person as he did me for Barry, you will keep on praying and working to reach that person.

Great is the difference betwixt a man's being frightened at, and humbled for, his sins. One may passively be cast down by God's terrors, and yet not willingly throw himself down as he ought at God's footstool.[2]
—THOMAS FULLER

Our ways parted. I married and started working for a growing evangelistic organization where I did radio work and moved up to a vice president position. Since I still lived in Baton Rouge, I occasionally saw Barry. After I moved to Haiti, however, I heard little from him until the day his wife, Debbie, called to tell me that Barry had been imprisoned in Honduras on an arms smuggling charge. Barry wanted her to come to Honduras but trusted only me to accompany her.

The decision to go was not an easy one. Association with Barry would not help my missionary image. Everything in me screamed, "Stay away. Don't get sucked into his world." But the Spirit of God kept saying, "Reach out to Barry. Reach out to him."

When God puts a person on our heart, He does not blind us to their sins. A God-given burden of intercession tunes us to an even clearer understanding of the person's sins, but that burden of intercession also carries an overwhelming love for the individual. This God-given love and the burden to intercede is not affected by time, distance, the person's actions, or even the person's vehement rejection of us. Although Barry had been arrested on a smuggling charge, I would have gone around the world to see him saved.

I flew to Honduras to visit Barry in prison three times. Each time I told him, "Barry, you have to get your life straightened out. You have to give your heart to Jesus." Each time Barry accepted the message without rancor. Each time Barry flew on toward his own horizon and ignored the one true horizon.

I continued to go after Barry with a strong and determined vengeance. I knew firsthand the skill, genius, and abundant talents that God had given him, and I knew that, if they were ever focused on God's work, Barry could impact the world for good.

FACT OF THE LAIR 4

THE LAIR OFFERS EXCITEMENT, PLEASURE, AND RICHES. THE TRAIL OFFERS SUFFERING. IN THE OPINION OF LAIR DWELLERS, ONLY THE FOOLISH WOULD CHOOSE THE TRAIL OF THE CROSS.

Following his release from the Honduran prison, Barry started smuggling drugs. It appears that he worked both sides of the law. He worked for the DEA (Drug Enforcement Administration) and CIA while running his own shipments of drugs. Venturing where few dared to go, Barry seemed to have a bizarre drive to fit into history. While most of the people in Baton Rouge had only a casual interest in Castro, the Sandinistas, and the Medellin cartel, Barry sought out their lairs and dined with the lions. Confidently, he entered their territory and took what he felt would serve the interests of his country and himself.

Barry soon owned a big home in Baton Rouge, a Rolls Royce, planes, and boats. Although we seldom saw each other, our friendship never wavered. When we did meet or talk, it was about memories of the past, planes, flying, our families, and his need to come to Christ. As always, Barry operated on a "need to know" basis. I didn't need to know about his business enterprises, and he didn't need to tell me.

Conclusions were drawn about my relationship with Barry, and some tried to recruit me in the fight against drugs flowing through the Caribbean. Emphatically I said, "I'm here to preach the gospel. I can do more to fight drug traffic by bringing people to Christ than by any other means." In my estimation, the efforts to stem the drug traffic by guns and sting operations were like charging hell with water pistols. I knew that changing people's hearts would stop the drug flow at both ends—at the producer level and the user level.

I maintained my friendship with Barry, but to all others related to his world I said, "You leave me alone. My only work is to preach the gospel and lead people to Christ." Knowing that some would always find it hard to believe that I could maintain friendship with Barry and have no connection to his world, I meticulously documented every flight that I made. Along with the normal date, time, etc., I logged details about the purpose of the flight in case I was ever questioned.

FACT OF THE LAIR 5

LAIR DWELLERS BELIEVE THAT THEY CAN
ALWAYS SPRINT TO THE LIGHT AND ESCAPE
BEFORE THE LION OVERTAKES THEM.

Barry saw no need for God because he was flying his own course with great success. It seemed that no matter what kind of scrapes he got into—plane crashes, failed parachutes, charges of smuggling explosives, arms, and drugs—he could always pull up in time and get out safely.

In all the operations Barry conducted, both for himself and for government agencies, he escaped all criminal charges except one. Some of his associates had been caught with fake Quaaludes in a sting operation called *Operation Screamer*. To lighten their own sentences, they had linked Barry to the drug deal.

In exchange for leniency, Barry tried to work out a deal with the DEA to act as an undercover informant. His offer was rejected, so Barry went over their heads to George Bush's Vice Presidential Task Force on Drugs in Washington. When Barry promised the task force the heads of the Medellin cartel and proof that the Sandinistas in Nicaragua were involved in the shipment of drugs to the United States, Barry immediately became the government's star informant.

From that time on, Barry used his ingenuity and his fearless zeal to destroy the drug trade. In an operation described in documentaries, books, magazines, newspapers, congressional reports, and the HBO movie *Doublecrossed*, Barry worked with the DEA and CIA to expose members of the Medellin drug cartel. Having won the trust of the cartel, Barry flew the *Fat Lady*, a C-123 military cargo plane, to Nicaragua. As crews loaded and unloaded his plane, Barry used hidden cameras to snap photos of government officials and cartel leaders who were overseeing the shipments. One of the photos taken by Barry was later used in a televised drug special. President Ronald Reagan displayed the photo as proof that the government of Nicaragua was involved in drug shipments to the United States.

Release of the story and the photos blew Barry's cover, and a $500,000 contract was put out on his life. He was offered witness protection but refused it. Without regard to personal safety, Barry infiltrated drug trafficking rings and then testified in court and in congressional hearings against drug kingpins and distributors. According to the U.S. Attorney General, Barry became the most significant witness in drug history. Barry seemed to be trying to pull up, trying to right some of the devastating wrong he had done by smuggling arms and drugs.

Although Barry had brought down the Medellin cartel and was exposing drug rings in the United States, the Caribbean, and Central America, one judge refused to drop the Quaalude charges. Federal officials pleaded Barry's case, and the sentence was reduced to time served and six months probation.

There was a catch.

Barry had to spend each night of his probation in a Salvation Army Community Treatment Center, and he could not carry a firearm or employ anyone who carried a firearm. The location and times of his stay were public knowledge. The judge had painted a bull's-eye on Barry that was visible all the way to Colombia, South America.

In 1985, Barry wrestled to regain control of his life, but he would never pull out of this downward spiral. With his cover blown and a half-million-dollar contract on his life, he was of no further use to the government. Since Barry had testified in congressional hearings about his lucrative drug flights, the IRS had decided that Barry must owe about $29,000,000 dollars in back taxes. By February of 1986 the IRS had seized his assets to pay the tax bill. Barry was nearly destitute of friends, money, and time to live. He was in a free fall, and no matter how hard he yanked his connections to the past, no way of escape opened for him.

During those months, Barry called me often, and we had long conversations. He seemed to have made peace with God and had accepted that the end could come at any time. I encouraged him to keep his trust in God. Among our topics of discussion were details of his funeral. He had a quotation that he wanted read at his funeral and etched on his grave marker. He asked if I would conduct the service, and I agreed to do it.

On February 19, 1986, Barry called in the morning. "Joe," he said, "they're closing in."

"Barry, keep your eyes on Jesus. Keep your eyes on Jesus." We talked for a while and then, before he hung up, I again said, "Barry, keep your eyes on Jesus."

That night Barry's brother, Ben, called. "Joe," he said, "can you come and preach Barry's funeral?"

Christ is inviting you to come: "Come unto me, all ye that labour and are heavy laden, and I will give you rest." Oh, may we all find rest in Christ now! Do not let anything divert your mind, but make up your mind this hour that you will settle this great question of eternity.[3]
—D. L. MOODY, "TOMORROW MAY BE TOO LATE"

When Barry had pulled into The Salvation Army parking lot that evening, two men had machine-gunned him to death as he sat behind the wheel of his white Cadillac. Barry's death was never ruled a homicide or a hit. It was ruled an assassination.

Standing before Barry's sky blue casket, I preached an evangelistic message and read the quotation that Barry had requested for the service. "A rebel adventurer, the likes of whom in previous days made America great."

While feeling profound grief that I had lost a friend, my deepest emotion following Barry's death was a sense of being robbed. I felt that I had been so close to bringing Barry into a relationship with God that could have used his talents and genius for the kingdom of God. At age forty-six, Barry would have had many years to serve God. While Barry couldn't have undone the harm he had done to those who bought the drugs and arms, he could have warned others before they took a similar route. There were so many places that Barry could have pulled up, but he kept flying his own course.

I walked away from Barry's grave deeply grieved over what could have been. Barry had believed he could outrun the lion and get to safety, but along the way he had consistently chosen the trails that led him further from God. When Barry finally decided to run, he found himself lost in a maze of wrong choices that led to dead ends. While I believe that Barry was plucked from the fire in the end, his life, with all its potential, crashed and burned, and his legacy was stained by corruption.

When God does not answer prayers the way you thought He would or could, you must guard against anger directed to God. Keep in mind that, no matter how much you care for a person, God loves that person more. The Lord is not willing that anyone should perish. He wants all people to come to repentance. God alone knows the best way to bring the person to Himself. In the end, though, neither you nor the Lord, nor the angels in heaven, can choose eternal life for that person. That person alone can say, "I am sorry for my sins. With Your help, I am turning from sin, and I am going to walk with You."

CHAPTER 10

DANGER IN HIGH PLACES

STAYING SAFE IN HIGH PLACES CAUTION 1

STAY ALERT IN LION TERRITORY. THE SLIGHTEST DEVIATION FROM TRUTH CAN LEAD TO DESTRUCTION.

O NE LION TRACKER said, "If you make a mistake with a lion, the lion will make you pay dearly." Among pilots there is a saying, "There are bold pilots. There are old pilots. There are no old bold pilots." A mistake in lion territory and in the air can cost you dearly.

Tuesday, May 14, 2002, "1 Finger May Have Prompted Lion Attack"

A zookeeper whose right arm was severed by a lion... might have simply wrapped her fingers around its cage to help pull herself up from a chair before the 364-pound animal lunged at her Sunday....Surgeons were unable to reattach her arm, which was severed near the elbow.... A wildlife investigator said the attack was quick. "One finger: That's what started the initial bite; that's when the animal pulled the arm in," he said. "Preliminary indications are it took less than 30 seconds."...The zookeeper...was "trained and proficient in our operating protocols."[1]

◆ ◆ ◆

In the Caribbean, sailors and pilots must cope with storms that seem to explode out of the ocean like sea monsters. Whether a calloused-hand fisherman or a captain of a 747, those who pilot vessels in the Caribbean must deal with a variety of dangerous weather systems.

Ubiquitous afternoon storms come quickly, fire the sky with noise and light, and leave in a few hours. Tropical depressions and tropical waves are like visiting relatives. Their first rains are often

140

welcomed, but they tend to stay too long.

The most dreaded storms, hurricanes, are the bullies of the Caribbean. As the pompous weather systems swagger across the Atlantic, they achieve name recognition, and island residents jump to prepare for their arrival.

Ever since witnessing Hurricane David's pounding of the Dominican Republic, I had kept a close eye on hurricanes. When Hurricane Gilbert struck Jamaica in 1988, Ken, a friend in Alabama, asked me to fly vital supplies to Jamaica for the Church of the Nazarene relief efforts. This was the first of many relief flights that I would do in the Caribbean.

As I approached Jamaica on that first flight, I discovered that the VOR was broadcasting wrong signals. Hurricane Gilbert had knocked the navigational aid askew. By using dead reckoning though, and tuning into weak radio stations that had gotten back on the air, I was able to find the right heading and make a safe landing in Kingston. The VOR, once a source of reliable guidance, had been shifted by the winds.

I have often thought about that Jamaican VOR. A pilot flying an outward-bound radial from the VOR would go further off course with each passing moment and eventually run out of fuel before reaching land. In much the same way, the winds of culture and the reemergence of old gods and philosophies have shifted the way to "spiritual life" slightly off Truth. The lines start at a point of Truth, seem to run concurrently, then gradually move further and further from each other. Gradually false gods and philosophies begin to emerge on the variant path.

There are no new gods. The old gods that teach "Be your own god" and "Whatever feels or seems good is good" are the same old gods with new identities. False gods have no problem sharing territory with other false gods. They lovingly promote tolerance of all beliefs and acceptance of all gods on an equal basis. On the other hand, Jesus says, "I am the Way, the Truth, the Life. I will share My glory with no one!" If you see Jesus appearing on the same radial as Buddha, Confucius, or Gandhi, you are on a false heading. The only bearing that leads to eternal life originates and remains focused on Christ alone.

STAYING SAFE IN HIGH PLACES CAUTION 2

YOUR FAITHFULNESS TO STAY ON COURSE WILL
LEAD OTHERS TO SAFETY. YOUR DEVIATION FROM
THE COURSE WILL NOT ONLY DESTROY YOUR LIFE
BUT ALSO THE SPIRITUAL LIVES OF MANY WHO
HAVE LOOKED TO YOU FOR LEADERSHIP.

For pilots who fly the Caribbean on a regular basis, there is little mystery to the disappearance of planes and boats in the Bermuda Triangle. Powerful storms can pop up so quickly that they defy detection by the most advanced avionics and the most weather-savvy pilots. They are in-your-face storms that strike before you can duck and get away.

I always kept an eye on the weather. Although I had a Cessna 421 with all the latest avionics and color radar, I continually evaluated the weather visually. After more than five thousand hours of flying, most of which were international flights, I practiced determining the weather visually before I verified it with radar and flight service.

In August of 1992, while flying a mission team to the States from the Bahamas, I noticed that in the distance cumulonimbus buildups went from twenty thousand to twenty-five thousand feet and had diameters of six to eight miles. This usual August weather pattern presented no problem, because the clouds tended to congregate in bunches and I could navigate around them. On this morning, however, the buildups were widely separated. "There's instability in the air," I told the young man who was sitting in the copilot seat. "Something is going to happen in the Caribbean."

We landed in Fort Pierce, Florida, and while the plane was refueled, unloaded, and reloaded, I grabbed a hamburger. It was a quick turnaround, about forty minutes. Before noon I was in the air again, taking another mission team to the Bahamas.

An hour and twenty minutes later, Nassau was in sight. To my surprise, the weather changed quickly and drastically. The scattered storm cells suddenly picked up speed and raced to link with each other over Nassau. I began a dash to Nassau, believing I could slip into the airport before the storm hit. The combining storm cells, though, had developed such intense circular motion that they sucked me into the maelstrom.

Caught in a blinding thunder squall, the plane bounced and soared and dropped like a leaflet in a wind tunnel. My passengers screamed and cried out to God and vomited. In all my flight experiences, I had never encountered such turbulence. In the rain I couldn't see to the end of the wing. The right wing shook so badly that I felt sure that the storm had ripped off an engine.

"Nassau," I radioed, "I've lost an engine."

We weren't alone in our dilemma. An American Airlines plane and a Delta airliner had also been trying to slip into Nassau ahead of the storm. Altogether, four planes had been sucked into the storm. They all reported being in extreme turbulence and were calling Nassau control for guidance either into the airport or out of the storm. Nassau control had no idea what to tell us. The storm had popped up so suddenly and powerfully that the controller didn't know where to direct our flights.

To my relief, both engines of my 421 were still attached and operating, but I wondered if we would get out of this one. To my advantage, I had a plane full of passengers who knew how to get in touch with God, and they were definitely talking to Him.

Suddenly, off to my right and below, I saw a clearing. "Nassau," I radioed, "I see a clearing, and I'm requesting a visual. I'm breaking off the approach."

"Do what you need to do to get your plane down safely," Nassau replied.

To the other pilots, I radioed, "About twelve to fourteen miles southeast there's a circular clearing that's about six or seven miles wide. Aim for it. I'm descending to two thousand feet."

"Roger," came the reply from voices that quivered with the turbulence.

Centering on the opening, I slipped through the tiny corridor into Nassau. The airliners landed behind me in quick one-two-three order. On the ground the pilots of the airliners thanked me for leading them to safety. A stewardess, with vomit all over the front of her uniform, said, "I have never in my life been through anything like that." We all agreed that the fast-popping storm had been uncanny.

I went away from that flight saying, "Something is brewing in the

Caribbean. There's an instability in the air that is not good." Five days later, Hurricane Andrew climbed into the ring of "Super Storms," and walked away from South Florida with a purse of over $25 billion.

In retrospect, I know that God opened a way of escape for me over Nassau that day. My response to that escape route not only saved my life and the lives of the mission team, but it also saved the lives of hundreds of passengers on those airliners.

As a leader on the trail, as one whom God has called to run to the roar, you have a special responsibility to keep close to the Guide. Although people should personally keep their eye on Christ, they see you as a flesh-and-blood representative of God. The longer you run to the roar, the more influence you will have on others on the trail behind you. Paul told the Corinthian church, "Now it is required that those who have been given a trust must prove faithful" (1 Cor. 4:2). As you run to the roar, keep in mind that the way you run will influence how others will run. Carelessness can quickly destroy you and those whom you influence.

As one in a position of leadership either by appointment or by familiarity with the trail, how should you live your life? No matter how carefully you walk, someone will criticize your lifestyle. The Scriptures give clear guidelines in doctrine and basic moral issues, but don't cover all the specifics on how to live a godly life. Paul handles differences in nonessentials by saying, "Make every effort to do what leads to peace and to mutual edification" (Rom. 14:19).

Where the Scriptures are silent, how can you set an example that edifies others without getting entangled in traditions and religious laws? A few guidelines will help you make wise choices.

- Know the boundaries of your own life. What activities create a sense of unease? Stay within the boundaries of God's peace.

- To whom have you given allegiance—a church, a denomination, a mission organization? Your lifestyle will reflect on that organization. You may not agree with all the standards of conduct, but if you join the organization, do your best to live within the prescribed boundaries.

- Respect cultural mores relating to acceptable behavior. Shorts and a T-shirt may be acceptable attire in a South

Florida church but would be unacceptable in a Mayan village church.

· Where has God opened doors of ministry to you—street kids, retirement villages, entertainers, public school teachers, mechanics, carpenters, doctors? Wherever God is opening doors to ministry, live freely but keep in mind your personal boundaries.

Be the best example of a Christian that you can be, and remember, you will never meet the expectations of all people. Even Jesus fell short of meeting the expectations of religious leaders.

Staying Safe in High Places Caution 3

Rejoice in the hard lessons on the trail. They train and enable you to discern good from evil.

In late 1983 when the ink was just dry on my new instrument rating, I had a beautifully equipped Cessna 206, complete with color radar. I was wrapping up a year of about seventy *JESUS* film crusades, and I was emotionally exhausted. After giving and giving and giving, I left Haiti to return to the States for some reoccurrence flight training in Virginia Beach. A pastor friend recognized my physical, emotional, and spiritual exhaustion and invited me to his church. This time the invitation was not to speak or give out, but to receive and find replenishment.

To this day, I look upon those days as one of the spiritual highlights of my life. That brother poured so many spiritual truths into me that I felt they were like a massive dose of antibiotics that came knocking all kinds of infection out of me. By the time I was ready to leave his home, I felt nourished and revitalized.

As I planned a flight from Virginia Beach to Baton Rouge, Louisiana, I tracked the passage of a rather severe cold front that had been crossing the eastern United States. It was to pass through Virginia that night, so I planned to leave in the morning. When morning came, I opted to wait and give the front more than adequate time to pass. By late afternoon when I departed Virginia Beach, the skies were clear, and I could see no problems with the weather. I filed an IFR flight plan, and since my departure was late in the day,

I planned to end the first leg in Raleigh-Durham where a Howard Johnson's hotel was almost on a taxiway.

I took off confident of the aircraft, confident of my ability to fly at night, and especially relaxed about the weather. Besides allowing more than ample time for the front to pass through, I had obtained the latest weather briefing. A ridge of high pressure was forecast to follow the front.

As the winter sun set and the shadows blackened the ground, I scanned the instruments and radar. I always enjoyed flying at night, and on this night I thanked God for the wonderful plane He had provided. The color radar swept the sky looking for the pilot's enemy—thunderstorms. Each sweep came up free of storm cells.

The roaring exhaust of the three-hundred-horsepower engine, the tips of the propeller cutting the air at nearly supersonic speed, and the pull of the two-thousand-pound air frame through the air were music to my ears. Air vents, directed toward my face and feet, kept the cabin filled with fresh air, and the soft glow of lights on the instrument panel added to the familiar cozy atmosphere of the cockpit. The sense of acceleration and movement through the sky was as enjoyable as relaxing in a Stratolounger. After being revitalized physically, emotionally, and spiritually, the evening flight was pure joy—at least for a while.

It's when things are going just right that you'd better be suspicious. There you are, fat as can be. The whole world is yours and you're the answer to the Wright brothers' prayers. You say to yourself, nothing can go wrong....Best you not believe it.[2]
—ERNEST K. GANN

I began to feel that something wasn't quite right. I couldn't put my finger on it, but something wasn't right. The Cessna was flying like a dream. The radar was working magnificently, and I was right on schedule with my IFR flight plan, but still I had that deep feeling in my gut that something was wrong. I picked up the mike and called the closest flight watch, which happened to be Rocky Mount, North Carolina. It was fifteen to eighteen miles away from my position.

"Listen," I said, "the cold front that came through...all passed yet?"

"All passed."

"How do things look between here and Raleigh-Durham?"

"Look fine. No problem at all. Looks like a ridge of high pressure is going to come in behind it. It's looking just fine."

"OK, thanks."

For some reason his reassurances didn't reassure me.

"Tell you what; I'm going to come in and take a look at the radar myself."

"Fine. Come on in. I'll put on some coffee."

I spiraled down and landed at Rocky Mount, North Carolina. It was typical of flight stations that peppered the United States before automated flight stations took over. The operator beckoned me to the radar screen and said, "Come on over. Take a look."

The trail of the cold front was visible on the extended radar range, and the front had indeed cleared the area several hours previously. The area between Rocky Mount and Raleigh-Durham was clear. I did not see a single storm cell in my flight path.

The nagging sense of foreboding persisted, but I could see no reason to abort the flight to Raleigh-Durham. I was a well-trained professional pilot. The weather was clear. The plane flew perfectly and was equipped with instruments, a stack of King radios, and the latest in weather avoidance radar.

After taking a few minutes to finish my coffee, I refiled my IFR flight plan for an altitude of six thousand feet and took off for Raleigh-Durham. Although some mountains lay below, the six-thousand-foot altitude was a safe level.

Twenty minutes into the flight, turbulence began to buffet the plane. I began to pay very, very careful attention to the radar, especially when I noticed it had pulled up some rain showers. The showers intensified on the radar. This was not supposed to be, and yet here it was.

The showers then turned into thunderstorms. Lightning ripped the clouds ahead. I could not continue on my course. I requested a course deviation and began turning to the south. The radar flashed red, highlighting very intense thunderstorms.

"Thank You, Lord," I murmured, "for onboard radar." A single-engine plane flying IFR at night over mountainous terrain and through intense thunderstorms would have no way of finding safe passage without onboard radar.

Radar, very much like art, though, requires interpretation. The best of radars can spot a thunderstorm and give an all-clear signal beyond the cell. In spite of what the radar says, a more intense thunderstorm can be hidden or imbedded in the obvious cell. To properly understand the radar's message, you may have to search for a different viewpoint by making a turn or adjusting the tilt of the wings to peek around a corner to fully understand what the radar is telling you. Reading radar properly is actually a lot like reading the Bible. You can read one verse out of context and get an all-clear signal to charge ahead, but if you read the verses around that one and compare it to other verses, you might get a totally different viewpoint. On this night, I was thanking God that I knew the intricacies of reading radar properly. When I maneuvered the plane to get a more accurate radar reading, my sense of foreboding became the reality of fear. The clouds ahead contained more than evening showers, and I was glad that I had taken time to check all aspects of the radar reading before proceeding.

I radioed Raleigh-Durham to request another deviation heading.

No one responded at Raleigh-Durham, but other aircraft in the area began reporting intense weather. As I persisted in radioing Raleigh for a course deviation I dodged a thunderstorm to my right and saw a clear passage straight ahead that kept me clear of another cell. The controller finally came on, and with a slow drawl gave me clearance to change my heading.

"Thank God for onboard radar," I murmured again as I watched the radar screen and slipped around a fiery cell into a clear space. But I had no preparation whatsoever for what happened next.

"Jesus!" I screamed.

A fire-hose stream of water blasted my face, taking my breath away.

The windshield! The windshield must have blown out! Water driven by 140–150 mph speeds blasted my face, and I gasped to breathe. Water hit my feet and legs and drenched my feet.

Terror seized me. *What's happening?*

It was as if I had hit a hard wall of water. A quick glance verified that the windshield was intact, but water poured through every opening to the cockpit and sloshed over my feet. The instruments and radar were still operating. The plane leaped in an updraft.

Silence filled the cockpit.

I ripped off the headset. The engine had died.

The sense of forward acceleration and movement ceased, and my stomach plummeted as the plane started dropping. A downdraft sucked the plane so rapidly that soda cans in the rear of the cabin exploded. The aircraft was free-falling toward mountainous terrain below.

Jamming the headset back on, I called, "Raleigh-Durham Approach, One Double O Three Victor."

The drawl came back, "Stand by, One Double O Three Victor. Delta 437, turn right to a heading of zero niner zero. Contact departure on 124 decimal 7."

With fifteen to twenty seconds before slam down I called, "Raleigh-Durham Approach, One Double O Three Victor. I just lost my engine. I'm going down. I'm declaring an emergency. I need help immediately."

"Everybody stand by. One Double O Three Victor, squawk ident."

I squawked the transponder code, which immediately identified me on the radar screen.

"Comanche 493 Yankee," the controller said, "you've got a 206 just beneath you and to your left. Look and see if you can spot him."

"Approach, I've got him just beneath me," the Comanche came back.

"Keep an eye on him." To me he said, "One Double O Three Victor, you've got a Comanche above you."

"Raleigh-Durham, what is that rotating beacon beneath me?" I asked.

"That's Raleigh-Durham East. Be careful. Big slope on runway."

The runway was on the side of a mountain, but with downdrafts accelerating my descent, I had no other option. I started to set up an approach to the runway.

"How bad's the slope?" I asked the tower.

"It's a big one."

As I started a quick, modified spiral down to the runway, I realized my speed was way too fast. Although experience as a bush pilot enabled me to stick planes into tight places, there was no way I could stick the plane in on that short of a distance and at my free-falling speed.

For the second time that night I cried out, "Jesus!"

The fewer the words, the better the prayer.[3]
—MARTIN LUTHER

Water sloshed over my feet, rain lashed at the windscreen, and the lighted runway rushed to meet me. My mind tried to squeeze the plane onto the fast approaching strip because there was no other choice, but I knew that there was no way to make a safe landing. I was too high and too hot, the runway had a bad slope, and trees probably hedged the end of the runway.

Noise burst from the plane for a split second.

The water-saturated engine had come back to life. It had lasted only about five seconds, then died again, but it had given me a surge of power.

"Come on, baby. Do it again. Do it again," I pleaded.

"*Bahh!*" It fired again and lifted the airplane.

Each time it fired, those precious seconds of power gave me more options.

"Come on, baby, do it again!"

With just a little more power, I wouldn't have to squeeze the plane into that downhill, hot, fast approach. "*Bahh!*" The engine roared again, giving me hope that I could set up a proper landing. If the engine kept firing, I could do an 80–260 reversal approach, which is similar to the maneuvers sailors use to retrieve a person overboard.

"*Bahh!*" I had to make a quick decision. I could keep on the same landing approach or change the approach and gamble on the engine giving me more power. If I could get a little more out of the plane, I had a chance to come down over the strip, do a downwind down the middle of the strip, then do a tight left turn, and come back in approaching the runway from the opposite direction. That would give me an uphill landing. With no time to deliberate and neither option guaranteeing a safe landing, I put my trust in the engine and started down the middle of the strip.

"*Bahh!*" Every three to five seconds the plane would belch power. I put the plane into the 80-degree left turn. When the compass registered the change, I made a 260-degree turn to the right. Each power burst gave me time to bleed off altitude and set up a saner approach.

By the time I had completed my turn, I was at a good altitude. I passed over trees near the threshold and whistled in noiselessly. Had I approached high and hot from the opposite direction, I would have never been able to stop and would have hit the trees doing 100 knots.

I rolled to the end of the runway. For a few minutes I sat thanking God for a safe landing. My desperate prayers had consisted of one word, "Jesus," but God had heard those prayers.

I keyed the mike and said, "Raleigh-Durham Approach, this is One Double O Three Victor. I'm down safe."

The plane was a mess. Flight charts, clothes, and upholstery were soaked. Cola from the ruptured soda cans spotted the ceiling. When I opened the door of the plane, a couple inches of water whooshed out of the cockpit.

◆ ◆ ◆

We never know when the lion will ambush us in an unexpected moment. When the lion comes so close that you can smell his breath, you don't need to run to the roar—YOU ARE AT THE ROAR! There's no time to strap on armor. It must already be in place. The sword must be in hand as you take your stand against the lion. On that North Carolina flight, I had no time to consult a manual or even anyone on the airwaves. I had to use all that I learned in previous years to land safely.

When we think of *sudden* happenings, our minds often shift to the Second Coming of Christ. On the day when our Lord suddenly comes, the world forecast will be, "All is well," and the news radar will read, "All clear." Christ said, though, that the day should not surprise us. He has given us signs of the season—not the day or moment, but the season. If we stay alert and familiarize ourselves with His Word and the developing signs, we will be prepared for that sudden appearing. Paul said that we are, "Not in darkness so that this day should surprise you like a thief…but let us be alert and self-controlled" (1 Thess. 5:4, 6). Stay alert. Familiarize yourself with the signs that Christ gave concerning His return. And on the day that He returns, when others faint with terror, you will safely reach your destination. (See Luke 21:26–28.)

◆ ◆ ◆

For years the events of that stormy night perplexed me. Why had my radar failed? I related my story to many pilots, but I never found a plausible answer until four or five years later. In the late eighties I attended a weather radar seminar conducted by Archie Trammell. Trammell was recognized around the world as a leading expert in weather radar systems. He developed radar training programs for major airlines, government agencies, and the military.

Early in the session we told of our flying background and experi- ence. During a break in the eight-hour course, I told Trammell, "I had a very strange thing happen to me ...," and I described the events of that night.

He began interrogating me about the type of radar, weather conditions, and all the elements of the flight. After taking in all the information, he looked off in the distance as if processing the data; then he let out a little whistle.

"You know," he said, "you hit something that in all of my years of flying I've only seen two or three times. Let me ask you another question. You said you were a missionary pilot. You've flown into the islands many times, haven't you?"

"That's right."

"If you take your weather radar and tilt it toward the ocean, what do you see?"

"Nothing."

"Why is that? It's water, isn't it? And radar reads water. It reads the rain, right?"

"Right."

"Well, there's a big difference. If you point your weather radar straight down at the ocean, you're looking at a whole body of water. When you look at a body of water, it doesn't paint anything.

"When rain falls," he went on to explain, "it falls as water drop- lets, and those water droplets create an electrical charge as they fall, thus creating a readable image. When you look at a solid body of water, there are no droplets. It is a solid body of water. Joe, what you ran into that night right outside of Raleigh-Durham is a most unusual weather occurrence. Have you heard of incidents where five to six or even eight inches of rain fall in a few minutes?"

I nodded.

"That's exactly what you ran into. You ran into a solid wall of water. It doesn't happen often. In fact, it rarely happens, but in that night, and in that location, you hit the wall. That's why the water poured through the vents into your airplane. Engines require fuel and air, and your internal combustion, fuel-injected engine with its induction system died because it ran into a solid wall of water. There was no air in that wall. We don't know how many planes have been lost when they've hit those walls. You are very fortunate to be standing here telling this story. You had all the elements of a disaster—flying at night, flying IFR, a single dead engine, and massive downdrafts. Young man, you were going down."

I survived that night because I sensed danger. I did not grow careless and trust only what was easily visible. I maintained alertness in spite of reassurances, and I used all the means of determining the source of danger that were available to me. When the danger came, years of experience in responding to danger kicked in, and the Lord stepped in to give me wisdom and favor beyond my abilities.

STAYING SAFE IN HIGH PLACES CAUTION 4

KEEP YOUR EAR TUNED TO THE SLIGHTEST WHISPER FROM THE GUIDE.

As you spend more time with the Guide, you will discern His voice more easily. Jesus said, "I am the good shepherd" (John 10:11). About the good shepherd, He said, "The sheep listen to his voice. He calls his own sheep by name and leads them out. When he has brought out all his own, he goes on ahead of them, and his sheep follow him because they know his voice" (vv. 3–4).

The closer and the longer you walk with God, the more easily you will recognize His guidance. The psalmist said, "Do not be like the horse or the mule, which have no understanding but must be controlled by bit and bridle or they will not come to you" (Ps. 32:9). The Lord delights in those who readily respond to His guidance. The King James Version says this: "I will instruct thee and teach thee in the way which thou shalt go: I will guide thee with mine eye" (v. 8). God's eye is on you as He guides you.

When you travel deep into lion territory, a tracker does not direct by yelling, "Don't do that! Get over here!" The tracker whispers softly or uses a nod, a pointing finger, or even an eye movement to keep those in his charge from danger. In the same way, our great Guide guides us by a whisper, a nod, or an eye movement as we travel in lion territory.

One afternoon while en route to the Bahamas, it seemed that my Guide dropped His hand and motioned me to stay and not move ahead. I could see no reason to stop on the trail, but I responded to His guidance.

That afternoon I sensed that something was wrong. I couldn't see it, but I could feel it. I scanned the instrument panel again. Level at 16,500 feet, the Cessna 421 cruised at a little over 200 knots. All systems registered green. There was no reason for the uneasiness I felt in the pit of my stomach. My eyes swept the instrument panel again.

I glanced at René, my copilot, to see if he detected any problems. He appeared relaxed. Under the pretense of stretching, I surveyed the passengers in the cabin behind me.

The French businessmen who had boarded in Cap-Haïtien, Haiti, seemed preoccupied with processing the information they had discussed at lunch and mentally preparing themselves for dinner with the prime minister of the Bahamas. No one in the cabin seemed uneasy.

I settled back in the seat. Off my left shoulder, Dreamsicle-orange clouds smeared an otherwise clear sky. Shielding my eyes from the setting sun, I checked the sea. Ragged white beaches of familiar islands were right where they should be. We were on schedule and on course. It seemed that the evening and the flight could not be more perfect. There seemed no logical explanation for the gnawing unease. Maybe it was just my imagination. Maybe stories about the Bermuda Triangle made me a little more sensitive to apprehension. I had flown through the Triangle too many times and heard too many stories to ignore this uneasy feeling. I, along with other pilots, had watched the compass and instruments go crazy for no reason when we passed through this area. I scanned the instrument panel again, watching for the slightest variation since my last check. Other than the normal drop in fuel supply, the instruments appeared stuck in place.

I decided, though, to call Nassau for an update on weather conditions. The Triangle often spawns notorious, rapid-rising, hard-hitting storms. In this area only a year ago I had encountered one of the deadliest storms of my flying career.

"Nassau Radio, Nassau Radio, this is November Seven O One Alpha

Mike." No one responded.

"They should hear us," René said. "We're well within range."

After several unproductive calls to Nassau, I radioed, "Is anybody on 124.5? This is Seven O One Alpha Mike looking for a Nassau PIREP (Pilot Report)."

The airways were dead.

René shrugged and said, *"C'est la vie."* Ordinarily I would have responded in the same manner to the erratic communications that were so common in that area, but today the silence troubled me.

The orange horizon had blackened near the sea. Day was closing down fast. The dropping sun would also shut the door to landing options. After sundown, landings were only permitted on two airstrips in the Bahamas—Nassau and Freeport.

I tried Nassau again. No response. I scanned the radar. Clear skies for 150 miles. Something inside, though, warned me against going on to Nassau. It was more than a vague feeling. It was more like a still, small, insistent voice. I wrestled with responsibilities.

I couldn't abort a flight because of a *feeling.* I had a responsibility to get these men to a meeting with the prime minister. Their cruise-line discussions would involve millions of dollars and thousands of jobs. Why wouldn't Nassau speak to me? Why wouldn't someone out there answer?

"What time is sunset tonight?" I asked René.

"It's about twelve minutes from now."

René still showed no sign of apprehension. This decision was mine. Whatever came of it, I would bear the responsibility. If I chose to land, it would have to be within the next ten minutes. If we were forced to land later at an unauthorized airport, it could cost us a five-thousand-dollar fine and possible seizure of the aircraft.

I radioed Nassau again. Still no response. I scanned the instrument panel again. Plenty of fuel to make either Nassau or Freeport. The radar sweep came up clean. All signs read *Go.* And yet, I felt uneasy about continuing the flight.

I had found that allowing God's peace to guard and direct my life was the safest and most rewarding way to live. I had learned that when I sensed inward unrest, it was time to pause and evaluate my direction. Above all, I had learned that unrest was a warning to avoid reckless charging ahead with my own plans.

To wait on God, no time is lost. Wait on.
—AUTHOR UNKNOWN

On this perfect flight I could not explain *why*, but inward unrest was building like a late afternoon thunderstorm. I felt that if I continued I would be going on alone—without God's protection.

"René," I said, "we can't go to Nassau tonight." Instantly his eyes swept the instruments.

"Why not?" he asked.

"Something inside is telling me not to go. It's real hard to explain."

"The PM will have a limousine waiting for us," he said.

"You know I've been trying to get a weather report with no response. I think we ought to just land at Exuma International and stay in Georgetown."

"You're the pilot. If you think we shouldn't go in, then I'm with you."

I turned and looked into the cabin and calmly told the executives, "We won't be able to reach Nassau tonight. We'll be landing here in the Exumas at Georgetown. We can send a message to the prime minister that we'll see him in the morning." They started to inquire further, but I quickly overrode their objections. "It's better that we land before dark. We'll get an early start and be in Nassau by nine in the morning."

They looked at me a bit strangely but accepted my judgment. I was glad they couldn't read my mind and know my doubts about the decision.

There was just enough time to bleed off the three miles plus of altitude without damaging ears and engines. When I called Exuma International to advise them of my plans, I asked, "Can you contact Nassau for me? I can't reach them."

"We can't raise them either," the tower replied.

We touched down three minutes before sunset. After tying down, I climbed the steps to the control tower and asked permission to contact Nassau. After keying the mike a couple times, I finally got through. I gently chided them for not getting back to us. In a stiff British accent weather service replied, "We've been a bit busy. Pretty foul weather about." I felt somewhat relieved about the decision to land.

The next morning, we flew across serene seas of aquamarine and deep turquoise and landed at the airport in Nassau just before nine o'clock. The prime minister's limousine pulled up at exactly nine o'clock. René and I told our passengers good-bye, and we began refueling the plane. During the refueling, I heard a Bahamian pilot ask the fuel attendant to add an extra forty gallons for the "search."

"Search!" For a pilot, *search* means bad news. *Search* means someone is lost.

"Who's lost?" I asked.

"Man, where were you last night?" the Bahamian pilot asked. "Didn't you hear? Last night two planes went down in the worst storm anyone can remember. A real killer. No trace of the planes yet."

"I was inbound, and something told me not to come in, so I put down at Exuma International."

The pilot grinned and said, "Good decision. Somebody up there's watching out for you."

"Add an extra fifty gallons to mine," I told the fuel attendant.

René and I joined the search, but it was futile. The killer storm, surpassing all tales of Triangle squalls, had ripped both planes apart in midair. All passengers had died instantly. Our projected flight path would have put us in the vicinity of those planes at the exact same time.

I don't know if the pilots of the other planes felt the same sense of warning or not, or why God would spare our lives and not spare others. I was thankful, however, for the inward unrest that had warned me against continuing to Nassau that evening.

There is no place for overconfidence or carelessness in the cockpit or in lion territory. You must stay alert. The Guide has posted warning signs for travelers all along the trail.

- "Be self-controlled and alert. Your enemy the devil prowls around like a roaring lion looking for someone to devour" (1 Pet. 5:8).

- "Let us not be like others, who are asleep, but let us be alert and self-controlled" (1 Thess. 5:6).

- Even with full armor on and sword in hand, Paul says, "Be alert and always keep on praying for all the saints" (Eph. 6:18).

At high altitudes, a moment's self-indulgence may mean death.[4]
—DAG HAMMARSKJÖLD

No matter how high you have climbed in your spiritual life, someone has gone higher and fallen. King David, a man after God's own heart and the author of sword-whetting psalms, decided he was tired of battling the Ammonites, so he stayed home while his army went out to fight. Unexpectedly the lion attacked while David was relaxing on the roof of his palace. Instead of quickly picking up his sword, David invited sin into his life. David, conqueror of many lions, had forgotten that you must always stay alert when living in lion territory.

Chapter 11

Attack!

O NE DOUBLE O Three Victor was all that I had hoped for in an air-plane. The Cessna 206 had an impressive King Silver Crown avionics package, color radar, and room for five passengers. This faster plane with additional passenger seating allowed me to fly mission teams throughout the Caribbean, where members took part in *JESUS* film crusades. Once, while taking five short-term missionaries to an island off Haiti, I ran into unexpected trouble.

SURVIVOR TIP 1

A THREATENED LION WILL ATTACK YOU.

About fifty miles offshore the aircraft's instruments started spooling. High voltage raced through the electrical system of the plane, spinning the instruments at ten times their normal speed. Gyros screamed like a cat at night and then shattered like crystal. I immediately hit the master switch to turn off all electrical power. The master switch did not respond. In horror I watched the $10,000 color radar spool and then collapse with a *phut* sound. One by one the instruments shrieked, then popped.

As soon as the first instrument had shattered, I had made a 180-degree turn back to land. By the time I got the plane headed back toward land, every electrical instrument in the plane had blown. The only instruments that did not fail were the gauges (which ran off vacuum), the compass, and my watch. Fully aware of how serious the electrical failure was, I pushed the power.

Smoke started curling out of the instrument panels. Along with the smoke, small flames appeared. The flames darted very close to fuel lines. I poured the coals to the airplane to get as much speed as I could because at fifty miles out and flying at 140–150 knots, it would take twenty minutes to reach land and an airport.

159

"We need to get our life jackets on," I told the passengers. I didn't have to tell them to pray. They understood enough of what was happening to know it was time to pray.

"Hold the life raft on your knees," I told the person sitting in the aft seat. After quickly briefing him on how to inflate the life raft if we had to ditch the plane, I turned back to the instrument panel. Without electricity, we had no radios or navigational aids except the compass.

The cabin filled with smoke, lessening visibility. I flew with my hand on the instrument panel in order to detect an increase in the heat. Some of the plastic started warping.

A fire in an airplane is not pretty, and when you are fifty miles out at sea, you don't have a lot of options or places to go. Stepping the airplane right down on the deck, I flew at about fifty feet above the water. If more flames surfaced on the airplane or inside, I would have to immediately stick it in the water before the fuel tanks exploded. It would be the only way to save our lives.

The minutes crept by. With no radio to inform me of other air traffic, I scanned the area for other planes. The unpleasant smell of burning electrical wires filled the cabin. Finally, the twin peaks just west of the Cap-Haïtien airfield came into view.

"When we land," I told the passengers, "stay calm, but get out of the plane immediately. Don't try to take any belongings or luggage out. The most important thing is to get out of the plane and move a safe distance from it. The fuel tanks may explode."

I flew above the runway and waved the aircraft's wings to warn the tower that I was coming in without radios. At the end of the runway I pulled up, eased around, and landed.

The mission team exited the plane quickly and took off for the terminal. I moved about thirty feet from the Cessna and stood cringing, hoping that she wouldn't explode and burn. After a few moments, I realized that no signs of smoke or fire were evident.

Cautiously, I returned to the Cessna and began pulling the cowling off to find out what had happened. My attention went straight to the main ground strap—a one-and-one-half-inch steel-braided cable that was bolted to the frame to ground the entire system.

The cable had been cut!

Someone had obviously tampered with the plane. Enough strands had been left to enable takeoff, but the natural jostling of the plane in flight parted the last strands. The master switch had shorted into the *on* position, thus making it impossible to stop the electrical surge.

Was it sabotage? Certainly. Who did it? I choose not to speculate about who did it. All I know for certain is that you cannot go into spiritually dark places and not expect to be a target. We had threatened the lion's control of the people in the lair, and the lion had responded. But God had heard our prayers for help and spared our lives.

◆ ◆ ◆

Why has my life been spared when other pilots have perished in sabotaged planes, wind shear, and Bermuda Triangle storms? I think that the answer might lie in the comment that the apostle Paul made about King David. Paul said, "When David had served God's purpose in his own generation, he fell asleep" (Acts 13:36).

I believe God has preserved my life to accomplish a work He has given me to do. For almost two decades (1979–1997), my mission service was in the Caribbean with a few crusades in Central America, South America, and Africa. A vision, though, burned in my heart to take the message of Christ beyond those boundaries. It has been the roar toward which I have run.

On a trip into Northwest Haiti, I expressed this burden to Allen Reesor, a fellow missionary. We were grinding our way up a mountain to one of those remote villages that missionaries describe as "not the end of the world, but you could see the end of the world from there." The four-miles-per-hour trip left us with plenty of time for conversation.

"Allen," I said, "God has given me a vision to take the message of Jesus around the world. I don't know how it's going to happen, but God has given me that vision. Maybe He will give me some type of business that will shoot me around the world to talk to men. I don't know how it's going to happen, but I do believe that somewhere down the road it will happen."

SURVIVOR TIP 2

BE AWARE: A GAP CAN OCCUR AT ANY
PLACE IN THE SECURITY FENCE.

The years between the vision of taking the gospel around the world and the beginning of the fulfillment were years of lion attacks. Erroneous assumptions abound about the level of protection and provision that the Guide supplies. It does seem that in response to our obedience that God builds a security fence around our lives and prospers us in many ways. But the security fence can come down at any point. Satan called that security fence "a hedge" (Job 1:10).

For reasons beyond our comprehension, God sometimes allows the hedge to come down and a lion to charge our path. At times a wide area of protection may come down, and many lions may assault us. Sometimes human error and sin bring down the security fence, but that isn't always the case. Job "was blameless and upright; he feared God and shunned evil" (Job 1:1), and his entire security fence came down. Job was left sitting on an ash heap scraping boils. He didn't understand why God allowed the hedge to come down, but he still trusted God, as revealed in his words, "Though he slay me, yet will I hope in him" (Job 13:15).

While in Haiti the security fence around my marriage and family began to bulge. My being away from home on crusades stretched the weakened area, but other factors that had been there since the start of our marriage had also stressed the marriage bond. I limited my crusades to two or three weekends a month. The rest of the time I did day flights, ministry in the local area, or worked in my home office. With the exception of the crusades, I pretty much went to work and came home like any other working husband. Had we been able to deal only with the lion that threatened our marriage, we might have possibly saved the marriage, but in early 1986 the security fence around our life began to come down all around us. The lions came at us in such ferocity that we could not focus on mending our relationship. All we could do was focus on survival.

Late in the fall of 1985, Haiti began to stir, and we saw evidence of political rebellion against the Duvalier dictatorship. Missionaries lived with packed suitcases (passports, cash, and valuables) beside their beds. Schools closed, reopened, and closed again due to violence in the streets. In January, when the American embassy began evacuating all nonessential personnel, I decided that it was time to fly my family to safety in Florida.

Jean-Claude Duvalier fled in February, but the political situation did not stabilize, so we made the decision to stay in the States and operate the ministry from Florida. Our family needed a break from the tension, and living in Florida would also allow my wife and me to get marital counseling.

Our family, like many other missionary families in Haiti at that time, had been living in a state of apprehension for three months. Fuel shortages, strikes, riots, fiery blockades, gunfire, and bodies on the streets had left adults jumpy and children frightened. The move to Florida added to the stress on our family. Overnight, our children had left familiar schools, church, and friends. They struggled to shift from a third world culture to an affluent one. Then the real battering began. In rapid succession lions leaped over the downed security fence. During one three-month period we endured an incredible mauling as several events occurred in quick succession.

Two weeks after the Haitian government fell, Barry Seal was assassinated. His death hit me hard. I grieved deeply. A close family member committed suicide, my father-in-law died, both my mother and sister were diagnosed with cancer and died in a short time, and one of my ministry planes crashed, leading to an intense FAA investigation.

SURVIVOR TIP 3

REALIZE THAT SOMETIMES YOU CAN'T AVOID
BEING MAULED. YOU WILL BEAR SCARS.

No matter what traumas affected our lives, I still had the responsibility to work and operate our ministry—Air Mobile Ministries (AMM). In spite of the difficulties, the ministry prospered, and we rented a terminal building in Titusville, Florida. At the ministry peak, AMM had three planes and leased five others from time to time. The staff included pilots, mechanics, office personnel, and twenty-five volunteers. With additional planes and pilots, AMM flew mission teams to the Caribbean, Central America, and South America. AMM also handled relief flights, and I trained MAF pilots to show the *JESUS* film.

My wife and I worked together in the development of AMM and went through serious marital counseling. In 1990 I stepped back from conducting *JESUS* film crusades that would take me away from home for more than a day. During the next two years I focused on making sure I was never away from home more than twenty-four

hours at a time, but in July of 1992 the marriage ended. I truly loved
my wife from the first day that I laid eyes on her, and losing her was
one of the bitterest disappointments of my life.

I was devastated. I never really thought that God would allow this
to happen. I thought that in some miraculous way the marriage
would hold together. Some divorces are amicable, but ours was not,
and my children stayed with my wife. I not only lost my children and
wife, but I also lost the hopes and dreams of a happy family life.

◆ ◆ ◆

How could the Guide allow me to face such devastating defeat in
the area of my marriage? When I was trying to follow His footsteps,
how could He allow this to happen?

We must accept the reality that the Guide may allow a hole to
develop in the security fence and the lions to charge through the gap.
No matter how spiritual we are, the fence can come down at any place.
We may face divorce or have a child kidnapped or murdered. We may
be horrifically injured and physically scarred, our daughters raped,
our mates unfaithful, our business wiped out by a hurricane. We may
lapse into dementia. The fence—the hedge that God places around
us—can come down at any point. We may bear some responsibility
for the gap, but often we have little control over the opening in the
security fence. How do we handle these debilitating attacks?

When we see the gap widen beyond what we can mend ourselves,
we often hold out hope that God will work a miracle. The child will
be found safe, the cancer will disappear, and the frivolous lawsuit
will be dropped. At some point, you must face the point that no
miracle is going to happen. This gap will never close. You eventually must face the reality that life will never, ever be the same again.
One person said, "You have to find a new normal."

In one afternoon my "normal" life ended. It was as if a nuclear
device had exploded in my whole being. All I had left of value was
the Lord. In times like this we try to find a reason or assign blame.
I knew that I was not blameless in the disintegration of our marriage. Little holes in that fence had existed from the start, but I
hadn't seen them as a real danger. I had failed—not in my relationship with the Lord, but in recognition of the seriousness of our
marital problems. Through ignorance, lack of parenting skills and

knowledge of my mate's needs, and yes, even stubbornness and pursuit of my own dreams, I had failed, and my marriage had ended.

I had to accept that the marriage had ended, and I had to find a "new normal." Although I hadn't been doing international flights that took me away from home overnight, I had been arranging crusades, handling logistical details for mission teams, keeping AMM planes and pilots operating, and providing purchasing and aviation services to missionaries. Now, Christian friends counseled me to get back into my international ministry. I began to fly teams to crusades in the Caribbean. I couldn't preach, though. I spent my days walking the beach, praying, and reading God's Word—trying to sort out what had gone wrong. Along with my family, my dreams of taking the gospel around the world lay on the ash heap. The stigma of divorce would shut many doors to me.

SURVIVOR TIP 4

THE KEY TO SURVIVAL IS EMERGING FROM THE BATTLE STILL HOLDING THE GUIDE'S HAND.

When the hedge develops gaps and lions assault from every side, you either emerge alone, or you emerge holding more tightly to the Guide's hand. If you can see a purpose or reason for the lions, you can accept the mauling a little better. When the *Challenger* disintegrated in a fiery explosion, NASA scraped the bottom of the ocean to find the reason for the accident. They found the reason. You may scour your mind, actions, and the Scriptures to find a reason that lions mauled you, but sometimes you will never find a sensible reason. What is, is. It doesn't make sense. You didn't think your Guide would allow you to face this situation, and you are left sitting on an ash heap scraping your wounds. In this critical moment of your trek through lion territory, you will face a trust issue. Do you *still* trust the Guide? Do you trust Him to lead you through the next stretch of the trail? Faith that holds on to the Guide's hand in this hour is the faith recounted in Hebrews 11. You see, some were delivered. They "conquered kingdoms, administered justice, and gained what was promised." Through faith they even "shut the mouths of lions, [and] quenched the fury of the flames." They "escaped the edge of the sword…and routed foreign armies" (Heb. 11:33–34). God seemed to double the security fence around these people and shoot every lion that tried to jump over.

In perplexities—when we cannot understand what is going on around us—cannot tell whither events are tending—cannot tell what to do, because we cannot see into or through the matter before us—let us be calmed and steadied and made patient by the thought that what is hidden from us is not hidden from Him.[1]
—FRANCES RIDLEY HAVERGAL

Others, though, seemed to have a security fence made of spider webs. They "were tortured…faced jeers and flogging…were chained and put in prison. They were stoned; they were sawed in two; they were put to death by the sword. They went about in sheepskins and goatskins, destitute, persecuted and mistreated.…They wandered in deserts and mountains, and in caves and holes in the ground" (vv. 35–38). Talk about lions coming through the security fence! Whether the security fence stayed up or went down, "they were all commended for their faith" (v. 39). They all walked out on the other side of the trial holding on to the hand of the Guide.

You cannot choose whether gaps come in the hedge or not. You cannot select the lions that may come through the gap. All you can do is choose to keep hold of the Guide's hand.

I grieved over the direction my family was going and the choices they were making, but I could not choose their path. All I could do was keep a grip on the Guide's hand. As Job, I emerged on the other side of the traumatic events with only my trust in the Guide left intact. I knew that "the LORD blessed the latter part of Job's life more than the first" (Job 42:12), but I didn't expect any such treatment from God. I was happy to survive each new day. Little did I know how many of Christ's riches still lay in store for me.

SURVIVAL TIP 5

PROMISES OF QUICK CURES APPEAL TO INJURED PEOPLE. RECOGNIZE YOUR VULNERABILITY DURING THE HEALING STAGE.

Following the divorce, I focused on flying and ministry. In Haiti, overthrow of the elected president resulted in a crippling embargo. I couldn't fly teams to Haiti, but I was able to do occasional relief flights. One day, a friend, Marjorie Wright, said, "I'm concerned about Cindy Perron." Cindy was a single missionary in Haiti with a three-year-old daughter, Angelica. Cindy and her father had flown with AMM a couple times, and I had conducted a *JESUS* film crusade in their village. On another occasion my copilot had stayed with the Perrons for a couple of days and had expressed admiration for Cindy's dedication to serving the Haitian people. She lived without modern conveniences—including electricity—and walked to her mission school, which was three miles from her home. Other than what people had told me, though, I knew little about Cindy. I assured Marjorie Wright that I would pray for Cindy's safety and then promptly forgot about Cindy.

In Haiti, Cindy was going through old newsletters and found an AMM newsletter. By candlelight she wrote asking if I could return and do another crusade in her village. I tucked the letter away and thought, *I'll do that sometime after the embargo lifts.* Soon after, Marjorie Wright contacted me again. "I'm really concerned about Cindy. I'm concerned about her safety."

"I just got a letter from Cindy," I said. "She asked if I could do a crusade. I'll try to get out to her village sometime."

Not long afterward, Marjorie called again. "Cindy is safe in the States," she said. "She is on a speaking tour with her daughter and a Haitian pastor. She is going to be at your church Sunday."

"Which service?" I asked. My church had three services.

I didn't attend the service that Cindy spoke in, but the missions pastor stopped me and said, "Could you take Cindy to lunch?" This was a normal request. Visiting missionaries always had to be entertained. I agreed to meet Cindy at a restaurant, and the pastor made the arrangements.

When Cindy sat down across from me at the table, I looked at her and thought, *Man, oh, man!* Her dark long hair, blue eyes, and energetic manner immediately seized my attention, and my heart kicked into a little pitter-patter rhythm.

"Is there a Mr. Cindy?" I asked.

"No. Just me, my daughter, and my dog."

"Interesting possibilities," I said, and was immediately embarrassed by my brashness.

She looked at me in a very proper way that said, "The nerve!"

At that point I really backed away from Cindy. I made a disciplined decision to really, really back away from Cindy, but my heart was still going pitter-patter. We finished the meal in a very formal way, and I chose my words carefully. I had made enough gaffes for one day.

Cindy's background had some similarities to mine. A registered nurse holding an executive position at a hospital, she had walked away from a high-paying position to answer the call to mission work. I knew that I was looking at a woman of faith. A single woman with a small child does not walk away from financial security to follow a whim. Cindy had made a deliberate choice to walk in obedience to the Lord and trust Him with the care of her daughter and herself. At the close of the meal I assured her I would be praying for her as she traveled in the States, and we parted ways.

◆ ◆ ◆

Traumatic or life-changing events may make you vulnerable to life-damaging decisions. You may teeter between an effort to break free from old restraints and start a new "normal" life *and* a need to preserve part of your familiar past. You hurt and crave comfort, and your pain may blind you to reality. And the devil is always breathing in your ear, "After all you've been through, you deserve..."

As a single person, I knew I had to set strict moral boundaries and stay within those boundaries. To avoid making regrettable mistakes, I had determined to block all the "Cindys" out of my mind and life unless I sensed God's hand in the arrangement. I made a special effort to forget this Cindy.

She called several weeks later. "Joe, I have an emergency. The Haitian pastor's visa is expiring, and he must return to Haiti."

"Cindy, there's a major embargo in force. I don't think I can get clearance."

"Look, I really must get this pastor home. The airlines aren't flying, and you are the only one I know who can fly him home in time."

"You're really serious about getting him home, aren't you?"

"Yes. Yes, I am."

"Well, you're a nurse, aren't you?" I asked.

"Yes."

"OK, Cindy, if you want to get him home, you'll have to work at it. I'm going to give you an assignment. I have a list of medical supplies that need to go to Haiti. I'll give you the number of a Treasury Department contact, and you convince him that we need to get these medical items into Haiti. If you are able to get the authorization for this flight, I'll fly your pastor to Haiti."

"I'll do it," she said. She also made it clear that she and her daughter intended to use this opportunity to return to their mission work in Haiti.

Since I had made the brash comment to her four months previously, I had purposely drawn a line in the sand and told God, "If You want me to see more of Cindy, You will have to make it happen." I knew that left to my own desires, my emotional and physical side could muck this up, and I could make a decision based on my interests, not on God's plan for my life.

I wasn't rude to Cindy, but I determined to keep our relationship on a business level. If she wanted to fly to Haiti and get her Haitian pastor home, she would have to carry out the assignment. I wondered how many phone calls she would make before abandoning the idea. In August 1994, during the height of the embargo, it would almost take an act of Congress to get permission to fly into Haiti.

Cindy was on a speaking tour in Ohio and Michigan. This was before cell phones were in use, and she had to use pay phones to call the Treasury Department. She faithfully plunked money into pay phones, making eighty calls before Lloyd Bentsen, Secretary of the Treasury, personally signed our flight authorization.

I had to admit, "This girl is good."

SURVIVAL TIP 6

IN THE GUIDE'S TIME, HE PROVIDES A HEALING
BALM. YOU HAVE ACCEPTED THE PAIN OF
THE TREK; ACCEPT HIS HEALING GIFT.

We planned to leave for Haiti at 4:30 a.m. from Stuart, Florida. At 10:00 p.m. on the night before the flight, Cindy, Angelica, and the Haitian pastor showed up at my house. I had been working on the plane's brakes up until an hour before they arrived, and in the August heat I was dirty and sweaty. A nasty gouge in my hand, full of lithium grease and covered by a filthy bandage, made me appear even scroungier.

When I opened the door to Cindy and her entourage, I said, "Ah, the medical team arrives. Cindy, take a look at this hand."

"This is terrible," she said as she began unwinding the bandage.

She fixed warm soapy water, and when she took my hand and lowered it into the bowl, my heart started that crazy pitter-patter rhythm.

"Just let it soak for a little while," she said. "Soak some of the grease and dirt out of that cut."

There is no situation so chaotic that God cannot from that situation create something that is surpassingly good. He did it at the creation. He did it at the cross. He is doing it today.[2]
—BISHOP HANDLEY MOULE

I was thinking, *This is downright scary!* I suddenly saw Cindy as someone I could truly be involved with for the rest of my life. A phrase from an old song started through my mind, *Please help me I'm falling*... But God seemed to bring me up short. He seemed to set up a shield and say, "Don't mess this up." As she cleaned and bandaged my wound, I kept thinking, *Don't mess this up. Don't mess this up,* and we talked of logistical preparations for the flight.

On the flight to Haiti, I learned more about Cindy and her ministry and found that we shared the same passion to lead others to Christ. She considered her ministry in the mud-hut village on Haiti's south peninsula as a blessing, not a sacrifice. To her, the embargo made it imperative that she return to her village and continue the school program that fed five hundred kids.

I struggled more and more with my feelings for her. When we landed in Haiti, I said, "Cindy, I know you need to go out to your mission. I have to meet with some contacts here."

"Wait a minute," she said. "You haven't flown me all the way in here just to drop me at the airport. I need your help."

"I have other things to do," I said. I knew that I couldn't handle being with her much longer without expressing how I felt about her.

We were gathering the boxes and bags to go through customs

when she said, "I did all that work and made all those phone calls to get that medical stuff in here, and you aren't going to leave me to handle my work alone! We'll do it together. I'll help you with your stuff, and you can help me with mine."

"Cindy, you can go your way and I'll go mine. After all, we aren't married!" She later told me she muttered under her breath, "Yet."

Finally I relented. "All right, Cindy, if that's what you want, I'll go out to your mission with you, but I've got to get back to do my work here."

I had brushed off association with Cindy at every step. I hadn't bothered to attend the service that Cindy had spoken in at my church, I had not asked her to lunch that Sunday, and I had definitely not gouged my hand so that she could hold it. I had predicated the flight to Haiti on an impossible assignment, and now I had resorted to bickering to get away from her. Without any effort on my part to make it happen, I realized events beyond my control were moving this special woman into my life.

When we showed up at her little house in Gressier, her helper, Madame Yvette, had made a spaghetti dinner. We ate the spaghetti dinner by candlelight—no electricity! Afterward, we walked outside where it was a bit cooler. The moon had risen, and we moseyed out to the end of the road. I had not pursued Cindy, but it seemed that during the last months the Guide kept allowing her to walk on the path with me. I had been fighting my feelings, afraid that in my own flesh I would make a wrong decision, but on this moonlit evening I felt as if the Guide walked with us.

There was a little protrusion in the bay, and we made a little turn on the road and passed behind a wall. I pulled her into my arms and kissed her—and that was it. I could not ignore my feelings for her any longer. Instantly, completely, and absolutely, I knew that I loved her and wanted her to know it. I wanted to spend the rest of my life with her. I didn't give her a little peck on the cheek; I kissed her and I kissed her! We walked a little further down the road and perched on the wall by the sea.

"You know we're probably going to get married," I said.

"You move pretty quickly."

"Well, it's probably going to happen."

She paused, then said, "Yeah, it probably is." We married in November of 1994.

CHAPTER 12

A MAP FOR THE JOURNEY

MAP READING TIP 1

GOD DOESN'T PUT LEGENDS OR SCALES ON HIS MAP.
HE ALONE KNOWS THE LENGTH OF THE JOURNEY
AND THE BREADTH AND DEPTH OF THE VISION.

I NEVER FORGOT THE vision of taking the gospel around the world. As one looking for a buried treasure, I kept looking for the map that would lead to a global ministry. I had shown the *JESUS* film in the Caribbean, Central America, some parts of South America, and Africa, but in my heart I believed God had more for me to do.

Along with marriage came a union of two mission organizations: my Air Mobile Ministries and Cindy's New Hope Mission. We affectionately called our combined ministry Air Hope. Together, we conducted *JESUS* film crusades in Haiti, and together we operated the school, which continued to grow. While obligations to our current ministries temporarily shelved the possibility of "taking the gospel around the world," God was at work cutting and shaping pieces of the vision.

MAP READING TIP 2

ON OUR SMALL MAPS WE SEE ONLY GOD'S OBVIOUS
PURPOSES. ON HIS MAP HE SEES HIDDEN PURPOSES.

For the apostle Paul, letter writing was a means of communicating God's Word to Christian believers in newly established churches. Paul died without realizing God's greater hidden purpose for his writings. The letters, a significant part of the New Testament, have guided the church in doctrinal beliefs and Christian living for over two millennia. As in viewing an iceberg, we often see only a portion of how God is working in our lives.

In 1996 Cindy and I were serving as missionaries in Haiti, and an event took place that benefited our mission work immensely. At that time I viewed the events as God's provision to continue our work in Haiti. I certainly didn't recognize it as a key piece in the vision to take the gospel around the world.

Cindy directed a school and feeding program for five hundred children in Haiti. Just before the school year started in 1996, I noticed that the printer cartridge was almost out of toner. Since the upcoming registration required a lot of printing, I went to Port-au-Prince to buy a couple cartridges. The $250 price for each cartridge staggered me. Our school was funded by my flying ministry and interested sponsors. The $250 price was simply unacceptable.

Since I flew mission teams, I asked team members to bring cartridges from the States. Customs officials, though, either imposed high tariffs or poked and punctured the cartridges until the toner ran out. I checked with hospitals, schools, and other mission organizations in Haiti to find a cartridge supplier that had reasonable prices. All the organizations, however, were paying exorbitant fees that seriously affected their nonprofit budgets. I decided that I had to find a solution. After researching remanufactured toner cartridges, I invested $500 in a kit and training video.

One day when an ocean breeze cooled our nonelectric home, I cleared the red-vinyl covered dining room table and laid out the parts of the kit—a special vacuum cleaner, bottles of toner, wiper blades, rags, alcohol, cotton swabs, a special set of pliers, and a training video. I fired up the generator, made sure the voltage was regulated, and projected the picture on the stucco dining room wall. During the next hours, I started and stopped the video, muttered and sputtered, and started and stopped the video. At 7:15 in the evening I popped a remanufactured cartridge into our printer.

It worked!

Euphoric, I grabbed the two-meter radio and contacted a nearby mission station that had the same type of printer and was also struggling with paying for high-priced cartridges. "I did it!" I excitedly told my friend. "I broke the code! I remanufactured a print cartridge."

The neighboring missionary, not given to emotion, was silent for a moment, then said, "That's great! That is just great news! It's going to help a lot of people."

That evening I fell asleep with a tremendous sense of accomplishment. I could remanufacture the cartridges we needed and possibly help other organizations. I didn't comprehend the significance of that day at the time, but there in a Haitian village between the sea and the cane fields...in a house without electricity and running water...and at a red-vinyl covered table...I had birthed a multimillion-dollar business that would start me on the way to taking Jesus around the world.

The next morning I awakened early to our dog's barking. A big box had been set on the front porch. It held a dozen empty print cartridges. Word had gone out that "Joe could recycle print cartridges."

◆ ◆ ◆

Take a "running to the roar" attitude toward solving daily problems. Rather than marking off a problem or difficulty as hopeless because you don't see an immediate solution, make an effort to solve the problem. In Haiti scores of nonprofit organizations had been paying exorbitant fees for print cartridges. Rather than find a solution, they had accepted the high costs. I viewed the cost as a problem that could be solved. Did I find immediate success? No. Efforts to bring cartridges into Haiti failed, but I kept working until I found a solution that worked.

What problems do you and your friends, neighbors, or business associates share? What is the obvious problem? What are the underlying causes? Have you tried to change the problem? If initial efforts have failed, try something else. Who said it would be easy? Solving the problem will require work, time, money, and patience. It may require several attempts, but few problems have no solutions. Just as many problems have hidden causes, the resolution to most problems produces hidden benefits.

When I produced the first recycled print cartridge, I thought I saw only the benefit of providing affordable printing for our Haitian school. By morning, though, I had the first of endless orders to remanufacture print cartridges. Filling these orders required little time but provided income for aviation fuel, food, and education for the school children; it also provided income for our family. Little did I know that even more benefits lay beneath the resolution of this problem.

MAP READING TIP 3

DON'T RUSH PAST "POINTS OF INTEREST." SOMETIMES THESE END UP BEING A HIGHLIGHT ON THE JOURNEY.

When I first arrived in Haiti during the 1970s, the only violent crime was conducted by the government. Oh, you could get robbed, but thieves outwitted victims rather than harmed them. You just had to stay alert and keep a tight hold on your wallet and briefcase. By 1996, though, violence had become commonplace. Road gangs and bandits had attacked us physically nine times in twelve months. We had fought our way out with pepper spray. Kidnappings, break-ins, and armed robberies abounded. Within a mile of our property, several people had been brutally murdered and dismembered. The violence seemed to go in tides. The country would be calm for several months, but then violence would rock the capital, and thugs in our area would see it as a license to rob and murder.

The personal attacks had been scary, but since the ministry was doing so well, we accepted the danger as part of the assignment. New Hope school was educating more than five hundred children and providing more than seven thousand hot meals a month to the students; many Haitians were coming to the Lord through the *JESUS* film crusades; and the cartridge-recycling business had relieved us of financial pressure. During lulls in the violence, we brought mission teams in to participate in *JESUS* film crusades and help in other mission work. *Missionair*, under the leadership of Dr. Rob Helmer, often flew the teams from Florida to Haiti. Times were difficult, but that was nothing new in Haiti. As long as God was blessing the work, we planned to stay in Haiti.

One day while I was waiting at the Port-au-Prince airport for Dr. Helmer's DC-3 to arrive with supplies and a fifteen-member mission team, Barbara Walker joined me. Barbara, a frequent guest in our home, had never accepted the idea that women are the "weaker sex." If something needed to be done—like moving a wandering bull off the road—she would take the bull by the horns and move it. The word *helpless* was not in her personal vocabulary even after major surgeries. Her ministry, however, focused on the truly helpless—orphan children in Haiti. She tracked down helpless and hopeless children and arranged for their adoption by American couples.

Today, as usual, she had a child in tow. While we waited for the plane, I watched the adorable three-year-old girl energetically climb on the railing outside the door to customs. When I caught her eye, she smiled shyly. Barbara had brought many orphans through our home, but this one seemed special. I felt a special tug at my heart when she smiled at me.

"What's the story on her?" I asked Barbara.

"She's from Sous Chaud (translated "hot water") on the northwestern coast."

"I've been there," I said. "Barren mountain ranges, cracked earth, mud huts. They have to walk an hour and a half or two to get water."

"More like three hours," Barbara said.

"What happened?"

"Her mother died while giving birth to her tenth child. The baby died, too. No one knows who her father is. She's the youngest child, and there is no one to care for her."

Thank God, Barbara found her. I didn't know how she did it, but she found these little ones and rescued them. We talked, and I watched the little girl bounce around. Then I asked, "Barbara, is she spoken for?"

"Yes, I already have a family for her."

"Have they seen her? Have they had any contact with her yet?"

"Not yet."

"Find another little girl for those people."

Barbara turned and looked at me with raised eyebrows.

I just smiled.

The plane landed, and we loaded trucks with supplies and team members and headed for Gressier. Barbara, as she often did, accompanied the team and me. No matter how well organized, chaos reigns during the first hours of a team's arrival. Unloading supplies, giving instructions on water, toilets, showers, and sleeping accommodations, and answering the same questions fifteen times generate noise and confusion.

While I put supplies away and focused on directing team members to their accommodations on the porch, in tents, or under the stars, Cindy and Barbara, with the little girl at their heels, prepared food for the travelers. In the kitchen, I saw Cindy nod toward the little girl and ask Barbara questions. Cindy appeared to show a special interest in the child.

I knew that with a team in our home, days would pass before Cindy and I could have a normal, relaxed, uninterrupted conversation, so I stopped storing supplies and said, "Cindy, could I speak with you a minute?" I nodded toward our bedroom. In our room I asked, "What do you think of this little girl?" Cindy looked at me like—well, we knew at that very moment we felt the same about her. "What do you think?" I said.

"I think we need to adopt her," Cindy said.

"So do I."

From that moment on, we considered ourselves the parents of this little girl that we named Juliet Joy. Barbara agreed to find another child for the adopting couple, and we began the process of jumping through legal hoops to adopt Juliet.

In our home, Angelica was a little bewildered with the new roommate who grabbed her toys, but the girls soon adapted and played together. Somewhere during the process of adoption and adaptation, Cindy became pregnant.

MAP READING TIP 4

PULLING INTO A REST STOP DOES NOT MEAN THAT YOU HAVE LEFT THE TRAIL. WHEN CIRCUMSTANCES FORCE YOU TO TAKE A BREAK FROM YOUR WORK, REMEMBER, HE PUT THE REST STOPS THERE WHEN HE DESIGNED THE TRAIL.

Cindy took extremely good care of herself, even forgoing coffee that she dearly loved. In spite of proper health care, including prenatal vitamins, Cindy developed a painful kidney stone that required stateside medical care. Cindy and Angelica immediately flew out, and Juliet followed, accompanied by Barbara Walker. I stayed to tie up loose ends at the mission, then went to Florida.

While Cindy was taking a walk with the girls, she sprained her ankle severely, and a dangerous blood clot formed. Doctors placed Cindy on a therapeutic level of heparin administered in twelve shots a day. Each shot left a big black bruise where it was administered. Soon she ran out of "real estate," a bruise-free spot on the body that could be used for the next shot. It was a dreadful time. I watched as she grew progressively worse. Since doctors had ordered complete bed rest, I was Mr. Mom. From afar, I ran our mission the best that I could, but Cindy's father and a Haitian pastor had to oversee day-to-day operations of the school.

◆ ◆ ◆

We have time lines on our life maps. We mentally put little black numbers above small spans of time: graduate from high school; graduate from college; get married; have first child; buy a home; buy a recreational vehicle. We place big red numbers between major change points in our life: education completed; marriage; children gone from home; retirement. We measure our life and goals by a scale of one lifetime equals seventy plus or minus years.

God works with a sliding scale. Try as you may, you will never figure out God's time management plan to cover the trail and fulfill the purpose He has for your life. You may look at the map and see a long tedious stretch and find that you arrive almost overnight. On a short-appearing stretch you may mark off years of asking, "Are we there yet?"

When a rest stop is a short-term goal, you look forward to stopping for a while. If you feel strong, alert, and energized, though, you will want to breeze past the rest stops because you don't want to lose time. The Lord, however, seems to have no regard for our personal schedules. You must set goals to reach the vision God has put in your heart, but along the way you must also accept the "stops" along with the "goes."

While we were in Haiti, donors provided most of the income for the mission school to operate, and I provided income for our family by remanufacturing toner cartridges. In the States I had no means of income, and we soon ran out of money. Our ministry had some assets, but we could not conscientiously touch those to meet personal needs. A couple of weeks after our arrival in the United States, I pulled up to the stop sign at the edge of our subdivision. When I pressed the accelerator to go on, the engine just spun. The transmission on the Mercury Sable station wagon had completely burned up, and the vehicle would not move.

I didn't know what to do. With Cindy far along in the pregnancy and dealing with the complications of blood clots, I had to have a vehicle. A friend loaned us a car for a couple of days, but it inconvenienced him dreadfully. His wife had to take him to work very early in the morning, and it just didn't work. Unexpectedly, a friend who was in the U.S. Army called. "Joe," he said, "I was surfing the Web and found round-trip tickets to Haiti for $82. I've never seen anything like it."

"What is it? Air Condor?" I asked. Air Condor was a notorious airline that kept getting busted for cocaine smuggling.

"It's American Airlines."

"There must be a mix-up. That's an unheard of price, but I'll call and ask about it."

When I called American Airlines, the agent said, "It's true. It's right here on the books. I've never seen anything like it, and no one can explain it."

"Book me," I said. I was desperate and had to find some way to get the car fixed, and I had an idea of how I could do it. Incredibly, I found a car rental business that was running a promotional rate of one dollar per hour. I drove from Orlando to Miami in four hours, topped off the fuel for six dollars, and took the courtesy shuttle to the Miami International Airport. In Port-au-Prince I got my little diesel van that I had left at a Texaco station and started toward Gressier.

All along the route to Gressier I stopped at every nook and cranny that used print cartridges. People had been sad about my leaving and were delighted that I had come back. They gathered all their empty cartridges and broken printers and copiers. By the time I arrived in Gressier, I had a van full of work.

I fired up the generator and worked all night Friday, all day Saturday, all night Saturday, all day Sunday, and Sunday night. Before the sun came up on Monday morning I started back to Port-au-Prince. On the way I delivered printers, copiers, and cartridges and shoved the money from each stopping place into my pockets. By the time I reached the airport to fly home, my pockets were full of cash. I had no idea how much I had until I reached home and tallied it up. From Friday evening through Sunday night I had made two thousand dollars, the amount needed to replace the transmission.

I never cease to marvel at the unique ways God provides for us. I left the richest country in the world, traveled to one of the poorest, and in one long weekend made enough money to put a transmission in my car back in the rich country. Getting the transmission in the car was good, but that didn't come near to solving our problems.

The second overdue notice from Florida Power and Light notified us that they would be cutting off our electricity. We were going from one crisis to another, and I was totally bewildered. Why was God allowing all these things to happen to us?

We had to stay in the States until Cindy delivered the baby and until the blood clots cleared. As soon as possible we would return to Haiti or possibly work in the Dominican Republic until the Haitian political situation stabilized. I couldn't take a job in Florida and then leave suddenly when we got ready to return to mission work. I had left Cindy and worked in Haiti one weekend to pay for the transmission, but I wasn't about to leave her again just to go make money. We were stuck, not knowing which way to go, *and* we had to find a way to pay the electric bill.

> **Christ sometimes delays His help that He may try our faith and quicken our prayers. The boat may be covered with the waves and He sleeps on; but He will wake up before it sinks. He sleeps, but He never oversleeps; and there are no "too lates" with Him.[1]**
> —ALEXANDER MACLAREN

I was crying out to God when it dawned on me, *I can call Florida Power and Light and offer to remanufacture enough cartridges to pay my utility bill.* It seemed like a great idea to me. In Haiti I had bartered for eggs, aviation fuel, hotel rooms for guests, and just about everything else imaginable. Why not trade cartridges for my electric bill? It made perfect sense to me.

When I called the Florida Power and Light office, a lady listened very carefully to my suggestion, then said, "Would you please hold for a moment?" She transferred me to a supervisor, and I gave my story to her about being a missionary pilot and my wife's complicated pregnancy.

"I remanufactured cartridges to support my family on the mission field," I told her. "I would be more than glad to remanufacture enough cartridges to cover my electric bill."

She sounded really, really interested in my proposal. "I've never heard anything like this before in my life," she said. "Let me discuss this and see what I can do."

Two hours later she called me back. "Mr. Hurston," she said, "I've presented your proposal and I think we have a good solution for you. I would like for you to call this person, but do exactly as she says to do. I think we can find a way to make some arrangements."

This is great! Frankly, I knew America operated on a different system than the barter system, but it looked as if my proposal was going to work.

I did exactly as the Florida Power and Light woman told me to do. I called a woman, and since it was a direct line, I had no idea to whom I was speaking. I started to explain my situation and the proposal to remanufacture cartridges when she said, "Yes, Mr. Hurston, I'm fully aware of your proposal. I think we have a solution, but you will need to come to my office immediately."

"I'll be glad to do that. What is the address?"

The address was not familiar, but I quickly drove there. I pulled into a large and elaborate facility and went to the exact room to which she had directed me. The room held a table on which were five bags of groceries. My electric bill lay on the table stamped "PAID." Florida Power and Light had directed me to Catholic Relief Services.

"But," I said, "I thought I was going to be remanufacturing cartridges."

She looked at me with compassion and said, "Mr. Hurston, would you please accept this as our gift to you to help you through this time? We know how difficult this is."

Their incredible act of kindness left me speechless. These people had given me what I needed but kindly and sweetly guarded my dignity. Their gift humbled me, but it also reminded me that God was watching over my family and me. One bag held a turkey, and that night we had a true Thanksgiving meal. Time after time during our "in between worlds" time—we weren't quite functioning in the United States and we certainly weren't in Haiti—God provided for our needs.

As Cindy battled the blood clots, we wondered if God was signaling us to move over into the exit lane and pull into a rest area. We thought a brief rest might be good, but we both wanted to get back on the trail and return to Haiti as soon as possible.

Just before Cindy's delivery date, the doctor treating the blood clots ordered one more sonogram to check for clots. The report came back negative. Cindy's obstetrician, however, had reservations about the accuracy of ultrasound to detect blood clots. She sent Cindy to the hospital to have a venogram. The ultrasound had indeed missed a significant clot. Cindy needed immediate surgery to have a microscopic screen placed in the vena cava vein leading from her leg to her heart. A few hours later she went into labor and delivered Peter James Hurston.

We thanked the Lord that Cindy had made it safely through the surgery and delivery, and we rejoiced over our perfect baby boy. I held Peter for a few moments, and then nurses took him to the nursery. While Cindy rested I watched my son in the nursery. Suddenly he seemed to start breathing hard and fast. His tiny chest was going up and down more rapidly than the other babies. I quickly brought it to the nurse's attention, and she immediately called a doctor. Their actions confirmed my suspicion that something wasn't right. They hurriedly placed Peter into a little capsule-type carrier and sent him by ambulance to Arnold Palmer Hospital for Children. Peter was going into respiratory and cardiac distress. Respiratory and cardiac arrest would follow.

I followed the ambulance, and since the hospital allowed parents to scrub and observe the care of their children, I was soon watching doctors work on Peter.

Peter flatlined.

The doctors worked frantically and brought him back. Later, after Peter had stabilized, I called Cindy. "We almost lost him," I told her.

During the next days, I shuttled between the two hospitals visiting Cindy and Peter. As soon as Cindy was able to move, she was up and dressed in scrubs and ready to visit Peter.

At Arnold Palmer hospital, Peter's doctor told Cindy, "Mrs. Hurston, your son is very, very, very ill." Beta-Strep had invaded Peter's body, and he was on a respirator. We couldn't touch him. All we could do was pray as we watched him lie there between life and death. During the next days the work of doctors, the prayers of many, and the mercies of God brought Peter through; he would grow into a healthy normal boy.

Somewhere during those nightmarish days Cindy and I both began to realize that we weren't going back to Haiti. Peter was too fragile and Cindy's blood clots had proven to be quite serious. Essential medical treatment for their health conditions simply did not exist in Haiti. We had not pulled off into a rest stop. Our road had come to a dead end!

Map Reading Tip 5

God doesn't mark all the dead ends on the map.

Together, Cindy and I had ministered in Haiti. Together, we made the heart-wrenching decision not to return to Haiti. It wasn't easy to walk away from a combined total of thirty-five years of ministry there, or to place the school of five-hundred-plus children in someone else's hands, but we knew that we couldn't return to our work or operate it from the States.

A dead end doesn't mean failure on your part to follow the Guide or the map. A dead end doesn't mean the Guide momentarily forgot about you or abandoned you. When young people face dead ends, they usually buckle on climbing gear and start up the face of the cliff. They expect to find another path lying at the top of the rock wall. Older people that have devoted their lives to one employer or even one ministry react differently if that long-term employment relationship ends abruptly. They tend to do more self-evaluation and take long looks at the "roads not taken."

How do you handle these dead ends? Accept that you are part of the human race—a flawed race that makes mistakes and has no way to determine the future. Sometimes the Spirit of God will seem to encourage you or give you a warning check as you make some decisions. Other times He is silent. All you can do is to try to stay sensitive to His leading and use your best judgment. Every indicator—the guidance of the Spirit, Scripture, counsel of godly people—may be aligned to signal a clear "go," and still you can find yourself at a dead end.

Just as you can't find reasons for gaps in the fence, you may find no sensible reason to run smack into an impenetrable wall. It's just there! You can't go back and remake earlier decisions. The only way to go is up the face of the cliff. Again you face that deep theological question on which faith hinges: "Do you still trust the Guide?"

Your faith may never waver. You may quickly tackle the mountain and trust the Guide to show you footholds and handholds as you go. Or you may anxiously search for assuring handholds before approaching the mountain.

Some scan the rocky face, and if they can't see a way up, they distance themselves from the Guide. They shrivel into bitter, resentful, people who die blaming the Guide for their plight. You can sit on the ash heap and moan that all is lost and life will never be the same again. Or you can have a young person help you buckle on the climbing gear and ask the Guide to show you the first handhold on the rock.

Often at the top of the rock wall, energetic and visionary youth fall in step with mature and seasoned travelers, and together they reach new goals that would have been unreachable by either traveling alone. Actually, the trail really doesn't reach a dead end. It just goes up the face of the mountain.

When the route to Haiti shut, I faced a massive wall of uncertainty about my future. Surprisingly, after the first shock, I felt relief. The longer I stayed out of Haiti, the more I realized how battered we were emotionally and physically. Cindy and I both needed rest, but I was going to have to find a way to support us before I could stop to rest.

Every assignment is measured and controlled for my eternal good. As I accept the given portion other options are canceled. Decisions become much easier, directions clearer, and hence my heart becomes inexpressibly quieter.[2]
—ELISABETH ELLIOT

At first I considered the airlines. In a surprising move, the airlines had begun to train and hire pilots again. With an airline transport rating, more than six thousand hours of flying, and a lot of time in multiengine planes and in international flights, I had a good chance of being hired. My age worked for me, too. I was old enough to be experienced, but too old to accumulate a large retirement liability to the airlines. A friend with United Airlines said he could help me get on at United if I chose. A new airline, AirTran, was starting up, and I was told that I had a good chance of getting on there. AirTran flew domestic flights, so I would only be away from home one or two days a week at the most.

When I thought of being away from my family, though, I knew I didn't want to be away even for short periods of time. Furthermore, my older children were having difficulties, and I wanted to be available to them. I didn't have peace about applying with the airlines. I kept looking at the cartridge business and wondering, *Could I make it here?* To be honest I was afraid to try the cartridge business in the States. In Haiti, advertising was by word of mouth, and I had no competition. In the States, the cartridge companies had slick advertising brochures and promotional plans. I had been out of the U.S. business scene for a long time and was totally out of sync with business advertising and promotion.

Finally, with the encouragement of friends and some investors, I started a cartridge remanufacturing plant on the Florida Space Coast. In January 1998 we incorporated under the company name of Cartridge Source of America, and I began the long process of building a business from the ground up.

In April 1998 I heard about an opportunity with NASA (National Aeronautics and Space Administration). Contractors for NASA periodically met with small business owners. NASA had a small business liaison at the edge of the Kennedy Space Center, so I went there and met with the representative. She was a very helpful, professional young lady who urged me to sign up to meet the contractors.

"Our next available opening is in June," she said, "so if you are interested, sign up now."

I signed up for the June meeting and left confident that from April to June I could pull together a decent marketing proposal.

Several hours later she called me at my office. "Mr. Hurston," she said, "we have a cancellation, and I wonder if you could meet with the contractors this Thursday?"

"Doesn't give me much time to get ready, does it?" I answered. It was already Tuesday evening.

"The next opening is in June. I just thought you might want to speak to them earlier than June."

"I'll be there," I said. I hung up, and it seemed that I heard the swish of a lion's tail behind me. *How could my team and I ever produce a professional, attention-grabbing sales pitch in thirty-six hours? Should I have waited until June? Would I blow my big chance by rushing to present now instead of waiting to do so in June?* I didn't know. All I knew was that the Guide had been with me as I had faced down lions of every size and strength, and He would be with me when I faced these lions.

On Thursday I sat across a large conference table facing representatives from major aerospace contractors, including Lockheed Martin, Boeing, and Johnson Controls. Their representatives had many questions about the proposals that others and I presented. I felt that my team had put together effective marketing material, but my competitors had prepared well also.

Following the close of the meeting, a young man named Mark approached me and handed me his card. "Call me when you get back to your office," he said.

"Thank you. I will call you this afternoon."

After everyone had gone, the young lady from the small business liaison said, "Now, Joe, you've made some good contacts today, but they will equate to nothing—absolutely nothing, 100 percent nothing—if you don't follow up on them. The real work is just beginning. You can make of it whatever you wish."

I remembered the challenges of getting into Cuba and the persistence required to get clearance from the U.S. Treasury Department, the U.S. State Department, and the Cuban Interests Section, and I thought to myself, *Young lady, if you think this is complicated and requires persistence, think Cuba. Now Cuba is difficult. I'll be back, and I won't quit.*

After thanking the young woman for her advice, I returned to my office and called Mark that afternoon.

He said, "I would like to give you an opportunity to make a presentation to my associates. I will arrange to get you cleared into Kennedy Space Center." Mark gave me instructions to the badging office and a time to arrive. A tiny crack had opened in the massive bureaucracy of NASA. I showed up right on time, and Mark accompanied me into the Kennedy Space Center. Following my presentation Mark said, "Joe, we'd like to give you a chance."

Cartridge Source of America (CSA) eventually became the main provider of print cartridges for NASA, the Kennedy Space Center, a major aerospace contractor, and for many Fortune 500 companies. An incredible perk—a pilot's dream come true—later came with my new work. I received clearance to board the space shuttles to scan for security vulnerabilities and to research new methods of printing in space.

During the establishment of CSA I was never totally out of ministry, but the step away from full-time ministry helped me get my bearings and determine business and family priorities. I envisioned growth of CSA that would allow expansion of the company into other countries and provide a means of income for tentmakers. As CSA grew, my excitement grew. CSA was going to enable me to "take the gospel around the world."

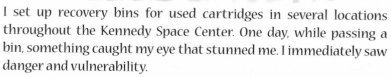

MAP READING TIP 6

P.S. DON'T FORGET ABOUT THE LIONS.

I set up recovery bins for used cartridges in several locations throughout the Kennedy Space Center. One day, while passing a bin, something caught my eye that stunned me. I immediately saw danger and vulnerability.

I stood holding the evidence in my hands, knowing that relaying this information could jeopardize my future. Besides losing contracts, I could get involved in months of paperwork to bring the problem to official attention. And who would believe that the "cartridge man" had discovered a security vulnerability? The security agents would listen to my warning with a smirk on their faces.

Just as there was no choice in delivering food to starving children, getting medical help for Dorothy Erdman, rescuing men at sea, and going after Barry—there was no choice about what I would do. I would have to deal with this lion.

When I pointed out the vulnerability to the head of security at the Kennedy Space Center, I also presented protective measures to guard against the problem. The security agent was amazed at the find and thanked me for bringing the matter to his attention.

"May I brief my clients and warn them of this vulnerability?" I asked.

He not only gave me full permission to brief my clients but also said, "NASA heads of security from all over the world are meeting here at Kennedy. Would you be willing to brief them on this vulnerability and advise them about protective measures?"

That briefing was the first of many briefings I would conduct. Before I could hardly pack my bags, I was booked to speak at National Security Agency seminars, interviewed by security magazines, and asked to conduct security sweeps for businesses. Briefings included officers in high government positions and agents on deep security levels. I became one of the leading authorities on this security vulnerability, which was considered one of the major security findings of 2001. Following the 9/11 attacks, the security find had even greater significance.

Facing this lion also put me into a new arena of Christian influence. No matter where I spoke, I never hid my faith. I started my presentations with, "I was a missionary pilot." I explained how missionary pilots constantly face danger. Since they have a plane and give away food and medicine, they appear to be extremely wealthy. In some cultures where compassion and generosity are equated with stupidity and weakness, the missionary appears to be a naïve, easy target. Add to these dangers the chaos of political upheaval.

"Being a missionary pilot," I told them, "trains you to constantly watch and assess everything around you in order to survive. That constant alertness to danger enabled me to see the vulnerability that I'm about to describe."

By the time I had explained the security issues that missionary pilots faced, they paid close attention to my briefing. The briefings gave me unimaginable opportunities to share and testify about the goodness of God. I always tried to give a unique presentation, and often listeners told me, "We've never heard a security presentation like this!"

During coffee breaks and lunch breaks, registrants would talk to me about flying and missionary work. Because I had climbed the forbidding cliff and faced the lion at the top that whispered, "Don't tell. Let it go," the Lord was giving me unimaginable opportunities to share the gospel. CSA was giving me an excellent ministry platform. To me, this was it! God was launching me around the world with the gospel, and I could hardly contain my excitement.

But, "who has understood the mind of the LORD?" (Isa. 40:13). Who would dare claim to know what the Lord is doing?

CHAPTER 13

TRAVEL COMPANIONS

SHARE THE PATH TIP 1
TAKE TIME TO ENCOURAGE OTHERS ON THE TRAIL.

WHEN WE USE a map to travel a long distance, we don't spread the entire map out. We fold the map to cover a section of the route. When God plants a vision or dream in our heart, He never shows us the whole map. He reveals just enough at first and during our "growing into the vision" to keep us going. At times you'll feel like the horse that keeps moving toward a carrot that dangles inches beyond your nose. You see the possibility of reaching your dream, but you can't quite touch it.

When all the segments of your dream begin to unfold, the results will probably be much larger than what you had imagined. Joseph envisioned being in charge of his family and their possessions, but when the vision unfolded, he was second in command of the world's greatest nation. Not only did his brothers bow before him, but also all of Egypt paid homage to him. If God would let us see the enormity of what He has for us to do, we would probably turn and run from the roar. The Lord, though, knows how to shape the pieces of the plan, shape us to fit the plan, and then slide the pieces together at the right time.

Those intricate pieces that form essential parts of our life picture often come to us through the hands of other people on the trail. In *Pilgrim's Progress*, travelers with names such as Interpreter, Prudence, Faithful, and Hopeful fell in step with Christian and encouraged him as he traveled.

One traveler who fell in step with me in late 1989 was from Germany. Speaking with a thick German accent, Rolf Engelhard called and introduced himself as a friend of a friend. "I am a missionary pilot," Rolf said. "I want to use my skills for the Lord."

189

I regularly get calls like this from people who have romantic pictures of a missionary pilot. The sweetness of his voice, however, made me listen closely as he told of his flight training in one of the best flight schools in the world. As he continued, I knew that he would not have enough flying hours to make my team, but I wanted to do what I could to encourage him.

"My instructors call me the Red Baron," he said. His voice bubbled with enthusiasm. "They say I'm one of their best students," he continued. "I know God has given me this gift for Him."

When I invited him to come and talk with me, he and his wife, Linda, immediately drove to meet me. They were a handsome, very professional-appearing couple. I would learn that he had been a partner in the largest solar and sauna business in Northern California. Following a near-death experience, his wife had become a Christian. She in turn had led Rolf to the Lord. Soon after his conversion, he decided, "I will sell my business and be a missionary pilot. I will get the best training in the world." He sold his part of the business, bought investment properties in California, moved his family to Florida, and had just completed a year of flight training.

Rolf had all the flight ratings but the bare minimum of flight time to obtain them—250 hours. He was so excited about working for the Lord that I hated to break bad news to him.

"Rolf," I said, "I have four airline captains with combined time of over 45,000 hours. I'm sure that you are a phenomenal pilot, but with only 250 hours of flight time, I couldn't even get you insured to fly my planes. I'm sorry, but I just can't do it."

He was crushed. "Oh, this is such a disappointment. I went to MAF and they told me the same thing. I went to JAARS* and they told me the same thing."

"Don't feel bad," I said. "You have joined the elite ranks of the rejected. They wouldn't have me either. I had to start my own aviation ministry so that I could fly."

"Well," he said, "God has given me an idea for a water purifier, and maybe He wants me to work on that."

"A water purifier?"

* JAARS is a missionary aviation ministry that provides technical support and services for the operations of Wycliffe Bible Translators.

"Yes. God showed me. I know exactly how to do it."

I had met a lot of crackpot would-be inventors, but something rang true about Rolf's idea.

"Tell me more," I said.

"I see the way God purifies water. It goes through the ozone layer, and then ultraviolet light purifies the water. It's just God's purification system."

"That's good, Rolf. Please invent that." I had just finished forty-six relief flights in ten days, following Hurricane Hugo. I had flown tens of thousands of pounds of water. "We need a water purifier about this size," I said and held my arms up about twenty inches apart. "And it must have a pump motor because there will be no water pressure. It must work on 110, 220, 12 volts. Can you do that?"

"I think I can do that," he said. "Maybe God wants me to do that."

When Rolf called, I could have ended the phone conversation with a "Thanks, but no thanks" answer. Instead, I had taken time to meet with Rolf and Linda in order to encourage them to keep following the call of God. We left as friends, and I followed his progress as he took the invention to Europe, got it approved, and worked to modify and perfect it. In the process he made millions of dollars. Little did I know that Rolf held an intricate segment of the map that would enable me to take the gospel around the world.

SHARE THE PATH TIP 2

PITI, PITI, WAZO FE NICH LI—LITTLE BY LITTLE THE BIRD
BUILDS ITS NEST (HAITIAN PROVERB).
LITTLE BY LITTLE, GOD PLACES PEOPLE ON OUR PATH
WHO WILL HELP US REACH HIS DESTINATION.

Through flying, Rolf Engelhard and I had kept in touch and often talked for hours. He was flying a variety of planes and making deliveries as far away as the Fiji Islands. I advised him on handling characteristics of each plane, and we discussed weight and balance on heavy, fuel-laden aircraft. We also talked about weather—especially about hurricanes. "Pure water is so vital following a hurricane," I reminded Rolf.

Rolf took the basic idea that he had invented for households and began to modify it to work in disaster areas. He called the new water purifier the "Vortex Voyager." In 1999, a couple hurricanes swept over part of the Bahamas. Knowing the immediate need for pure water, I approached my pastor, Larry Linkous, and told him about the Voyager. "If we could get one of these to our missionary family there, they would have pure water and could supply water for others in their community." He thought it was a great idea and asked me to speak to the congregation on Sunday about the Voyager.

I spoke in the Sunday morning service, which was broadcast on radio. "We have an incredible water purification system," I explained, "and we want to get one to our missionaries in the Bahamas." The church, of course, was excited about the prospect of providing water following the hurricanes and funded a Voyager.

After I spoke, I took my seat in the congregation. About forty-five minutes later, an usher tapped me on the shoulder. "There's a gentle-man in the lobby who wants to see you right now."

I left the auditorium and met a very distinguished, dignified, southern gentleman who was wearing a Tuskegee Airman blazer. "Are you Joe Hurston?" he asked in a deep, rich voice.

"Yes," I said extending my hand in greeting.

"I'm Robert Decatur. I want to help you with your mission. I'm part of a group of aviators from World War II, and I want to help you."

"Oh, Mr. Decatur, I've heard of the Tuskegee Airmen. I would be glad to talk with you."

We exchanged phone numbers, and I called him on Monday.

"What are you doing to help people?" he asked.

I explained about the water purification units and mentioned that a friend, Rob Helmer, would be taking some units to the Baha-mas on a C-47 (DC-3).

"Oh, I flew right seat on a C-47," he said and launched into a list of planes that he had flown, including the Steerman, P-51, B-25, and P-47. Then he said, "I just want to do something."

I saw Judge Decatur as an elderly man but strong, clear-eyed, and determined to still make a difference in his world. I wanted to help him walk out his call, so I arranged a meeting for him with Dr. Rob Helmer. The judge did not go on the flight to deliver the units, but he did help load the DC-3. He also climbed into the cockpit and reminisced for a few minutes. Surprisingly, he showed an interest in CSA and often came over for a cup of coffee. He would come to my office and in his deep authoritative voice ask, "How is the erudite Joe Hurston, entrepreneur? I think you are going to be bigger than Bill Gates."

He always wanted to know about the business and gave me expert advice, especially on legal aspects of my business. For me, it was more than a business association. It was the development of a rich friendship and a walk through the History Channel. He not only had been a part of history, but also he had been a shaper of history. Decatur had been one of the architects of the Peace Corps and had traveled all over the world and met with kings and potentates. He had served under Presidents Kennedy and Johnson. Kennedy had asked him to take an ambassadorship, but before Judge Decatur could answer, Kennedy was assassinated. Judge Decatur had also been with Martin Luther King Jr. the evening before King was assassinated. We talked about our country that we both loved, we talked about business and flying, and we cried together when Rob Helmer died in a plane crash.

◆ ◆ ◆

When we read Romans 8:28, "And we know that in all things God works for the good of those who love him," we attach a negative connotation to the verse. If something bad happens, you look to this verse for hope that some good will emerge from the situation. God not only brings good out of evil, but He also works in the good things of our lives also. While we focus on the big "bads," God is busy slipping little "good things" into many parts of our lives that we don't even notice. Rolf Engelhard and Judge Decatur fell into the category of *good things* God slipped into my life. To me they were pilots, dear friends, and encouragers. To God, they were holders of map segments that I would need in order to fulfill God's purpose.

SHARE THE PATH TIP 3

WHILE THE ROAD AHEAD MAY HOLD NOVELTY AND EXCITEMENT FOR YOUR COMPANIONS, YOU MAY BE MUTTERING, "BEEN THERE. DONE THAT. DON'T WANT TO DO THAT AGAIN."

In May 2004, a flood swept more than three thousand people to their deaths along the Haiti-Dominican Republic border. I made note of it, but the pressures of being the CEO of a now multimillion-dollar cartridge recycling business had my full attention. I would never want to minimize the value of one person, but I knew that in Haiti the level of desperation ran so high that people would build houses in the riverbeds. They took risks that others would not take, evidenced by a group of people who packed 180 people into a 29-foot sailboat and made a 700-mile journey in search of a better life. Because of their desperate plight, they gave no forethought to the future. The flood was a terrible tragedy, but the people had built in the riverbed, not taking into account that someday the waters would rise and sweep them away.

In my determination to think ahead about the welfare of CSA, I was focused on the challenges of a large contract I was negotiating. Working on the contract one evening, I had one eye on the clock, as it was getting late and I needed to get home in time for dinner. The phone rang, and when I answered, Judge Decatur, in his deep eloquent voice, said, "Brother Joe, have you heard about Haiti?"

"Yes, I have."

"What do you think about it?"

"They cut down all the trees, and then they built their houses in the riverbed, and the rains came and they all got swept away."

Silence.

When the silence became very uncomfortable I said, "That's probably not the answer you wanted to hear."

"No, Joe. It's not what I wanted to hear."

"You want me to do something about it, don't you?"

"Yes, I do. As a matter of fact, I feel like God tapped me on the shoulder and said, 'Robert, you've got to do something about those poor people suffering way down there.' I took that quite seriously. I thought about it. And all I could think about was to call my good friend Joe Hurston."

At that point my mind began to race. I was trying to think of someone that I could hand him off to. My initial reaction was, "Rob, why did you have to die? I could have handed the judge off to you."

The judge and I had developed a true and honest friendship, and so I said, "You realize, Judge Decatur, that you have totally ruined my evening. You realize, sir, that you've really messed up my whole thinking. Right now I am up to my elbows in alligators with a major contract challenge. I don't have time for this. But don't go anywhere. I'll call you back in about ten minutes."

I broke the connection and dialed Rolf Engelhard.

"Rolf," I asked, "do you have any Voyagers left?"

"You are not going to believe it. I have a hanger full of parts. I think I can put a couple together for you."

"Could you put a couple together like…right now?"

"I think so."

"Let me call you back."

I called the judge and said, "OK, Judge. Tell you what. I just talked to Rolf Engelhard, the inventor of the Voyager."

"That water thing?"

"I can't make any promises. As I said before, you've totally messed up my day."

"I know. I know you're having contract challenges."

"You say God tapped you on the shoulder?"

"Yes. Yes, He did."

"I'm going to try to pull something together. You're going to have to find some money to buy these purifiers, and we'll see if we can get some to Haiti."

Together we raised the money ($4,200) for two purifiers, and I located a pilot and plane. I called Judge Decatur. "We have a plane. Let's put it together. We need to leave soon. Do you have any good press connections? How about *Florida Today?*"

He knew the managing editor, who sent a reporter, John Torres, with us.

At noon on the day before departure, I was eating at a Chinese restaurant with my son Christian when the pilot called. Due to an urgent personal need he canceled the flight.

"Christian," I said, "I have the judge, a reporter from *Florida Today,* missionaries in the DR to pick us up and take us to the flood site, and now we've lost the plane."

I hadn't really chosen to do this trip. It had chosen me. This path was looking very familiar. Planes, mud, displaced people—and I wasn't sure how involved I wanted to get. I wanted to take Jesus around the world—not water. Suddenly the Guide was shoving the map to relief ministry in my hands, and I didn't even have the necessary tool—a plane—to conduct the work.

I sat in the Chinese restaurant, holding my phone and wondering, *Where can I find a plane?*

"What are you going to do?" Christian asked.

"Don't call anybody. Don't say anything."

I went in search of a plane to rent but could find nothing. Back at the office, I prayed like crazy. Finally I called Marlin Moudy, an old friend down in Stuart. The phone rang and rang, and finally Marlin picked up.

"Joe, Joe, I was just walking out the door to fly to the Bahamas."

"Are you going and coming right back?"

"Yes."

"How is old 402 flying?"

"Oh, I'm keeping it patched together."

"Marlin, I need you; I really need you. I'm scheduled to leave tomorrow at 5:00 in the morning for the DR. Would you let me use the 402? Would you fly with me?"

He paused and then said, "Yeah, I will. I'll fly to the Bahamas and be back tonight. You gonna come to Stuart?"

"We'll come to Stuart."

Marlin flew to the Bahamas, returned that evening, and topped off the plane with fuel in preparation for the next day's flight. At 3:00 a.m. the next morning, I picked up Judge Decatur and John Torres, and we drove to Stuart.

Marlin said, "Joe, I'll let you use the plane under one condition. I'm dog-tired. You fly the plane. I won't touch the controls. You fly the whole thing. I don't really want to do this trip, but I feel like God wants me to do it."

"Marlin, I owe you one."

"Yes, you do. Do you have any money to pay for this?"

"Not very much."

"I figured that. How much can you afford?"

"Not nearly what it's worth. Marlin, I don't have any money for this. We're just going down to help these people."

"You haven't changed, have you?"

"No."

Witnessing the aftermath of the flood left a lasting impression on both John Torres and Judge Decatur. John wrote a powerful account of the delivery of the water purifiers that ran on the front page of

Florida Today. The judge determined to raise money to buy and send more Voyagers to Haiti. For me, the trip refreshed memories of other relief flights. No matter how busy I was with CSA, I was going to have to take time to do some relief flights when the need arose.

After the Haiti trip, I realized that the Voyagers were the answer to critical water shortages following disasters, and I told Rolf that we were going to need more units.

"It will take a while to put them together," he said. "All I have is junk bits and pieces and parts." During the summer months, Rolf worked on assembling more Voyagers, and I traveled to his home in Arizona and entered an agreement that would allow CSA to manufacture Voyagers. Previous attempts to market the Voyagers to American homeowners had fallen short of projected goals. I could see, though, that the Voyager—about the size of a briefcase, weighing about twenty-five pounds, and operating from solar, batteries, or electricity—would appeal to first-responder relief and humanitarian agencies.

In September 2004, when Tropical Storm Jeanne ravaged the north coast of Haiti and three thousand people died in the Gonaïve area, I told Rolf to pull together every unit that he could. During the next six weeks, he took a pile of parts and extracted twelve working Voyagers.

On September 23, Marlin let me use his plane, and Judge Decatur, Rolf, and I took in three Voyagers. The Orlando ABC-TV affiliate picked up the story and sent a filming crew along. Fifteen years after Rolf and I had discussed his being a missionary pilot and inventing a water-purifying system, he was flying as my copilot on a missionary relief flight to deliver Voyagers. I marveled at the way God had slid the simple contacts with Rolf and Judge Decatur on my path to form a water-delivery mission.

Upon landing in Port-au-Prince, we linked up with Barbara Walker, who had the perfect relief vehicle. She had a Toyota four-wheel drive diesel crew cab with a platform on the top. The truck bed had seats along the sides and was enclosed by a metal cage for security of both possessions and passengers. After loading the vehicle, which looked like a boat, we headed up the coast to Gonaïves.

In Gonaïves, a city of two hundred fifty thousand, more than three thousand people were dead or missing, and two hundred thousand had been left homeless. To complicate relief efforts, a 1.6-mile wide lake covered the highway with water four feet deep,

isolating Gonaïves. Small and large vehicles had tried to cross and
had slipped off the crumbling berm and lay partially submerged in
the muck and water. After making the crossing I dubbed the road
"Sweaty Palm Pass." On that first trip into Gonaïves, we placed two
units with missionary pilots and set one unit up in a hospital just in
time for a doctor to use pure water for a baby delivery.

> **I find doing the will of God leaves me no
> time for disputing about His plans.**[1]
> —GEORGE MacDONALD

By this time I was seeing myself pulled deeper and deeper into relief
work. Through Hurricanes David and Frederic, God had unstopped
my ears and enabled me to hear the cry of hurricane victims, but
relief ministry had been an on-again, off-again part of my life. My
dream was to take the gospel around the world, not water! The doors
to take the gospel around the world, however, had not opened, but
the means of providing clean water for Haitians had developed.

I could have ignored the doors opening to disaster relief ministry. I knew from experience that disaster relief doesn't give you
many warm, fuzzy feelings. You stifle tears, choke back vomit, have
nightmares, contract death-borne disease, and struggle with personal survival. As I contemplated a greater involvement in disaster
ministry, I heard the lion roar, but the low, raspy wail of lost children was louder. The dream to take the gospel around the world
would have to wait while I did the job at hand.

Waiting. Doing the job at hand. The stronger the vision, the harder
the waiting. You feel as if you are at the end of the runway, doing a
run-up of the engines. Instead of taking off into the great adventure
that you know God has for you, He aborts the flight and you must
taxi back to the terminal. Solomon said, "Hope deferred makes the
heart sick" (Prov. 13:12). Be aware, if God has a great work for you to do,
it will require a lot of waiting as He prepares you for the work and as
He moves all the necessary parts of the plan into place.

◆ ◆ ◆

Upon my return to Stuart, before I even left the airport, Doug
Rodante called. He was a noted journalist and film producer. I had

been renting planes from him to do flights related to NASA space shuttle launches, but we had never met.

"Joe, what are you doing after all these hurricanes? I heard all about these hurricanes, and I just wanted to know what I could do to help people in Haiti. I've been through tough things in my life. What can I do to help?"

"Doug, I want to go back next week, and I need to get some more water purification units. Do you want to come with me?" Doug not only agreed to go on that trip, but he also provided his plane for the next four trips to Haiti.

SHARE THE PATH TIP 4

THE STUMBLING BLOCK THAT YOU HELP ANOTHER MOVE MAY TURN INTO A STEPPING-STONE FOR YOU.

By my return on October 3, Sweaty Palm Pass had disintegrated further. We linked up with Barbara Walker again and headed to Gonaïves in her "relief vehicle." Heavy trucks had chewed up the weak roadbed, and a UN transport was among the vehicles that lay on their sides in the water. The previous crossing over and back had terrified me, and now I stood looking at it and trying to evaluate whether I really wanted to cross it again. The water was still three feet deep. Out of the corner of my eye I noticed a camera crew, which wasn't unusual. Everybody was coming to the big disaster. A couple minutes later, a cameraman said, "Do you think we can make it over in that?" He pointed to a Jeep Liberty.

"Not with any equipment," I said. "You might get over, but with your equipment you'll swamp."

"Oh, man," he groaned.

"I'll give you a ride."

"What are you driving?"

"That four-wheel drive Toyota with platform on top." I nodded toward the Toyota.

"Great, man. Thanks. When are you going?"

"When I see something about the size of my truck make it across, we'll go."

The men, John Goheen and Pat Woodard, introduced themselves, and John returned to his driver and said, "We're going to take out some of our vital equipment and go with him. We'll meet you over on the other side." Even with the lighter load, their Liberty took on water that destroyed film worth a thousand dollars.

John rested a one-hundred-thousand-dollar camera on his shoulder, and as we waited for a vehicle comparable to mine to make a crossing, he asked, "Do you mind if I ask you a few questions?"

"No, go ahead." We talked for about ten minutes, and he filmed the conversation.

After safely crossing Sweaty Palm Pass, John asked, "Where are you going?"

"On a mission up the road," I said.

"Mind if I come?"

He accompanied me to the hospital where we had previously set up a unit, and I explained how the Voyager worked.

John and Pat continued with their driver, and I never thought a whole lot about the encounter. Through the years, many reporters and cinematographers had chronicled my relief work. A few weeks later I received a video of the Gonaïves flood from HD Net. I was shocked to see my face throughout the video. Unknown to me at the time, John Goheen and Pat Woodard were top TV journalists with hundreds of awards, including twenty-seven Emmy awards between them. Their story had run on HD Net World Report. Friends around the world contacted me saying, "I saw you! I saw you on TV. I turned on TV and there you were!" I called John and Pat and thanked them.

"It's a good story," they said.

◆ ◆ ◆

You can often move a stumbling block from someone else's path through a simple act of kindness. Yes, it will take time and may disrupt your schedule, but those stumbling blocks often turn into stepping-stones for you further down the path. The apostle Paul said, "Let us not become weary in doing good, for at the proper time we will reap a harvest if we do not give up. Therefore, as we have opportunity, let us do good to all people, especially to those who belong to the family of believers" (Gal. 6:9–10). Taking time to meet Rolf Engelhard, to go with Judge Decatur to Haiti, and to give John Goheen a ride across Sweaty Palms Pass were simple acts of "doing good," but these events would place key stepping-stones to enter other parts of the world.

Never give up. Keep on doing good. In God's time you will reap a harvest.

There is an important time factor to our dreams and visions. For even after we make sure they really have come from God, we must also make sure we are on God's timetable. Both the dreams and their schedule need to come from Him.[2]
—DAVID SEAMANDS

◆ ◆ ◆

Just before Christmas, I delivered ten more units to Haiti. These ten units were the first ones manufactured by CSA, and all the parts were new. Judge Decatur informed me that a wealthy friend had made a commitment to fund five hundred units for Haiti. I was settling into a relief ministry to Haiti and enjoying it immensely.

The year of 2004 was ending well for me. My children came home for Christmas, CSA sales had steadily increased, Voyagers were now being manufactured by CSA, and I was once again flying and doing mission work that I loved. On the night of Christmas Day, I fell asleep with warm, fuzzy feelings of great contentment. The next day, the world awakened to a deafening roar.

CHAPTER 14

THE ROAR HEARD 'ROUND THE WORLD

O N DECEMBER 26, 2004, I got up early because I had been keeping an eye on news in Haiti. I went to the normal news channels and stopped dead in my tracks. Cindy wasn't quite awake yet, so I said, "Honey, wake up. There's been a monster earthquake. It's an 8.7 (later determined to be 9.0–9.3), and it's in the Ring of Fire. They are saying three thousand, maybe four thousand people have died."

As we got ready for church, the death toll continued to climb, passing the ten thousand mark. "This is horrible," I told Cindy.

As I saw and heard the news of the tsunami, memories began to resurface of hurricane and flood relief flights. Faced with memories of muck, debris, bewildered expressions, and the haunting background sound of children who had cried until their voices were cracked and hoarse—well, there are some lions you must run to, and I knew that I would have to run to this one.

In the afternoon, a reporter from the ABC affiliate in Orlando came and asked, "Joe, what do you plan to do about the tsunami?" In the past, I had been able to borrow, rent, or beg a plane to make a short flight to the Caribbean; now, though, the disaster was half a world away.

"Man, I don't know," I said. "It's so big! I don't know how we will do it, but I will tell you this, Air Mobile Ministries will be there with Vortex Voyagers."

LEADERSHIP POINT 1

YOU ARE HERE FOR SUCH A TIME AS THIS.

God places each of us in unique positions in the history of our families, our communities, our countries, and the world. We have opportunities to effect change that will go beyond our immediate scope of influence and our lifetime. In Jewish history, Mordecai told

Queen Esther of a plot to kill the Jews and asked for her assistance. He said, "Who knows but that you have come to royal position for such a time as this?" (Esther 4:14).

Wherever you are, keep your eyes open to the needs and opportunities that surround you. What is happening in your family? What fears do your neighbors or friends face? What challenges confront your business or place of employment? What problems create conflict in your community? God has placed you here for such a time as this. Look to Him for guidance on how He wants you to enter that need and give assistance.

He who breathes into our hearts the heavenly hope, will not deceive or fail us when we press forward to its realization.[1]
—STREAMS IN THE DESERT

As the tsunami news swamped the world, I knew that all the previous experience in distributing the Voyagers had been preparation for "such a time as this." But what could I do? What could one man do in such an enormous catastrophe? Many journalists held back because they didn't know where to begin. They said, "It's so big, we can't wrap our arms around it. We don't even know where to start with our stories."

I determined to take twenty Voyagers to an area that needed water. In the chaos of the catastrophe, I would never see the units again if I tried to ship them. I needed *water mules*. The Voyagers would have to be hand carried, but who would be willing to spend a couple thousand dollars of their own money to be a water mule? Who would have a good reason—other than carrying a Voyager—to go?

I started by calling John Goheen at HD Net. "I'm going, John. Do you want to go?"

"I'll call you right back."

Less than an hour later, John called and said, "I'm in. We didn't know how to go and even approach this. We were looking for someone going in that we could follow. You are perfect. You have given us something to latch onto."

Other team members were John Torres (*Florida Today* reporter),

Doug Rodante, Cindy, Cherie (my daughter), Martha VanCise (writer), and Chris Stamper (Voyager technician). The team and I arrived in Jakarta on January 10, a little over two weeks after the disaster.

LEADERSHIP POINT 2

SOMETIMES YOU WILL STAND ALONE IN YOUR DECISIONS AND METHODS OF HANDLING A CRITICAL ISSUE.

When we landed in Jakarta, we had a pretty good idea of how we would implement the Voyagers. John, through United Methodist contacts in Jakarta, had identified Nias as an isolated island that needed help. Due to John's influence, Methodists leaders in Indonesia had pulled off an extraordinary feat in getting us a flight to the island, ground transportation, and accommodations. We would fly from Jakarta to Medan the next day, stay overnight, and then go on to Nias.

The evening we arrived in Jakarta, leaders from the Baptists met with us, and I demonstrated the Voyager to them and explained our plans to help the people in Nias.

"We've had people in Nias," one Baptist missionary said. "The damage there is minimal. One hundred were killed, but their basic needs for water and food are being met."

One hundred deaths are a lot until you compare it to forty thousand, one hundred thousand, or two hundred thousand. I would never minimize the death of one person, but I thought, *I've come eleven thousand miles and am still traveling hundreds of miles further to give assistance where water needs have been met.* With a sinking feeling, I began to realize that we weren't really needed in Nias.

The thirty-hour flight began to take its toll. Martha and Doug had boarded the flights with colds, and by the time we reached Jakarta, Martha was having a hard time keeping up with the team, so she opted to stay in Jakarta. We cut our luggage to bare necessities, piled the excess in Martha's room, and boarded a plane to fly a thousand miles to Medan.

The hours of nonstop flight and the upending of my internal clock, along with taking doses of prophylactic medications and vaccinations just before our departure, were assaulting my body like a sledgehammer. I was beginning to lose ground physically, but I had to keep going.

In Medan, the Methodists had reserved rooms for us where no rooms were available. The modern hotel that catered to business people and tourists was packed with reporters, relief workers, and other NGO (non-government organizations) from all over the world.

Through John Goheen, we met Jeff, a courageous missionary who works with the persecuted church. Jeff said, "Nias received very little damage. The really devastated area is Melauboh. Melauboh is being passed over by everyone because of the extreme difficulty to get in. No planes can go in because the runway was broken up in the quake. The earthquake destroyed bridges, and the overland route to Melauboh is infested with separatist rebels. Until they put protection on the road, about the only way in is on a helicopter."

"We'll go to Melauboh," I said.

When I said that, John Goheen looked at me, and I could see the disappointment and the legitimate questioning of my leadership. His experience in wars and disasters far exceeded mine, and he knew that both high-ranking church and government officials had put their reputations on the line to make arrangements for the team and me. In the presence of this news giant, I couldn't help but think, *How would he have handled this?* No matter his response, I had to take responsibility and make the decision I felt was best. Whether our fears are real or imagined, we must take responsibility to make critical decisions.

◆ ◆ ◆

In the Old Testament, Esther was the only Jew who had access to King Xerxes, and when Mordecai asked her to speak to the king about the danger to the Jews, she said, "All the king's officials and the people of the royal provinces know that for any man or woman who approaches the king in the inner court without being summoned the king has but one law: that he be put to death. The only exception to this is for the king to extend the gold scepter to him and spare his life" (Esther 4:11).

Mordecai, though, convinced Esther to approach the king. She acquiesced by saying, "If I perish, I perish." After three days of prayer and fasting by the Jews, she appeared before King Xerxes, and he extended the golden scepter to her.

As the person that God places in a position for a particular task, you will often stand alone. Ask for the counsel and prayers of respected people, but accept your responsibility to make the final decision. Some decisions may carry unpleasant repercussions. If, after praying, you believe that you are choosing the best course of action, then move boldly and accept the outcome. Sometimes you have to plunge into a decision with an "If I perish, I perish" attitude.

The vision must be followed by the venture. It is not enough to stare up the steps; we must step up the stairs.[2]
—VANCE HAVNER

After telling the team that we would be going to Melauboh, I went up to the Singapore military command center and talked to one of the young Singapore officers that spoke excellent English about getting seats on the helicopter. Hundreds of people, representing big names like Red Cross and the UN, were trying to get to Melauboh on the Singapore military helicopters, which seated fourteen or fifteen people only.

"There is a CMAC* meeting at 9:00 tomorrow," the officer said. "Be sure to attend." As I walked away, he said again, "Sir, I want to stress…be at that meeting tomorrow morning."

Before going to my room, I called the Methodist leader who had set up the trip, and I canceled our flight to Nias.

"You can't do this," she said.

"We can't go to Nias."

"You have no idea what I've gone through to get this flight for you. I have pulled out every government connection. You can't do this to me."

"I'm sorry."

"What are you going to do?"

"I don't know." I hung up, went to my room, and collapsed on the bed.

John came to the room and said, "I just got a call saying that you canceled the flight."

"Yes," I said. "Yes, I did."

---

* CMAC is an acronym for civilian and military joint operations.

"Are you sure you know what you're doing?"

"If you want to go to Nias, go ahead. I'm going to Melauboh."

"How are you going to do that?"

"I don't know, but I'm going."

There was open, clear, and very vocal disapproval of my decision. One woman had interrupted a major regional conference to make scores of phone calls to get us on the flight to Nias. She had pulled every string and called in every favor to get us on that plane. I had arrived in Indonesia following the worst disaster in modern history, and I had made some of the leaders of the church and the country very, very angry.

LEADERSHIP POINT 3

WHEN YOU MAKE A FUTURE-ALTERING DECISION, EVENTS OFTEN GO DOWNHILL BEFORE THEY GO UPHILL AGAIN.

After Moses finally got the Israelites out of Egypt, events went downhill real fast. The Egyptian army chased the people to the Red Sea, and the terrified people responded by screaming at Moses, "We told you to leave us alone! Why did you take us to the desert to die?" Within a few hours of his departure from Egypt, the hero, Moses, had lost friends. However, Moses' faith had never been in his own ability to deliver the people. He had tried and failed miserably at that. His faith rested in God, who had commissioned him to lead the Israelites out of Egypt.

In Indonesia I was running out of friends quickly and running out of physical stamina. I lay down to sleep and awakened an hour later in a pool of sweat with a temperature of 103 degrees and diarrhea. I stayed awake all night long. Several times Cindy urged me to try to get to sleep. I tried, but stayed awake all night feeling sick and horrible because I had brought prominent people into Indonesia and torpedoed their guaranteed ticket to get into the tsunami site. It was not good. It was not at all good, and I needed confirmation from the Lord that I was not making a big mistake.

I wasn't drifting in and out of sleep. I was wide-awake. A little before 3:00 a.m., I lay thinking about a packet of high-dosage, high-energy vitamin C and my water bottle. *I ought to get up and take that vitamin C,* I thought, but it seemed to be too much effort. As I lay in bed, suddenly a light turned on in the room. Two little high-beam lights shone directly on the vitamin C packet and my water bottle. It was not a hallucination, because the sudden light partially awakened Cindy.

"Thank You, Jesus," I said. I got up, poured the vitamin C into the water, and drank it. I still could not sleep, but after I took the vitamin C, I lay there in incredible peace. His assurance came: "My grace is sufficient for you, for my power is made perfect in weakness." And, "When I am weak, then I am strong" (2 Cor. 12:9–10).

LEADERSHIP POINT 4

GOD'S PLANS ARE NOT OUR PLANS. WHEN WE RUN OUT OF PLANS, HE WILL SHOW US HIS PLAN.

When Gideon started out to fight the Midianites, he had thirty-two thousand soldiers. Even then, Gideon double-checked the orders from the Lord by putting out a fleece. Per Gideon's request of the Lord, the fleece was wet one night and dry the next. With God's assuring fleece signs and thirty-two thousand soldiers following, Gideon felt confident of victory. God couldn't give Gideon victory, though, until the troops were reduced to three hundred men. No doubt about it, God was going to get the glory for this battle, because there was no way Gideon and three hundred men could win. Against Gideon's human judgment, and probably against the advice of everyone in his hometown, Gideon asked three hundred men to stay with him and told the rest of the army to go home. Through those three hundred men, God brought great victory to Israel, and the glory went to God.

While reporters on my team had willingly served as water mules, their main purpose in making the expensive trip to Indonesia was to write eyewitness stories on the tsunami. My cancellation of the Nias flight had stripped the reporters of certain success. Furthermore, I had thrown away my only guaranteed chance to install Voyagers in a tsunami area. I, like Gideon, had reduced an opportunity for victory to probable defeat. However, the great need for the Voyager lay in Melauboh—not Nias. If God could help Gideon defeat the Midianites with trumpets and lights inside of pitchers, He could get us to Melauboh.

God's most common method of answering prayer is giving us

clear vision and understanding of what will work and what won't work. During the preceding hours in the bathroom, I had seen a lot of the crud-crusted black waste can in the bathroom. Strangely, the can began to look like a ticket to Melauboh.

At 5:30 a.m. I called Cherie and told her to gather the team for a 6:30 a.m. meeting in my room. I told them that we would not be going to Nias, but we were going to find a way to get to Melauboh. I believe they all had reservations about my leadership at this time. "Chris and Cherie," I said, "I want you to set up the Voyager in the lobby downstairs."

I pointed to the nasty, little black garbage bucket that sat in the bathroom and said, "Take that with you. I will do my demonstration with that." I emptied the can but did not clean the accumulated buildup of crud inside. "I'll fill this with tap water, pump it through the Voyager, and drink it."

In the gleaming lobby of soft, reflected light, marble floors, deep-cushioned settees and chairs, towering flower arrangements, uniformed hotel personnel, and soft piano music, we plunked down the gross waste basket and set the Voyager up where military officers and NGO members would pass. The wastebasket was familiar to them all. "Do you know where this has been?" I would ask. "Do you know how much filth and disease have been in this can?" And then I would catch a cup of water pouring from the Voyager spout and drink it.

A few minutes before 9:00 a.m. John Torres and I went up to the CMAC meeting. At the meeting they asked for a show of hands to determine who was doing what type of work. We discovered that 35 percent handled food, 35 percent worked with shelter, and 35 percent worked with sanitation, but not water. Only a couple people supplied water. It was obvious that pure water was needed and hard to come by. This was why we had come.

Following the meeting, I was more convinced than ever that the place we should go to was Melauboh. I continued the demonstration in the lobby and talked to everyone that would listen. "I must get these units into Melauboh," I said. A young Singapore Armed Forces (SAF) officer passed by the demonstration, and I asked, "What do I need to do to sign up for a flight?"

He returned with a form and said, "Fill out this." I filled out the form and included all seven team members.

"You want seats for seven?" he said.

"Yes, I have seven on my team. I need seats for all."

"We can't do that. Not for seven." I still filled in the information for seven and returned it to him.

About ten minutes later he found me and said, "You need to fill in these lines. You left out lines thirteen and seventeen." One line required a phone number, so I used Jeff's cell number.

I told John Goheen to feel free to go wherever he wanted to go. I'm sure he had wrestled with his own decision the night before, but he stayed with me faithfully and shot footage of the Voyager demonstration in the hotel lobby. When I told him I had no guarantees that we would get to Melauboh, he said, "I'm gonna stick with you." Cindy and the rest of the team had gone to a refugee camp with Jeff, and soon after the CMAC meeting, I went to bed and slept for several hours.

Later that afternoon, Jeff organized a meeting of ministries. He had us bring in a Voyager and demonstrate it. Near the end of the meeting, Jeff's cell phone rang. He was speaking to about fifty people, but held up his hand and said, "Excuse me," and stepped behind a screen to take the call. He rushed out from behind the screen and said, "Joe, you are to be at the airport tomorrow morning. You and your whole team are going to Melauboh on a SAF Chinook."

◆ ◆ ◆

Why did I shut open doors and pound on closed doors? I knew that Melauboh was a neglected lion. Just as Esther did, I knew lives depended on my response. Esther didn't have assurance her life would be spared. She prayed and felt that if God willed it, she would live. I didn't know if God would get us to Melauboh, but stories of the desperation there surrounded me, and I knew that the Voyager was for such a time as this. Esther said, "If I perish, I perish." I had felt that if God didn't come through with a flight, then He didn't come through. The fate of our trip had been in His hands.

I hadn't thought beyond transportation to Melauboh, but we would need a place to sleep. Instantly the missionaries who had been there since the disaster, and who had been unable to travel further, came asking me to do things for them in Melauboh. One major organization had nineteen million rupiahs, which is about

$2,500, to rent a house for a command center for Christian groups that would be arriving. They told me they had made a payment to hold the house and that if I would take in the money and rent the house for them, our team could stay there.

After giving the Air Mobile team the news, I went back to my room and slept like a baby. God really, really, really, really redeemed this leader, because we went against all the odds.

As we waited to board the helicopter, Sarisma, an Indonesian woman, joined the small group of passengers. She wore a yellow tunic. An aqua and yellow scarf, piped with silver, covered her head. She appeared to be a middle-class woman who carried her less-than-five-foot frame with strength and poise. Two sons, about eight and ten, stood with her. She spoke a few words of English and smiled at us. When I made eye contact with her, I crossed my hands and placed them on my heart. As I patted my chest, I enunciated in English, "I am so sorry."

She crumpled. The poise and inner strength she had been hoarding ran out before our eyes. She collapsed and fell on me, and she began to cry with deep, wracking sobs. All I could do was pat her shoulder and hold her. Cindy stepped closer, and Sarisma turned and fell on her, then turned back to me. John Torres had spoken to Sarisma through a translator and told us, "She was away from home when the tsunami hit. She lost forty members of her family, including her husband and three children. She's going back to see what is left."

In the helicopter, crates were lashed down the middle, and passenger seats lined the wall. I planned to follow Sarisma and see how we could help, but the chopper put down in a clearing short of Melauboh, and she and several other people got off. The last I saw of Sarisma was her flowing yellow tunic disappearing into the jungle.

When we landed in Melauboh, body hunters provided our initial transportation. These young college students and professionals had volunteered to recover bodies. They searched the rubble and muck for bodies, then laid them out alongside the road. Late in the afternoon, they loaded the truck with bodies, took them to a central location, and at 5:00 p.m. each evening they gave people an opportunity to view the bodies. By now, more than two weeks after the tsunami, it was just a ritual. The bodies had decomposed to unidentifiable masses of putrefaction. Following the obligatory display of bodies, they were buried in a mass grave.

LEADERSHIP POINT 5

FEAR ACCOMPANIES GREAT DANGER.
ACCEPT ITS PRESENCE AND FACE IT.

Fear is a legitimate life-preserving emotion. When the apostle Paul was en route to stand trial in Rome, the ship ran into prolonged hurricane-force winds. The seas had battered the ship so much that everyone had given up hope of survival. Paul told the crew to cheer up because an angel had told him, "Do not be afraid, Paul. You must stand trial before Caesar; and God has graciously given you the lives of all who sail with you" (Acts 27:24). Yes, even the great apostle had been afraid. When we run to the roar, we have no way of knowing what lies ahead. At times, we will experience fear. Our greatest fear is meeting something that we can't handle physically or emotionally. No matter what we face, the Lord has promised never to leave us. He will be with us in every situation.

Due to the very real threat of rebel separatists who had attacked convoys and troops trying to enter the area, a green zone had been established with military protection within the zone. When we asked the body hunters to take us to the house we were to rent, they knew exactly where it was, because it was one of the few remaining buildings. They took us down the main road, past the mosque, and a little beyond the green zone. No one was at the house, and we sat on the stoop hoping the owner would soon appear. Someone told us that he lived two hours away.

Massive destruction surrounded us. Melauboh, on the east coast of Sumatra, had been a heavily populated city with three-story buildings, a mosque, schools, dry cleaners, grocery stores, bakeries, banks, and hardware stores. Firm statistics were hard to come by, but it seemed that probably ninety thousand people lived there, and forty thousand were involved in the fishing industry. When the 9.3 earthquake, directly abeam of Melauboh, struck the first blow, buildings collapsed. After that, a series of waves thirty feet high traveled inland, then sucked everything back to sea. When the seas finally subsided, arms, legs, toys, chairs, boats, and empty baby strollers protruded from debris piles and the mud flats. Only the mosque and a few partial houses remained. Eighty percent of the city was leveled, and estimates ran as high as thirty-two thousand dead or missing.

The house that we hoped to rent had been spared because there was a slight hump in the road and the house had shared the same elevation. The surrounding mucky landscape was pocked with black water and protruding debris. The stench of decaying animal and human flesh forced us to pull on surgical masks.

In an effort to create a pure Islamic territory, the area had been isolated from foreigners for thirty years, and we white Americans attracted immediate attention. The gathering group of people seemed to be friendly and eager to try out their English. One group of young men took special interest in us, paying very close attention to all that we did.

The whole scene made me uneasy. Beyond the protective green zone, we were white strangers with cameras and oversized luggage that appeared to be heavy with supplies. Along with a backpack of nineteen million rupiahs, I carried U.S. dollars. People who had nothing else to lose in life surrounded us. As the afternoon shadows lengthened, I considered breaking into the house, but I remembered that breaking and entering carried a death penalty in some Islamic countries.

Quietly I said, "We need to pray."

The owner eventually appeared, and some young men helped us negotiate the balance due on the lease. I peeled off wads of money for him as the assembled crowd watched. After signing the contract, written in pencil on a piece of notebook paper, I took the keys and opened the house.

Mud and water had swept through the house when the tsunami hit, and a dirty line high on the wall marked the water surge. I found a well and set up a Voyager to provide safe water for the team. Cindy began to scrub and clean the place to make it more habitable and healthier. Nothing, though, could dull the stench of putrefaction in the muck that surrounded us.

That night, John Torres, Doug, and Chris lay down on cushions, couches, and love seats that fell short of supporting their bodies. Cindy and I slept on a mattress that was so filthy that we put on extra clothes to make sure that our bodies didn't come in contact with the dirt. Cherie stretched across the foot of the bed. John Goheen, trained by covering civil war and famine in Somalia, Desert Storm, and news on every continent, pulled a thin mat from his luggage, covered it with a clean sheet, and lay down to sleep. My admiration for John grew each hour.

Every noise made me hold my breath and listen to determine the source. Flimsy locks and doorknobs that came off in your hands would never deter anyone who decided to see if the rich white foreigners had more than nineteen million rupiahs. If militant separatists decided to attack, our location, outside the protective green zone, made us a first target. In the other rooms I knew dirty, hungry, and apprehensive team members were sleeping fitfully—except John Goheen.

I had been running to the roar for several years and trusting God to stand with me and deliver me from the lion. Others had gone with me on some of these runs, but I had only taken them into familiar territory that carried no threat to them. The occasional lion encounter, such as the beach attack or the sabotaged airplane, had been sudden, unexpected, and beyond my control. On this night death permeated the air. I realized that I had purposely shut safe doors and lunged against closed doors to lead six trusting people deep into the lion's lair. These people included husbands and fathers, parents, and those dear to me—Cindy and Cherie.

**God incarnate is the end of fear: and the
heart realizes that He is in the midst... will
be quiet in the middle of alarm.**[3]
—F. B. MEYER

Have I made a mistake in pressing into the center of the disaster? I wondered. *Should I have stayed with the original plan that guaranteed us a clean place to sleep, food, safety, and transportation? Will God protect us through the night?* That night I heard the cough of the lion just outside the door.

A scripture began to repeat itself in my mind. "Never will I leave you. Never will I forsake you" (Heb. 13:5). I lay awake repeating the promise: "Never will I leave you. Never will I forsake you." Whether God provided protection or not, I knew He would not forsake me. He would be with me whatever happened this night.

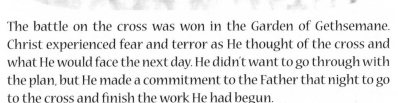

LEADERSHIP POINT 6

GREAT SPIRITUAL BATTLES OFTEN PRECEDE GREAT ACCOMPLISHMENTS.

The battle on the cross was won in the Garden of Gethsemane. Christ experienced fear and terror as He thought of the cross and what He would face the next day. He didn't want to go through with the plan, but He made a commitment to the Father that night to go to the cross and finish the work He had begun.

I faced several battles for Melauboh. I faced one on a night when fever raged, and I had no idea how God would provide a way into the tsunami area. And I faced one on this night as I lay awake listening for sounds of dangers in the tsunami zone. Each time I had to make the decision to keep going toward the roar.

When we awakened after that first night in Melauboh, we were sore and stiff, and I knew the days ahead would be physically and emotionally rough, but the spiritual battle had been fought and won. God had provided a way to get to Melauboh and had protected us during the night. Now, we could do the work that we came to do.

We ate trail mix and granola bars and made preparations to attend an NGO meeting at 8:00 a.m. Attendance at the meeting was essential. We couldn't just wander out and set up the Voyagers in a pile of rubble and pump water. If we were to make a difference in the area, we would have to deploy the water purifiers in strategic places where they would meet the needs of many people. I especially wanted to place the units in the hands of medical personnel who had mobile clinics.

At the NGO command post, I set up a Voyager, and a Filipino doctor with Operation Blessing said, "I was intending to leave, but if you will give us a Voyager, I'll spend another week here." He immediately recognized the strength and the ability of the Voyager to provide necessary pure water for medical treatment. Other contacts included UNICEF and Samaritan's Purse (Franklin Graham's organization). When we later hooked up with the body hunters, we set up a unit for them. They had been working in the fetid, tropical heat and drinking horrid water from a variety of sources.

Melauboh had been 80 percent destroyed, and survivors were

trying to salvage what they could from the muck and survive in the few damaged places that still remained. They bought water if they could find it or boiled brown contaminated well water. As they worked, they of course kept one eye on the activities of the strangers. Their friendliness, openness, and determination to deal with the disaster impressed us. Sadness rimmed their eyes, but they also smiled.

We went in search of a well and found one with dark brown water. I began to assemble a couple Voyagers. I liked to use two at a time, so that no break, machine malfunction, or maintenance issue would stop the constant flow of water. Almost instantly, the machines began to pull water from the well and pour out clear, pure water that I caught in a cup. I held the cup as if toasting those who had gathered closer, then I drank the contents. The crowd burst into spontaneous applause. They needed to see that I felt it was safe enough to drink. Once they were convinced that the water was safe, they started bringing battered pans and bottles and pitchers to be filled. Cindy cleaned the vessels with pure water before filling them, and some drank from the pitchers greedily as they moved away from the line. As I watched them gulp down pure water in this incredibly putrid setting, all the difficulties in getting the team to Melauboh disappeared. This was why I ran to the roar. Yes, obstacles to our return home still lay ahead, but what did it matter? With pure water to drink, these people could avoid many of the life-threatening diseases that the tsunami was generating. On this afternoon I kept brushing away tears of joy. I felt that I had conquered the trophy lion and stood with my foot on his head and my sword lifted to the heavens.

Enough fresh food had come into the area to provide for a primitive market. Cindy bought vegetables, eggs, and noodles, and we had a hot meal. That evening we fell into an exhausted sleep. A team of doctors and nurses from Bless Indonesia Today arrived at 11:30 p.m. They were part of a first convoy to reach Melauboh by land. The trip had taken almost twenty-two hours. For the first time in days, I was sleeping soundly and barely knew they had arrived. In the morning, I set up a Voyager for them to use in their medical work. We placed all but two units in strategic places where they would be maintained properly and serve many people. The two remaining units had failed, and I knew that modifications needed to be made on the units. No matter how intense and complicated lab simulations, you cannot put the same demands on equipment that tsunami muck and debris do. Melauboh was a testing ground for the development of an even newer and more improved Voyager.

We had distributed the water purifiers, interviewed people, and filmed footage, and we were ready to go home. We still, though, had no promise of a flight to Medan in less than two weeks. By now the Singapore army officers had come to know us pretty well. I had demonstrated a Voyager to them, and we had gotten acquainted with a major. We had been able to get John Torres out the day before, but securing seats for six people on one flight appeared to be asking too much. Nevertheless, I tried.

"Why should I let your people go ahead of the others?" the officer asked.

"I manufacture the Voyager. I must get home to get production going on more. I plan to return with more purifiers."

"Have your team here at 11:00 a.m."

On the helicopter, John Goheen continued to film, and his camera caught the stark, ravaged emotions that none of us could hide. We could never fathom the depth of the people's suffering, but we had shared enough of their suffering to have emotions raw and sensitive to the slightest bump.

When we landed in Medan we quickly unloaded our bags in a state of daze. We had lost track of time, but we were vaguely aware that our flight to Jakarta had been booked for today. As we shouldered our bags, a man in a perfect-sized vehicle for our team asked, "Do you need to get back in town?"

"Yes, we do," I said. "We need to go to our hotel." I gave him the name of the hotel.

"I can take you," he said.

We noticed that a small Christian symbol hung from his rearview mirror. We couldn't believe that a taxi driver would make a public display of faith in this strong anti-Christian country. When we mentioned the symbol, he said, "I am a Christian, but this isn't a taxi. I just came to the airport today because I felt like that was what I was supposed to do. I had no idea why I should go until I saw your team get out of the helicopter."

At our hotel, we recovered our tickets and found that we had just enough time to make our flight. As the team was gathering items that had been left in a room at the hotel, John Goheen handled the checkout details.

"There is something I've got to do," I said and dashed off. I went up to the big double doors of a huge conference room where the Singapore Armed Forces had headquarters. I pounded on the door and burst into a conference room with about thirty people seated around it. "I want to talk to the man in charge, right now," I said.

No one said anything.

A major general spoke up. "I am deputy commander of the wing. I'm in charge."

I crossed to him and said, "Sir, I just want to say..." When I tried to tell him what his forces had done, I broke and started crying.

He reached out and patted me on the shoulder and said, "It's OK; it's OK."

I couldn't stop the tears but managed to get out, "You have no idea what your men did. I'm going to write your president and tell them how great your men have been. I want you to know that." With tears streaming down my cheeks, I headed for the elevator.

The minute I stepped off the elevator, Goheen was saying, "C'mon! C'mon!"

"I had something I had to do," I told him.

We arrived at the airport thirty minutes before takeoff. We had done it. We had faced dangerous, difficult, devouring lions, but we had persevered and reached the goal of delivering Voyagers to Melauboh—a place of desperate need.

Epilogue

There is no epilogue.

Yes, following devastating killer floods, I took water purifiers to India, New Orleans, and Mississippi. When Hurricane Rita came ashore, I had Voyagers ready to deploy at strategic locations. But those experiences do not constitute an epilogue to *Run to the Roar*. As William Shakespeare said, "What is past is prologue." When you choose to run to the roar, a greater adventure always lies beyond today.

You can live in the prologue believing God is preparing you today for an even greater work tomorrow. Or, if you choose, you can live in the epilogue, remembering the good years and tacking a few memorable experiences to the end of your life story.

The fulfillment of my dream to take the gospel around the world is taking place as I take Voyagers to disaster areas around the world. Jesus said that when we see someone hungry and feed them or thirsty and give them something to drink, that we are doing it for Him. Words cannot describe the joy I feel when I extend a cup of clear, pure water to a thirsty disaster victim. I feel as if, through the power of the Holy Spirit, I am extending the love of Jesus to that person.

God placed dreams in my heart, and He has placed dreams in your heart. Your God-given dreams and visions will only be realized as you face the difficulties that block the path. You can stay on the bus and mumble, "I've always wanted to…" or "I wish I had…," or you can leap into the great adventure of running to the roar.

What do you choose?

NOTES

CHAPTER 1—LIONS STILL PREFER CHRISTIANS

1. C. S. Lewis, *The Chronicles of Narnia* (New York: McMillen Publishing, 1979), 75.

2. John Bunyan, *The Pilgrim's Progress* (New York: Gilbert H. McKibbin, 1919), 70.

3. Quotes by Paul Eldridge, BrainyQuote.com, http://www.brainyquote.com/quotes/quotes/p/pauleldrid101460.html (accessed March 23, 2006).

4. Quotes by John F. Kennedy, The Quotations Page, http://www.quotationspage.com/quotes/John_F._Kennedy/ (accessed March 23, 2006).

CHAPTER 2—DO YOU HEAR THE ROAR?

1. Quoted in Mrs. Charles E. Cowman, *Streams in the Desert* (Los Angeles: The Oriental Missionary Society, 1944), "March 26."

2. Quotes by Frank Crane, WorldofQuotes.com, http://www.worldofquotes.com/author/Frank-Crane/1 (accessed March 23, 2006).

3. Watchman Nee, *A Table in the Wilderness*, American edition (Wheaton, IL: Tyndale House Publishers, Inc., 1978), "October 26." First published in 1965 by Kingsway Publications, Ltd., Eastbourne, Sussex, England.

CHAPTER 3—THE ULTIMATE GUIDE

1. Cowman, *Streams in the Desert*, "April 16."

2. Nee, *A Table in the Wilderness*, "February 25."

3. Charles Spurgeon, *Collections: Words of Cheer for Daily Life*, "A Harp's Sweet Notes," GodRules.net, http://www.godrules.net/library/spurgeon/NEWspurgeon_h22.htm (accessed March 23, 2006).

CHAPTER 4—PICK YOUR LION

1. Quotes by Raymond Spruance, on reputation, Quotationsbook.com, http://www.quotationsbook.com/quotes/34049/view (accessed March 23, 2006).

2. Dietrich Bonhoeffer, "Thoughts on the Day of the Baptism of Dietrich Wilhelm Rüdiger Bethge, May 1944," *Letters and Papers From Prison*, updated edition (New York: Touchstone, 1997), 298.

CHAPTER 5—WEAPON OF CHOICE

1. "What People Have Said About the Bible," Bernard Ramm, TheScriptures.org, http://www.thescriptures.org/quotes/index.html (accessed March 23, 2006).

CHAPTER 6—TRAINING FOR TRACKERS

1. Phillip Keller, *A Shepherd Looks at Psalm 23* (Grand Rapids, MI: Zondervan Publishing House, 1970), 101–102.

2. This material is taken from *My Utmost for His Highest* by Oswald Chambers, copyright © 1935 by Dodd Mead & Co., copyright renewed 1963 by the Oswald Chambers Publications Assn. Ltd., and is used by permission of Discovery House Publishers, Grand Rapids, MI 49501. All rights reserved.

CHAPTER 7—PERSEVERANCE PASSAGE

1. Quotes by Kirk Kirkpatrick, on opportunity, http://www.quotationsbook
.com/quotes/28714/view (accessed March 23, 2006).

2. William Shakespeare, *Henry V*, Act 3, Scene 7, http://www-tech.mit.edu/
Shakespeare/henryv/henryv.3.7.html (accessed March 23, 2006).

3. Dag Hammarskjöld, *Markings* (New York: Alfred A. Knopf, 1964), 66.

CHAPTER 8—THE LION'S LAIR

1. Quotes by Christian Nevell Bovee, American author and lawyer, http://www
.giga-usa.com/quotes/authors/christian_nestell_bovee_a002.htm (accessed February 28, 2006). Also listed on various quotation Web sites.

2. Francis Thompson, "The Hound of Heaven," *The Oxford Book of English Mystical Verse*, D. H. S. Nicholson and A. H. E. Lee, eds. (Oxford: The Clarendon Press, 1917).

3. Ibid.

CHAPTER 9—DEVOURED

1. C. T. Studd, Quotes and Notes, Echoes From Glory, WholesomeWords.org,
http://www.wholesomewords.org/echoes/studd.html (accessed March 23, 2006).

2. Thomas Fuller, *A Wounded Conscience* (1655), quoted in "Christian Quotation of the Day," April 15, 2002, http://cqod.gospelcom.net/index-04-15-02.html (accessed March 1, 2006).

3. D. L. Moody, sermon, "Tomorrow May Be Too Late," http://www
.biblebelievers.com/moody_sermons/m4.html (accessed March 23, 2006).

CHAPTER 10—DANGER IN HIGH PLACES

1. George Wilkens and Donna Koehn, "1 Finger May Have Prompted Lion Attack," *Tampa Tribune*, May 14, 2002. Used by permission.

2. Ernest K. Gann, *The Black Watch* (New York: Random House, 1989), 194.

3. Quotes by Martin Luther, ThinkExist.com, http://en.thinkexist.com/
quotation/the_fewer_the_words-the_better_the_prayer/150792.html (accessed March 23, 2006).

4. Hammarskjöld, *Markings*, 103.

CHAPTER 11—ATTACK!

1. Frances Ridley Havergal, *My King, or Daily Thoughts for the King's Children* (New York: Anson D. F. Randolph & Company, 1876), 90, "The Token of the King's Grace," quoted on http://delta.ulib.org/ulib/data/moa/594/9ec/07f/1f4/6ab/0/data.txt (accessed March 23, 2006).

2. Bishop Handley Moule, quoted in Christian Quotation of the Day, March 26, 2002, http://cqod.gospelcom.net/cqod0203.htm (accessed March 23, 2006).

CHAPTER 12—A MAP FOR THE JOURNEY

1. Quoted in Cowman, *Streams in the Desert*, "July 10."

2. Elisabeth Elliot, *Keep a Quiet Heart* (Ann Arbor, MI: Servant Publications, 1995), 18.

CHAPTER 13—TRAVEL COMPANIONS

1. Quotes by George MacDonald, Quotes by Author, http://www
.christiansquoting.org.uk/quotes_by_author_m.htm (accessed March 23, 2006).

2. David Seamands, *Living With Your Dream* (Wheaton, IL: Victor Books, 1990), 32–33.

CHAPTER 14—THE ROAR HEARD 'ROUND THE WORLD

1. Cowman, *Streams in the Desert*, "March 26."

2. Quotes by Vance Havner, ThinkExist.com, http://en.thinkexist.com/quotation/the_vision_must_be_followed_by_the_venture-it_is/345392.html (accessed March 23, 2006).

3. Quotes by F. B. Meyer, on fear, Quotationsbook.com, http://www.quotationsbook.com/authors/4967/F._B._Meyer (accessed March 23, 2006).